DATE DUE

DANGEROUS DOMAINS

DANGEROUS DOMAINS

VIOLENCE AGAINST WOMEN IN CANADA

Holly Johnson
Canadian Centre for Justice Statistics
Statistics Canada

Nelson Canada

I(T)P An International Thomson Publishing Company

Toronto • Albany • Bonn • Boston • Cincinnati • Detroit • London • Madrid • Melbourne
Mexico City • New York • Pacific Grove • Paris • San Francisco • Singapore • Tokyo • Washington

I(T)P"
International Thomson Publishing
The ITP logo is a trademark under licence

© Nelson Canada,
A division of Thomson Canada Limited, 1996

Published in 1996 by
Nelson Canada,
A division of Thomson Canada Limited
1120 Birchmount Road
Scarborough, Ontario M1K 5G4

Canadian Cataloguing in Publication Data

Johnson, Holly
    Dangerous domains

(Nelson crime in Canada series)
Includes bibliographical references and index.
ISBN 0-17-604877-4

1. Women – Crimes against – Canada.   2. Violent crimes – Canada.
3. Conjugal violence – Canada.   I. Title.   II. Series: Crime in Canada series.

EV6250.4.W65J64   1996   362.88'082   C95-933012 7

Team Leader and Publisher	Michael Young
Acquisitions Editor	Charlotte Forbes
Senior Production Editor	Bob Kohlmeier
Projects Coordinator	Heather Martin
Art Director	Liz Harasymczuk
Cover Design	Julie Greener
Production Coordinator	Brad Horning
Senior Composition Analyst	Alicja Jamorski
Input Operator	Elaine Andrews

Printed and bound in Canada
1 2 3 4   (WC)   99 98 97 96

To the memory of Michael D. Smith

Contents

Foreword xi
Acknowledgments xiii
Introduction xv

CHAPTER 1 ***Theoretical Approaches to the Study of Violence Against Women*** **1**

Individual-Level Explanations 2
Social Learning Theory 2
Sex Role Theory 7
Situational Theories 10
Evolutionary Theory 13
Societal-Level Explanations 16
Lifestyle / Routine Activities Theory 16
Resource Theory 18
Social Control and General Systems Theories 19
Feminist Theories 21
Summary 25

CHAPTER 2 ***Methods of Measurement*** **26**

Police Statistics 27
The Laws on Assault and Sexual Assault 29
Trends in Assault and Sexual Assault Statistics 32
Clinical Samples 37
Population Surveys 39
Measuring Sensitive Experiences 41
The Violence Against Women Survey 46
Constructing Definitions of Violence 47
The Prevalence of Violence Against Women 48
Ethical Considerations in Survey Research 52
A Word on the Conflict Tactics Scale 56
Summary 60

Foreword

Until the 1970s, the problem of violence against women was all but ignored by criminologists. Like female offenders, female victims were considered less prevalent and of less significance than their male counterparts.

Over the last two decades, however, interest in the problem of violence against women has grown exponentially. The impetus for much of this growth was the pioneering work of several feminist scholars and activists who focused attention on what they correctly viewed as a neglected area of study. Now it is commonplace to find the results of research on topics such as wife assault, sexual violence, and sexual harassment featured in the pages of mainstream scholarly journals. Moreover, the problem of women's victimization has come to occupy a prominent place in the mass media and on the agenda of many government policy-makers.

In *Dangerous Domains*, Holly Johnson provides a comprehensive and critical analysis of contemporary social scientific thought on male violence against women. She begins with the assumption that although this issue is part of the larger social problem of violence in society, it poses unique theoretical and empirical problems. Her substantive inquiry offers a detailed exploration of a range of topics, including women's fear of crime, stranger violence, dating violence, wife assault, spousal killings, and the ways in which women are affected by and cope with male violence. Throughout her analysis, Holly Johnson remains keenly aware of the theoretical diversity that characterizes the study of female victimization, and she is sensitive to the need to integrate insights from what many would see as competing or even antagonistic theoretical viewpoints.

Also given extensive treatment in the pages that follow is the empirical character of violence against women. Holly Johnson provides important commentary on the difficulties that characterize efforts to investigate this problem and on why so many of our traditional measures of crime have proven inadequate to the task. In this respect, her own analyses draw heavily on the 1993 Canadian

Violence Against Women Survey—a study regarded by many as ground-breaking in its scope and design.

It is probably safe to say that despite the large number of research studies that have been undertaken and the amount of theoretical attention that this subject has attracted, the study of violence against women is still in its early stages in this country. *Dangerous Domains* by Holly Johnson is, however, a significant step forward.

Leslie W. Kennedy, University of Alberta
Vincent F. Sacco, Queen's University
Series Editors

Acknowledgments

I have many people to thank for the support and encouragement I received during the writing of this book. The manuscript was written during a one-year research leave from Statistics Canada. I am indebted to Statistics Canada's Research Sabbatical Program for their financial support and for allowing me the opportunity to bring this book to completion. It could not have been attempted otherwise.

Many other people at Statistics Canada provided invaluable assistance and advice. I would like to thank Sange DeSilva and Doug Norris for their faith and confidence in my work all the years we have worked together and for reviewing earlier versions of the manuscript. Gilles Beaulieu, Michelle Toupin, and many other people at the Statistics Canada Reference Library cheerfully fulfilled endless requests for material on interlibrary loan. David Paton, Josephine Stanic, Orest Federowycz, Michael Martin, and Rebecca Kong spent considerable time providing and interpreting statistical data. A special thank you goes to Karen Rodgers for her enthusiasm and commitment with respect to every request I have made of her.

The Violence Against Women Survey and the benefits it offers to Canadians were made possible through funding from the federal Department of Health through a government-wide initiative aimed at combatting the problems of family violence and other crimes of violence against women. Elaine Scott, Katherine Stewart, and Carol MacLeod are but a few of the dedicated individuals who facilitated my work in this field and, by extension, on this manuscript. I would also like to thank legal beagles Renate Mohr and Hilary McCormack for sharing their considerable talents and for taking the time to review the legal references throughout this book. Louise Savage of the Department of Justice facilitated my research into the criminal harassment law. Notwithstanding their input, the accuracy of the text remains my responsibility alone.

A number of individuals shared their wealth of expertise and experience with me over the past few years, and to them I am extremely grateful. In particular, I thank Vincent Sacco and Leslie Kennedy for their generosity, counsel, and ongoing support, and for always being available. I also thank Helene A. Cummins, Brescia College, University of Western Ontario; Julian V. Roberts, University of Ottawa; and the other reviewers who provided suggestions and feedback on my work. Finally, I wish to thank John and Laura, just for being there.

Holly Johnson

Note to Readers
Readers wishing further information on data provided through the cooperation of Statistics Canada may obtain copies of related publications by mail by writing to Publications Sales, Statistics Canada, Ottawa, Ontario K1A 0T6, or by calling 1-613-951-7277 or toll-free 1-800-267-6677. Readers may also facsimile their order by dialing 1-613-951-1584.

Introduction

During the time I was writing this book, the well-known American ex-football star O.J. Simpson was charged with the brutal murders of his ex-wife, Nicole Brown Simpson, and her friend Ronald Goldman. These murders captured the imagination of the cable networks, which broadcast every detail of the motor chase that preceded Simpson's arrest through to the end of his trial and his eventual acquittal. Simpson—football icon, celebrity, movie star—was evidently a hero to untold millions who maintained their support for this man who allegedly beat his wife on many occasions prior to her death. For millions of North Americans, Simpson's violent private persona was irreconcilable with his celebrity status, his public image as the all-American hero. For these people his status as a public figure overshadowed the gruesome allegations that he had brutalized his wife for years and stalked her after she refused his pleas for reconciliation.

Throughout the Simpson trial, some concerned groups tried to keep the media focused on the issue of wife battery and to put the murder of Nicole Brown Simpson into perspective against the thousands of other women who are battered and killed every day by the men who profess to love them. In a typical year, 120 women in Canada are killed by their husband, ex-husband, or boyfriend (Canadian Centre for Justice Statistics, 1993b), and almost 450 000 are slapped, punched, choked, beaten, sexually assaulted, or threatened with a gun or knife (Statistics Canada, 1994a). In the United States, 1400 women are killed by intimate partners and one million are physically or sexually assaulted each year (Bachman and Saltzman, 1995).

In the early stages of the trial, the interest of the media in the plight of abused women seemed, on balance, to outweigh demonstrations of support for the accused killer. But in the end, the racial divisions within the country rendered futile any attempt by the prosecution to tie together the way Nicole Brown Simpson had been battered and stalked with the fact that she had been brutally slain. "There was no motive," one juror remarked, and declared further that the history of abuse laid out by the prosecution was "a waste of time" (Wente, 1995). To judge by the mass outpouring of support of Simpson's acquittal, this perception was not limited to the 12 jurors.

The outcome of this widely publicized trial—in which there was an almost complete denial of the interconnections among the motives and dynamics of wife battering, stalking, and homicide—is sure to engender pessimism among those who work with and for battered women across North America. However, it would be a mistake to let this one event overshadow the real progress that has been made over the past two decades in this country in exposing the brutality of wife battering and sexual violence and in breaking down some of the most destructive myths and stereotypes about violent men and their victims. Approximately 400 shelters for battered women and their children now exist in Canada, and over 200 crisis centres providing counselling and support to women who have been sexually assaulted. Approximately 124 treatment programs for abusive men have been established across the country. The Canadian Teachers Federation and various provincial Ministries of Education have developed curricula to facilitate classroom discussions about dating violence and abusive relationships. The Society of Obstetricians and Gynecologists of Canada has initiated a nation-wide program to identify women enduring violence and to educate its members, and eventually family physicians, about the symptoms of abuse. Some religious leaders have begun frank and open discussions about wife battering with their congregations. And many communities across the country have established procedures with the cooperation of the police, courts, hospitals, shelters, and crisis centres to ensure that sexual assault and battering cases will be handled compassionately and effectively.

With this increased awareness of the scope and magnitude of the problem of violence against women has come a greater understanding of the dynamics involved. Out of a multitude of research studies has emerged statistical and case study information with which to better understand the nature, extent, correlates, and consequences of the problem. The result is sure to be a more informed policy-making process. Theories originally put forth with one or two single causative factors have been elaborated to take into account the complexity of a wide range of factors and the social context in which battering and sexual violence take place. As research tools and expertise have evolved, so too has theory, which has stimulated yet more research ideas.

What has been slower to emerge and gain acceptance are integrated theories that address the parallels among different forms of violence against women and take into account the range of situations that women find threatening. A primary contention of this book is that acts of male violence against women encompass a wide spectrum that includes murder, wife battering, and sexual assault, but that also includes threats of violence, intimidation, and noncriminal acts of sexual harassment. All of these acts are alike in motive and dynamic that make them more similar to one another than to violence that occurs in other contexts. Wife battering, for example, has more in common with sexual assault than with other forms of family violence, and sexual assault has more in common with sexual harassment than with any other type of assault.

WHY STUDY VIOLENCE AGAINST WOMEN?

Public concern about violence, particularly youth violence, has increased dramatically in recent years. Sensational drive-by shootings and other senseless slayings have fuelled public fears about random violence on the streets. Police statistics reported a steady increase in violent crime between 1961 and 1990, with a levelling-off effect in the early 1990s; crime victimization surveys, on the other hand, recorded no increase between 1988 and 1993 (Ogrodnik, 1994; Gartner and Doob, 1994). Both these sources report that, while the majority of offenders are male, victims are equally likely to be male or female (Trevethan and Samagh, 1992). So why write a book on violence against women? If the potential for violence is a human attribute and affects us all, both men and women, why not write about violence more generally?

When we speak of violence in terms of its legal definition, we are talking about a tremendous range of acts, from schoolyard fights to a barroom brawl to a brutal rape to an assault during a hockey game. How each of these acts is interpreted and labelled depends to a large extent on the social setting in which the act occurs and the meaning it has for the victim, the offenders, and any witnesses or bystanders. Spanking a child has all the ingredients of a violent act, but few people consider it violence of the type that deserves public attention until it becomes severe or is committed by someone other than the parent of the child. Spanking is generally considered a legitimate way of correcting children and teaching them appropriate behaviour. Similarly, physical assaults during hockey games and other sports are tolerated because of the social setting in which they occur. These acts would have different consequences and different interpretations if they took place in almost any other setting.

Not only are they situation-specific, but the social definition of each of these acts of violence is subject to change over time as public tolerance shifts. Child development experts are beginning to rethink the wisdom of physical punishment, and citizens' groups have lobbied the federal government to make spanking a criminal offence. There are concerted efforts by parents, school boards, and teachers across the country to reduce the level of violence in schoolyards. The lines between tolerable and intolerable levels of violence and coercion among dating partners, as another example, are in transition as well. Acts that, a decade ago, might have been considered the young woman's fault because of her lack of prudence or caution, or as simply a case of a young man going too far, are increasingly being labelled "date rape" even though the legal definition of these acts has not changed. While it is debatable from available statistics whether the level of violence in our communities has changed, societal definitions of some of these acts have changed perceptibly. At the same time, however, increasing levels of violence are tolerated in professional sports and in movies and videos. Witness the newest phenomenon in combat sports in the United States, the Ultimate Fighting Challenge, in which male combatants go at each other with no protection and few rules until one or the other is knocked unconscious or gives up. While as a society we have developed a greater awareness of the dangers of witnessing and experiencing violence and profess to deplore it, depending on the social context, we are tolerating increasing violence in certain social settings.

The reason for studying violence against women lies in the context within which these events take place and the nature of these experiences for the women involved. The problem of violence against women is a problem of intimate violence. Few people would argue that women are uniquely vulnerable to sexual violence. Wife battering is also unique in that it occurs within a specific context that gives it a distinct meaning for the victim and the aggressor that is different from violence that occurs in other arenas. Because of the social context of the husband–wife relationship that historically has awarded men higher social status and authority over their wives and children, domestic assaults on women take on a significantly different meaning than the same acts perpetrated by one man against another, or by women against their husbands. Wife battering can have the effect of reinforcing the unequal status of the female partner, strengthening the husband's dominance and authority within the relationship, and more firmly entrenching her dependence on the abuser (Saunders, 1988). The same acts by women don't have the same outcome.

Not only is the meaning of these acts different for all who are involved, violence against wives differs from other acts of violence in type, frequency, and severity. Wife battering is typically accompanied by extreme possessiveness and jealousy, emotional put-downs that whittle away at the woman's self-esteem and decision-making abilities, restrictions on her freedom of movement, threats of future punishment, and sexual assault (Walker, 1984). The proximity of the victim to the perpetrator; the financial, legal, and emotional bonds between them; and the unequal social status and physical strength all mean that assaults on wives tend to occur more systematically and cause greater physical and emotional damage than violence in any other context, with the exception of child abuse.

The contention put forward by some researchers (Steinmetz, 1977–78; Straus, Gelles, and Steinmetz, 1980) that women and men use violence against each other in equal proportions is not supported by other statistical research, testimonials of battered women in shelters, police statistics, or homicide data (Dobash et al., 1992). In 1993, 90 percent of spousal assaults reported to the police in Canada involved wives as victims (Canadian Centre for Justice Statistics, 1993a), as did 72 percent of spousal homicides (Canadian Centre for Justice Statistics, 1993b). Women are also the victims in 90 percent of spousal assaults recorded by crime victimization surveys (Statistics Canada, 1993b). Men are by far the most likely perpetrators of violence outside the family as well, committing 85 percent of all nonspousal violence known to the police. Although twice as many men are murdered every year, most homicide victims are killed by men (87 percent). It is difficult to conceive of a theory to explain how women, who are undeniably more peaceable than men in public situations, could suddenly become as or more vicious than men in the privacy of their homes.

This is not to suggest that women don't have the capacity for physical aggression. Some women commit serious violence and even murder against their husbands, children, and other men and women. But few people would argue that men and women are evenly matched in physical combat. Generally speaking, girls and women receive neither the social training nor the encouragement for physical violence, nor do they have the physical strength to engage in violence, particularly against a much bigger and stronger male opponent. Men receive both the training and the social assurance that in certain circumstances aggression will be tolerated, including violence against one's wife. Despite recent advancements in job training and education for women, husbands also tend to have greater social and financial resources at their disposal that facilitate leaving an abusive partner. Men can also more easily walk away from an abusive situation without fear of being physically restrained. Studies that produce equal rates of violence by husbands and wives nevertheless indicate that female victims are three times as likely as male victims to require medical care for injuries sustained in spousal assaults (Kantor and Straus, 1990). Wife battering, and not husband battering, receives broader support from social learning theory, sex role theory, and theories of unequal social status for wives and husbands.

The focus on female victims is not meant to deny the very high rate of violence against men as a group and some men in particular, or to minimize the physical and emotional costs to the victims. Violence is socially learned, and boys more than girls pick up cultural messages that encourages them to use violence as a legitimate way to solve disputes and to prove one's strength and daring. Violence and aggression in boys is reinforced through participation in sports and through normal children's television programming, movies, and video games (Miedzian, 1995). This is accepted as a normal part of growing up male. It is not unusual in North America for some boys to have to defend themselves from other physically aggressive males at some point in their lives. In certain contexts, this is viewed as normal and good, as a legitimate way of proving one's manhood, and a large number of boys and men are victimized in the process.

The point of this book is that wife battering and sexual violence are unique aspects of the wider social problem of violence in general, and they demand unique attention and solutions. These are violent events that uniquely affect women and that have potentially devastating consequences for large numbers of women. Many books have been written on these subjects, but most have looked specifically at only one aspect of the overall issue. This book is not just about rape, wife battering, or sexual harassment. It is about all of these and more. It is about the interconnections among all types of physical and sexual violence—and the routine threats of violence—that keep women from achieving a status that is equal to men's. This book is about the fear and caution that permeate the lives of some women as a consequence of threats and violence and that interfere with their right to participate in a free society.

PRIVATE AND PUBLIC VIOLENCE

Most researchers working in this subject area at one time or another point to the extent to which many of women's experiences with violence remain hidden from public awareness. A minority of acts of wife assault come to the attention of the police, who have been the official record-keepers of criminal incidents. Until recently, reported cases tended not to be treated as criminal matters. In fact, the legal system has historically reinforced an acceptance of wife assault by making a clear distinction between types of behaviour that threaten public safety and types of behaviour that take place in the home. Historically, order on the streets was seen as the responsibility of the police and the state, while order in the home was seen as the responsibility of the man as head of the household. Acts of violence committed by men were subject to their interpretation, and very few found their way into the courts. Until very recently, women were not able to testify against their husbands and so, without a witness, no case of assault could be made.

In many ways, the O.J. Simpson situation is a classic case of wife battering. Friends and relatives noticed Nicole Simpson's bruises and injuries but seldom asked her about them. The police failed to make official reports of their many visits to the couple's home, laying charges on only one occasion. Mr. Simpson's friends and colleagues looked the other way. His employer, the Hertz Rent-A-Car Company, kept him on the payroll publicly endorsing their products. And Nicole did not leave her husband until years after the abuse had allegedly begun. By one account, police were called nine times to respond to calls about Mr. Simpson's violence against his wife.

Our past failure to protect battered women, and present-day attitudes that continue to tolerate men's use of force over women, can only be understood in light of history. The law has historically sanctioned the abuse of a woman within marriage as an aspect of the husband's right to chastise his wife and to confirm his ownership of her. This belief in a man's right to discipline and punish his wife has deep social roots. It springs from ancient customs about a wife's duty to "honour and obey" her husband and to stay in the marriage "until death do us part." Although women are no longer subject by law to endure their husbands' brutality, vestiges remain in the form of attitudes that tolerate a man's right to exercise a certain amount of authority over his wife and family. And little has changed for a great many women in terms of their economic propects—their ability to live independently of an abusive husband and to provide for themselves and their children.

The mythology around the all-American family, which has been embraced whole-heartedly by Canadian cultural norms, has put the family off-limits to intrusion by others and has protected the privacy of the violent man. This has allowed husbands the privacy necessary to beat their wives without fear of legal interference or other types of social sanctions. However, our romantic ideals about courtship and marriage are beginning to unravel. Gradually, an awareness is emerging that varying levels of violence and abuse exist in a great many intimate relationships, including dating relationships, common-law unions, and legal marriages. Once seen as providing a safe haven for all, the family has come under close scrutiny, and it has become clear that some of its more vulnerable members are suffering.

Sexual assault also remains hidden to a large extent because of the reluctance of many women to seek help from the police or other social agencies. The deplorable treatment of women in some highly publicized sexual assault trials has discouraged many women from reporting assaults to the police. But failure to report assaults is only one aspect of the problem. Equally problematic is the reluctance of many people to acknowledge that certain forms of sexual violence are harmful, even when these are prohibited by law. Sexual assaults in which the woman is not visibly wounded, or where there is a perception that her behaviour might have provoked the attack, often present difficulties for the police, bystanders, witnesses, and others she may turn to for help, as well as for the woman herself. Noncriminal forms of sexual harassment and intimidation are felt by many victims to be degrading and threatening, but these are frequently laughed off by both the perpetrator and bystanders. Women who object to such treatment are often admonished not to "take things so seriously." As recently as 1994, a prominent *Globe and Mail* columnist dismissed some of women's experiences of sexual and physical assault as "transient and insignificant conflicts of everyday life" because they don't conform to "truly violent behaviour as it is commonly understood by most people" (Wente, 1994). Consequently, many acts of violence and harassment remain private and hidden.

RESEARCHING VIOLENCE AGAINST WOMEN

A number of researchers have lamented the lack of empirical research that explores the full range of violence that women experience, including threats of sexual violence, sexual harassment, and sexual and physical assault (Kelly, 1987; Koss and Oros, 1982). For some time, there has been a need for representative statistical data describing the interconnections among women's experiences of violence over a lifetime. Traditional crime victimization surveys, with their narrow one-year reference period, have proven to be problematic for studying violence and fear among women. And the vast majority of empirical studies that look more closely at women's experiences of violence look at only one aspect—either wife battering, sexual assault, dating violence, or sexual harassment.

In the early 1990s, Canada's federal Department of Health recognized the need for an integrated dataset with which to expand existing knowledge about violence against women. Statistics Canada was commissioned to undertake a special survey, and it recommended a special focus survey based on the traditional crime victim survey approach. The methodology of these surveys, including the random digit dialling method of selecting respondents, techniques of telephone interviewing, complex weighting procedures, and questionnaire design, have been highly refined and could provide the necessary scientific rigour to obtain reliable data. Conducted in 1993, the Violence Against Women Survey interviewed 12 300 women by telephone about their experiences of sexual and nonsexual violence, and sexual harassment, and their perceptions of their personal safety. Details were gathered about violence committed by husbands and common-law partners, dates and boyfriends, other known men, and strangers since the women had turned 16. Survey respondents were asked about the physical and emotional effects of their experiences, their reactions, the reactions of others around them, and who they turned to for help. The primary goals of the survey were to gain a better understanding of wife battering and sexual assault within the broader social context of sexual harassment and women's fear of violence. The urgency of rethinking the common practice of measuring one-year rates of violence is underscored by the fact that *80 percent* of violent incidents reported to the Violence Against Women Survey occurred *before* the 12 months leading up to the survey (Johnson and Sacco, 1995). This was clearly a survey whose time had come. The results of this survey form a central component of this text.

FORMAT OF THIS BOOK

The topic of violence against women is extremely wide-ranging, and there are many possible ways to organize discussions around it. Women experience violence in a vast array of situations and circumstances, such as by their husbands in the privacy of their homes, on dates, in cars, in their places of work, and by strangers on the street. They experience threats of sexual violence, sexual and physical assaults, and combinations of these. These events occur with varying degrees of seriousness and consequences for the women involved.

This book begins with a synthesis of current theoretical explanations of male violence against women. Chapter 1 traces both individual-level perspectives (such as social learning, sex roles, conflict, and evolution) and situational factors (such as stress and alcohol abuse) and societal-level theories (such as routine activities, resource theory, social control and systems theory, and feminist theory). These theoretical accounts have a reciprocal relationship to research and public policy whereby they both shape and are shaped by research and public policy. By presenting theoretical debates at the outset of the text, readers will begin with a common understanding of how various forms of violence against women have been conceptualized and measured, and how societal responses have been developed in turn.

Chapter 2 describes in some detail the techniques that have been used to measure the prevalence and nature of various forms of violence against women by tracing the evolution of police statistics, clinical samples, and population surveys. Here, the methodology and the approach of the primary data source, the Violence Against Women Survey, is reviewed in detail, and its evolution is charted through other, earlier, national crime victim surveys.

Women's concerns about crime and safety have been a topic of study since the genesis of crime victim surveys two decades ago. Chapter 3 traces the links between women's perceptions of their personal security and their experiences of sexual assault, physical assault, and a wide range of potentially fear-inducing experiences of sexual harassment that do not involve an outright attack. It is argued that these noncriminal events serve to remind women in subtle and not so subtle ways of their vulnerability to sexual violence, and that these events can have negative effects on women's feelings of vulnerability that are similar to actual acts of violence.

Discussions about the prevalence and nature of sexual and physical violence against women in Chapters 4 through 6 are organized around broad relationship categories: violence by male strangers, dating violence, and assaults by husbands and common-law partners. Sexual and physical assaults are treated together within relationship categories because of the blurring between the two in some cases. Precursors or correlates of these various forms of violence are examined within a blend of theoretical and empirical evidence from the latest research on each subject, along with relevant Canadian court decisions and changes to the criminal law.

Chapter 7 follows with an examination of spousal killings. A majority of homicides involving marital partners have some evidence of previous violence against the woman, but it is frequently the husband who is killed in the fatal altercation. There is a growing recognition by the courts and by legislators of the complex situation many battered women face as their marriage deteriorates and the violence against them becomes progressively more severe. This chapter reviews some of the legal responses available to battered women in these situations.

The book ends with a look at the consequences of violence for female victims, the steps women take to obtain help from others, the role played by the criminal justice system, and recent innovations undertaken to improve the criminal justice response to abused women. Violence against women is not a private problem but a public issue that warrants public attention and debate. The aim of this book is to contribute to this debate.

Theoretical Approaches to the Study of Violence Against Women

While male violence against women is not a new phenomenon, attempts to explain it are relatively recent. Early theorists assumed that violence against women was quite rare because rapists and batterers seldom came to the attention of the authorities. From studying the small, extremely violent group of men who were charged by police and convicted for their crimes, researchers concluded that men who rape women or who beat or kill their wives must be mentally ill.

Men who were available for scientific study were actually a very unique sample. Early work in this area was based on interviews with men who had been imprisoned for viciously raping women who were strangers to them, or for killing or brutally assaulting their wives. These men were described as psychotic, paranoid, sociopathic, poorly socialized, or as having an extra Y chromosome that made them behave violently. Typically, the attacks were attributed to outbursts of uncontrollable aggression. Blame was often laid on the female victims, who were thought to be masochistic, provocative, or sexually promiscuous. Sexual assault victims were considered temptresses who were "asking for it" by their manner of dress or their lifestyle. Women who stayed with violent men obviously enjoyed being mistreated, otherwise why would they stay?

Researchers studying battered women and rape victims also noted a range of mental disturbances in these women. At the time, these were perceived to be the causes of their victimization, personality flaws that made certain women susceptible to violent attacks by men. Although mental distress is now understood to be very often a consequence of having been raped or battered, there was a widespread belief that women were responsible for causing the violence against them, for getting themselves into the situation, and for not being able to get out of it (Wardell et al., 1983). Solutions that followed from this line of thinking focused on changing women's behaviour in order to reduce their vulnerability to attack.

Over the past two decades, these assumptions have been widely criticized as, increasingly, researchers have found that abusive husbands and men who rape are, on average, no more likely to suffer from psychological disorders than men in the general population. Further, as more sophisticated techniques for measuring the prevalence of male violence against women have evolved, it has become apparent that wife battering and sexual violence are far too prevalent to be attributable to a small group of deviant men.

A wide range of theories have emerged to add to our understanding of the causes and correlates of male violence against women. Some have a psychological focus and stress individual characteristics of offenders and victims. These include explanations that centre on social learning, sex roles, situational factors such as stress and alcohol abuse, and evolution. Others have a sociological perspective and emphasize the importance of the social context of the players in the violent interaction. These include routine activities theory, resource theory, social control/ general systems theory, and feminist theory. Throughout the following discussion and the remainder of this text, it will be clear to readers that all the theories presented do not serve us equally well in explaining all types of violence, but all the theories make a contribution to ongoing debates about the causal factors at play.

Table 1.1 summarizes the various individual- and societal-level explanations discussed in this chapter and the principal tenets of each.

INDIVIDUAL-LEVEL EXPLANATIONS

SOCIAL LEARNING THEORY

According to social learning theory, people form ideas about how to behave and how to solve problems through observing influential people in their lives (Bandura, 1977). Violence becomes the way in which problems are solved if the consequences of using violence are perceived as positive, and if opportunities to learn more peaceful means are infrequent or unavailable. This is a popular explanation for the "intergenerational cycle of violence." A great deal of empirical evidence supports the theory that men who have been exposed to violence as children, either as witnesses to violence by their fathers or as victims of parental violence, are more likely to be violent toward their wives later in life (Straus, 1983; Straus, Gelles, and Steinmetz, 1980; Kalmuss, 1984; Hotaling and Sugarman, 1986; Fagan, Stewart, and Hansen, 1983).

The majority of social learning takes place within the context of the family. Family members exert a powerful influence over one another through modelling and through reinforcing some behaviours and punishing others. Murray Straus and Richard Gelles have identified certain features of the modern family that make it prone to violence. These include the intensity of the involvement of family members in one another's lives, the amount of time spent together, age and sex differences among members (both the generation gap and the battle of the sexes), the stresses of everyday life, intimacy among spouses, emotional involvement, and the privacy from outsiders afforded the family (Gelles and Straus, 1988; Gelles, 1979). Because all family members are affected in a similar manner by these factors, child abuse, sibling violence, and interspousal violence are all considered to be parts of the same phenomenon.

Images that condone violence as a way to solve life's problems are prevalent outside the family as well. Almost everyone is exposed to violence in some form, and some people are exposed to it on a regular basis through television, movies, sports, video games, music videos, and pornography. There is evidence that frequent exposure to violence can cause some individuals to model that behaviour and act aggressively toward others. Experimental research has shown that individuals will copy aggressive behaviour they see on television or in movies if it is performed by someone with whom they identify strongly or share some common characteristics (Bandura, 1977). Generally speaking, the more an individual's real-life situation matches the situation in which messages about violence are presented, the more likely these messages will be used as a guide for behaviour (Huesmann and Malamuth, 1986). Repeated exposure to messages approving of violence is likely to lead to changes in attitudes and behaviour, especially in children. The more violence children observe, the less likely they are to regard such behaviour as wrong. Over time, they can become desensitized as a result of repeated exposure.

According to social learning theory, the prevalence of violence in the larger society provides justification for the use of violence to solve problems among family members. While the primary values of the family promote a loving, caring atmosphere, abusive behaviour is also the norm. Physical punishment of children is a primary example of this (Straus, 1990b). Straus (1990b:185)

TABLE 1.1

Theoretical Explanations for Male Violence Against Women

Individual-Level Explanations

Social learning theory
- Violence as a problem-solving tool is learned through observing others and perceiving benefits or rewards to the behaviour.
- Examples that support the use of violence are prevalent in society and the family.

Sex role theory
- Men and women learn appropriate masculine and feminine behaviour through a process of socialization.
- Toughness, power, and control are valued masculine qualities.
- Sexual violence and wife battering are ways in which a man can reaffirm these masculine qualities.

Situational theories
- Violence is often a response to the high levels of conflict and stress among family members.
- Alcohol abuse causes men to act violently toward their wives.

Evolutionary theory
- Men use violence in certain social environments to gain status and respect from other men.
- Rape and other risk-taking is used significantly more often by low-status men with little or nothing to lose.
- Wife battering occurs as the result of a man's fear of losing status and exclusive control over his mate's reproductive capacity.

Societal-Level Explanations

Lifestyle/ Routine activities theory
- Exposure to high-risk situations varies according to a person's lifestyle, which is determined by age, marital status, employment status, and income.

	• Young, unmarried women suffer higher rates of violence from strangers and boyfriends because they have lifestyles that increase their proximity to potential offenders.
Resource theory	• Traditional norms give men greater status and power than women in society and the family. • Violence is the ultimate resource available to husbands to keep their wives in line.
Social control and general systems theories	• The rewards to men for using violence against their wives (a positive self-image of toughness) are greater than the costs. • Historically, men have been able to use violence against their wives without fear of retaliation or punishment. • Violence that is not sanctioned in the early stages will escalate.
Feminist theories	• Wife battering, sexual assault, sexual coercion, and harassment are the products of social institutions that historically have awarded greater privilege and authority to men over women. • Only a few of the most serious acts of violence against women have been considered by male-controlled institutions to qualify for punishment.

maintains that children learn four lessons as a result of routine types of physical punishment inflicted on them by parents:

1. Love is associated with violence, and those who love you also have the right to hurt you.

2. Physical punishment is used to train the child, which establishes the moral rightness of hitting other family members.

3. When something is really important, it justifies the use of physical force.

4. When one is under stress, tense, or angry, hitting is understandable and, to a certain extent, legitimate.

As the child grows up, these lessons are generalized beyond the parent–child relationship to other family relationships.

Reinforcement is an important part of the social learning equation: violence will increase in frequency if it produces the desired outcome (such as compliance or submission on the part of the victim, or feelings of control or power by the aggressor), and if it is not met directly with punishment. In the case of assaults against wives, social controls have been weak or inconsistent compared with the sanctions against assaulting one's boss or neighbour or practically anyone else. The legitimacy of using violence against one's wife is reinforced if, when the woman looks for help or support from other people, they fail to respond.

The greater the number of violent models in one's life, the greater the opportunities for imitating and acquiring similar behaviours. Children who receive physical punishment from their parents and who witness their fathers' aggression toward their mothers learn that violence is a legitimate way to settle differences. The number of children who witness violence against their mothers is larger than perhaps many people realize. According to Statistics Canada's national survey on violence against women, 2.6 million women in Canada have been assaulted by a marital partner, and in 39 percent of these cases, children witnessed the violence (Statistics Canada, 1993a). If each of these families had only one child, approximately 1.1 million children (many of whom are now adults) have experienced the trauma of watching their mothers being assaulted. The average number of children per couple is just under two, and since this has been higher at other times in our history, two million children, *at a minimum,* have learned some powerful lessons about the acceptability of using violence as a problem-solving tool.

The Violence Against Women survey found that men who witnessed their mothers being abused are three times as likely to be violent toward their own wives as men who grew up in non-violent homes (Rodgers, 1994). Having learned the techniques and rationalizations of wife assault, they were also significantly more likely to inflict more severe and repeated violence on their wives. Women who observed violence committed against their mothers also suffered higher rates of violence against them by their own husbands than women from violence-free homes, which suggests that some lessons are being learned about a woman's obligation to tolerate abuse from her spouse (Statistics Canada, 1993a).

With this evidence of learned violent behaviour, it is tempting to accept social learning as a simple causal explanation for why men batter and why women stay with abusive partners. However, it is important to note that the absolute number of men who did not witness violence inflicted on their mothers but were nonetheless violent toward their own wives was significantly higher than the number for whom this cause-and-effect pattern holds. In addition, a significant proportion of men who did witness violence at home were not violent toward their own wives. While intimate role models for violence may play an important role for some men, the fact that many men who abuse their wives had no such model, and many who had such a role model were not abusive, suggests that a much more complex dynamic is at work.

SEX ROLE THEORY

What are the messages in social learning through which men learn that women are legitimate targets for intimidation, threats, and violence? How is it that many men who are not violent toward their peers view aggression as an acceptable response to their wives? Sex role theory specifies the important role of gender in social learning that is necessary to answer these questions.

Sex role theory takes social learning theory one step further by incorporating the dynamics of male–female relations in explaining how some men learn to direct their anger, aggression, and violence toward women in particular. According to sex role theory, cultural messages that little boys and girls receive about appropriate male and female behaviour help explain why men are more aggressive and women are more passive and submissive in their social relations. Masculine toughness, power, and control are cultural messages that predominate in the rearing of boys, while girls grow up to follow submissive ladylike behaviour, to strive to maintain relationships, and to serve others. Male socialization that encourages toughness in boys is reinforced through peer pressure not to be a "wimp" or a "sissy." Boys who act in any way "unmanly" risk facing rejection by their peers.

Gender stereotypes act as a script through which men and women learn to act in social situations, and for the most part, male roles are awarded greater power and prestige. Television programs, advertisements, movies, and music videos often present women as having less worth and deserving less respect than men. Violent pornography conveys strong messages that men are to be sexual predators and sexually dominant in their relationships with women. Wife battering and sexual violence are seen by some as an extreme manifestation of these qualities that define masculinity and male–female relations (Clark and Lewis, 1977; Brownmiller, 1975; Russell, 1984).

Cultural stereotypes and attitudes about rape victims that blame the victims themselves for the violence they suffer have been found by researchers to co-exist with attitudes tolerant of rape and an expressed likelihood of committing rape. Among these are the beliefs that only certain types of women get raped, any woman who doesn't want sex can resist it if she wants to, women "ask for it" by the way they lead men on or the way they dress, and women cry rape when they engage in sexual intercourse that they later regret (Burt, 1980; 1991). This victim-blaming focus has been challenged over the past decade, and progress has been made in sensitizing men and women and anyone who interacts with rape victims about the damaging effects of these myths on women who are raped. However, attitudes about rape have been found to be strongest among people who hold traditional attitudes about male–female relationships, such as strongly held beliefs about stereotypical roles for men and women, distrust of the opposite sex, and belief in the legitimacy of violence and coercion in intimate relationships (Burt, 1980:229). In controlled experiments with college students, young men who accepted these myths about rape were more likely to say they would rape or force a woman into unwanted sex (Check and Malamuth, 1985; Malamuth, 1981a).

Some research has presented evidence of a connection between the consumption of pornographic material that depicts women as willing victims of sexual violence and the development of a willingness to rape. When sexual violence is portrayed in the media, there are often strong suggestions that the victim desires the degradation and derives pleasure from the violence inflicted on her, and no negative consequences ensue to the one abusing her (Malamuth and Briere, 1986). Images that present sexual arousal simultaneously with violence may condition the viewer to act aggressively to sexual stimuli. Studies have also shown that exposure to films that portray women enjoying rape can produce an increase in acceptance of violence against women, an increase in aggressive behaviour toward women, a desensitization to sexual violence, and an increase in reported willingness to commit rape (Linz, 1989; Check and Guloien, 1989; Check and Malamuth, 1983; Check and Malamuth, 1985). Those who don't actually commit sexual assault as a result of viewing pornography nevertheless may develop the belief that women are legitimate victims of violence and then lend support to their peers who behave abusively toward women. The fact that attitudes toward sexual violence can be learned through exposure to images that condone it lends support to the sex role theory.

Even in the absence of pornography, men who relate strongly to the masculine ideals of toughness and dominance may be more likely to accept it as their right to physically abuse their wives and to take what they want from women sexually. They may demand obedience and submission from their wives, dates, and girlfriends, and use threats or violence to achieve their demands.

Both rape and wife battering have been described as methods through which men overcompensate for underlying feelings of inadequacy and express their insecurities about their own power, strength, control, authority, and identity (Groth, 1979). Rape and battering are seen to represent extreme acting-out of these masculine qualities (Russell, 1984; Medea and Thompson, 1974; MacLeod, 1980; Clark and Lewis, 1977).

Psychologist Nancy Chodorow (1974) offers a helpful description of the early training boys receive to become abusive toward women later in life. She argues that because both girls and boys usually receive their primary care from a female, the formation of gender identity is different for girls and boys. Female identity formation takes place in the context of an ongoing relationship with someone whom the little girl sees as being much like herself. Girls see the world as comprised of relationships with and connections to others. Identity formation happens within a context of ongoing attachment to the most significant person in the young girl's life.

Boys also live the first few years with a strong attachment to their mothers, especially if contact with their fathers is infrequent or missing. But, in defining themselves as masculine, boys must separate from their mothers. During early formation of their gender identity, the emphasis for boys is on individuation and separateness. Later, when they perceive men to have greater power and prestige than women, boys develop a strong need to reject any identification with anything feminine. The result, according to Chodorow, is that the development of male gender identity depends on the rejection of all things female. Some men learn that to be truly masculine they must repress all things feminine in themselves and devalue them in others. They may try to prove their masculinity through displays of physical strength or daring that may involve violence. The stronger and more frequent these displays, the stronger they perceive their rejection of femininity to be and the more masculine they see themselves. Individual women, who personify femininity, are considered legitimate targets for aggression.

As Elizabeth Stanko (1985:73) points out, these feminine personality traits are important with respect to understanding women's reactions to abusive husbands. She writes that "if females are connected to the world through relationships, and particularly their relationships to men, they are likely to be confused by aggression exhibited toward them within their relationships. Perhaps they aren't giving enough, they might think, perhaps they somehow provoked a(n) ... encounter." Women are encouraged to look to their own behaviour for an explanation of male violence and aggression and to see the failure of the relationship as their own failure.

The man who must appear to be in control, powerful, and masterful at all times may retaliate for feelings of inadequacy or failure through violence against his wife. In this way, he attempts to reassert control, to prove that he at least is master in his own home. Sexual assault provides the same function—it enables a man to exhibit dominance over someone less powerful than himself, re-establish his masculinity, and demean femininity at the same time. Through battering and sexual violence he proves to himself, his victim, and the world that he is a real man. Men who feel secure in their masculinity, and about what it means to themselves to be male, have no need to rape or to assert their dominance over women.

SITUATIONAL THEORIES

Violence is seen by some researchers as a reaction to situational factors such as stress or family conflict. When faced with stressful situations, individuals seek to regain control over the situation, and violence is one possible response. The family is a group with inherently high levels of conflict and stress. It is constantly undergoing changes and transitions, and specific stresses felt by one family member will be felt either directly or indirectly by other members.

Some believe that domestic violence occurs predominantly among lower-income families, where stress and frustrations associated with poverty and low-status occupations are greatest. Others have challenged this assumption by suggesting that unemployment affects middle-income men more profoundly because it threatens their self-image to a greater degree, whereas lower-income men are more likely to expect and experience periods of unemployment. The image of abusive men as being from lower-income families may actually be due to their greater visibility to researchers and data-gatherers because of the limited options available to their victims apart from contacting the police or other agencies for help.

Straus (1990b) suggests that while stress is an important component of the dynamic of family violence, stress in itself does not directly cause violence. People are unlikely to respond violently to stress unless

1. the individual has learned to behave aggressively in response to stress;

2. such a response to stress is culturally recognized;

3. the man believes in male dominance, especially if he has achieved a position of power within the relationship; and

4. the situation is one that will likely produce rewards for aggression.

In most cases, the victim bears no direct responsibility for the aggressor's anger and violence but receives the brunt of it (Sebastian, 1983). According to the situational stress school of thought, efforts to reduce violence must target the stressful conditions under which many families live.

Alcohol abuse is a second situational factor thought to be linked directly to violence. Alcohol can alter judgment and reasoning and cause people to behave in ways they wouldn't normally behave. Many battered women describe how their husbands become "monsters" when they drink (Martin, 1981:55) and that their husbands are violent only when drunk. Although there is a link between aggression and alcohol in some people, there is considerable debate about the factors that mediate the effects of alcohol. There is little doubt that alcohol functions to reduce inhibitions, alter judgment, and increase the probability of socially unacceptable behaviours; however, most experts would also agree that the relationship is not a direct cause-and-effect one. For instance, people who have a tendency to act aggressively may drink, knowing that doing so will give them an excuse for their violent behaviour. Many people allow a "time out" to be associated with drunkenness, in which drinkers are excused and forgiven for socially unacceptable behaviour that occurs while drinking (Gelles, 1974). For example, bystanders, and often victims of violence, are willing to excuse the violence when the aggressor has been drinking alcohol. Interviews with women battered by heavy drinkers suggest that these women may have a need to attribute the batterer's violence to alcohol as a way to understand and excuse what has happened to them (Dobash and Dobash, 1979).

The legal defence of drunkenness continues to go in and out of favour in Canada. In 1994, the Supreme Court of Canada allowed the defence of severe drunkenness and overturned the conviction of a man who had been found guilty of sexually assaulting an elderly woman (*R. v. Daviault*, 1994). One justification of the court in granting this defence was that the degree of intoxication was so extreme that the situation would rarely arise again. In the months that followed, the same defence was successfully used in several acquittals of intoxicated men who had assaulted women. In 1995, Parliament passed amendments to the Criminal Code that disallow the drunkenness defence in most cases of violence involving women and children.

Despite conflicting opinions about the causal role played by alcohol abuse, there is empirical evidence that women who live with heavy drinkers run a far greater risk of violence, and that more severe violence is perpetrated by men who are drinking at the time of the assaults. According to Statistics Canada's Violence Against Women Survey, women who are married to or living with heavy drinkers are five times more likely to be assaulted by their partners than are women who live with nondrinkers (Statistics Canada, 1993a). Half of all batterers were usually drinking at the time of the assault, and women who suffered very serious abuse (being beaten up or suffering injuries that required medical attention) were almost twice as likely to state that the man was drinking at the time than women suffering less serious violence (Statistics Canada, 1994a). And, the more a man drinks, the greater the likelihood that drinking will be involved in incidents of assault against his wife: 28 percent of battered women who say their husbands rarely drink to excess (5 or more drinks at one time) nevertheless reported them to be usually drinking at the time of the assaults, compared with 68 percent of women who say their husbands regularly drink heavily. However, drinking is not the only factor at play, as a substantial amount of violence was perpetrated by abstainers and moderate drinkers.

Kantor and Straus (1990) point out that the link between alcohol abuse and violence may be spurious in that both the drinking and the violence may be caused by an underlying third factor. For example, cultural norms support both domination over women and excessive drinking as acceptable masculine behaviours. In their research, Kantor and Straus found that the combination of low occupational status, drinking, and approval of violence against one's wife is associated with the highest likelihood of violence. Men with these characteristics had a rate of wife abuse eight times higher than others, but the authors also point out that two-thirds of these men did not assault their wives. They found that men who claim to disapprove of a man slapping his wife nevertheless had higher rates of violence against their wives when they drank heavily, perhaps acting on a belief that drinking alcohol permits them to assault their wives, or a belief in a "time out" that permits them to deny responsibility for their actions. Briddell et al. (1978, as quoted in Russell, 1984:129), in experimental research with college students, found that although alcohol did not significantly affect levels of sexual arousal to depictions of rape, subjects who *believed* they had consumed alcohol were more highly aroused by rape scenes than those who believed they had consumed a nonalcoholic drink, regardless of the actual contents of the drink. These findings support the "time-out" theory, in which alcohol is used as an excuse for behaviour that would normally be considered unacceptable. The spurious third factor in explaining the link between alcohol abuse and acts of sexual assault and wife battering would seem to be cultural factors that increase a tolerance for both drunkenness and violence under certain conditions.

EVOLUTIONARY THEORY

Evolutionary psychology is concerned with the processes through which certain human traits come to predominate as a result of natural selection. As human beings have adapted to their environment and developed techniques for survival, certain characteristics that enhance the ability of the species to survive will surpass other, less adaptive, characteristics. Canadian psychologists Martin Daly and Margo Wilson have developed an evolutionary explanation for how men's use of violence can be an adaptive behaviour that helps them adjust to certain environmental circumstances, rather than being a purely deviant act.

From an evolutionary perspective, violence is functional behaviour, something that men in particular were designed to do through natural selection. Men have evolved to be effective users of violence because they have had to compete with other males for sexual access to females (Daly and Wilson, 1988). Throughout evolution, men of higher status have been assured of both easy access to females and respect from other men, and so men have competed for status with other males. Organisms (including human organisms) have also evolved to expend their lives improving the chances that they and their offspring will survive. This is achieved in the human world through marriage, sexual reproduction, and the cooperative rearing of offspring. In any species in which females spend a lot of time and energy caring for offspring, males will compete for exclusive rights to a female.

There are immediate and long-term costs of pregnancy, childbirth, lactation, and child rearing for women, and so to enhance their procreating efforts, women have had to be discriminating about whether and with whom they will mate. Women generally try to select men who are likely to produce high-quality offspring and will invest economic resources, time, and energy in them. Men, on the other hand, could afford to be less choosy and could copulate with a wider variety of mates because the costs of mating were lower for them (Shields and Shields, 1983). The genes of men who were able to copulate with large numbers of women eventually survived over those of less aggressive men.

Evolutionary theorists interpret violence against wives in light of the way males have had to compete for exclusive access to a female's reproductive capacity. If men can control women's reproductive capacity, they increase the opportunities for their own progeny, and one way to do this is through marriage. When the marriage bond is broken through adultery, it is more likely to be the man who is adulterous, yet men are more likely to feel that adultery, when committed by women at least, warrants divorce. The reason for this is that adultery has very different consequences for men and women. When women are adulterous, men lose exclusive sexual ownership over them and can never be absolutely sure about paternity, whereas maternity is seldom questioned. If his investment in parenting is to pay off, the man must be sure of his offspring, and therefore he must be sure that his mate is faithful to him alone.

Men of lower status who lack the resources to attract a woman for legitimate mating are more likely to take sex by force because they have little or no chance of reproductive success through socially acceptable means. Taking very dangerous risks to raise their status may actually make sense for males who have nothing to lose and no legitimate prospects (Wright, 1995; Daly and Wilson, 1988). Nonconsensual mating has evolved as a reproductive technique but is used more frequently among low-status men, because the social costs of rape are significantly lower for these men, the potential benefits of rape in terms of acquired status are greater, and other means of achieving status are unavailable to them. Evolutionary psychologists try to explain how human nature has evolved to respond to environmental clues in an adaptive sense. In some environments, violence is an adaptive tool available to men to raise their esteem in the eyes of their peers and improve their reproductive prospects.

From an evolutionary perspective, the great majority of violent incidents result from status competition among males (Daly and Wilson, 1988). Males display the power to invoke violence, and they assault and kill other males over challenges to their status. Status plays an important role in attracting a mate and so must be defended, even at the risk of injury or death. Of course, there are other means through which men can achieve status. In environments where violence does not enhance status, men often compete intellectually or through sports or other ways. But violence has commonly been used by men throughout human history as a tool to let other men know they are prepared to fight to defend their turf. Much violence and impulsive risk-taking are explicable once they are viewed within a larger social context of reputations, social status, and ongoing relationships and are not separated from the social environment in which they occur (Wright, 1995).

Violence and killings among family members may seem anomalous within an evolutionary perspective in that they violate principles of cooperative child rearing and reduced conflict among individuals who are related to one another. Spouses share common interests in the rearing of offspring that should reduce the chances of violence between them. This apparent anomaly is addressed by Daly and Wilson (1988:182) by what they describe as "male sexual proprietariness," or perceived right of certain entitlements over women, which is demonstrated by men's desire to control the activities of their wives. This proprietariness is cross-culturally universal and is central to understanding how and why men use threats or violence to establish and maintain control over their wives, even to the point of killing them.

In fact, male sexual jealousy has been found to be the leading motive in spousal homicide and spousal violence. In every society for which they were able to find a sample of spousal homicides, Daly and Wilson found that the majority of cases arose out of the husband's jealous, violent response to his wife's real or imagined infidelity or threats to leave him (1988:202). Adultery in many of the societies they studied has been construed to justify a man resorting to violence or even homicide against his wife (1988:194).

Many of the same motivations have been noted in cases of nonlethal assaults on wives. The simple suspicion, or in some cases the *apprehension,* of adultery as the man faces a loss of control over his wife has been cited as a greater incentive to violence than any other factor (Dobash and Dobash, 1979; 1984; Martin, 1981; Pagelow, 1981; Walker, 1979; 1984). Statistics Canada's Violence Against Women Survey found that jealous and controlling tactics were used against wives by three-quarters of violent men and by virtually all men who inflicted the most serious violence against their wives. Most common were jealously guarding her contact with other men, demeaning her through name calling, and attempting to control her whereabouts and isolate her from family and friends. Suspicions of infidelity represent a challenge to a man's respect, and violence is a way to regain this respect, particularly if he finds support and increased esteem in his peer group. In extreme cases, such a man can barely stand to let his wife out of his sight lest she leave him for another man. In the majority of such cases, the suspicion and jealousy are unfounded.

SOCIETAL-LEVEL EXPLANATIONS

LIFESTYLE/ROUTINE ACTIVITIES THEORY

A number of theories have emerged that take into account the interaction effect of victims and offenders in explaining the differential rates of victimization among members of the population. They are known as *routine activities*, *lifestyle*, or *exposure* theories. The central component of these theories is lifestyle, which refers to the ways in which people distribute their time and energies across work, leisure, and recreational activities. Lifestyle differences are affected by certain personal characteristics, such as marital status, age, employment status, and income.

Lifestyle is an all-encompassing concept that affects how visible and how accessible one will be in particular places and times as a potential target of predatory crimes. The higher rates of violence suffered by young single women compared with older or married women are said to be a consequence of the fact that young women enjoy a less structured lifestyle with fewer social constraints. Young single women tend to be freer of family and household responsibilities and enjoy greater leisure time and opportunities to spend time away from family members in public places. They are vulnerable to sexual assault because they frequent places, such as bars, parties, and fraternity houses, also frequented by young single males, who are the group with the highest rates of offending.

Miethe, Stafford, and Long (1987) have argued that the routine activities theory has stronger relevance to property crime than to violent crime because the nature of the two differs significantly. They maintain that while property crime is motivated by material gain, violent crime often involves interpersonal conflicts or disagreements, involving players known to one another, that are spontaneous and emotional in nature. The perpetrators of violent crimes, therefore, do not fit with the theory's assumptions about offenders who rationally calculate opportunities to achieve their goals. Kennedy and Forde (1990) counter this argument with an analysis of the lifestyles and violent experiences of young single males, concluding that the very public lifestyle of this group creates exposure to risky situations. They claim that although violent crime may be spontaneous, the victims of violent crime are more likely to be found without adequate protection in places where conflict flares up.

Three criteria must be satisfied before a crime can occur: there must be a motivated offender, a vulnerable target, and an absence either of capable guardianship or of factors that offer protection to oneself or one's property (Cohen and Felson, 1979). To the extent that a person's lifestyle increases her or his proximity to motivated offenders or attractiveness as a target, or diminishes guardianship over her or him, the chance of being a victim increases. Bars, parties, and nightclubs are places where sexual aggression is likely to occur and where the ability of young women to protect themselves is diminished. By comparison, the lifestyles of older women are likely to encompass interaction with other older women in locations where the risk of violent victimization is low. Rates of violence reported by older and married women are low as a consequence.

Cohen and Felson explain crime rates as a by-product of broad societal factors such as smaller households, increased labour force participation and university attendance for women, and increased consumerism. Over the past few decades, there has been growing tendency for people to pursue leisure activities away from the home among nonfamily members. Women, in particular, have joined the workforce and entered postsecondary institutions in increasing numbers, which has brought them into more frequent contact with motivated offenders in both work and leisure domains. This shift in routine activities has created greater opportunities for those motivated to commit crimes while exposing greater numbers of women to the dangers of the public sphere.

Routine activity theorists do not try to explain offender motivation. That there are motivated offenders is taken as a given. Instead, theorists maintain that variations in the number of motivated offenders are a necessary but insufficient explanation for differences in the rates of victimization. Equally important are variations in the opportunities to commit crimes. Opportunities are influenced by the exposure of individuals to high-risk situations, which is influenced in turn by lifestyle. Exposure to risk, coupled with the presence of motivated offenders and the absence of capable guardianship, increases the likelihood that victimization will occur. The value of this theory will be demonstrated when we turn to discussing violence by strangers and dates in Chapters 4 and 5.

RESOURCE THEORY

Resource theory is based on the premise that the strong and powerful will dominate the weak and less powerful. For centuries, there was support in law for men to assume control over and responsibility for women in all decision-making within the family and society. Within families, men were permitted to use the level of force necessary to correct or punish their wives and children (Dobash and Dobash, 1979). While laws governing the chastisement of wives have changed, certain norms and customs continue to award men greater status than women in many aspects of modern life.

According to resource theory, men have retained power over their wives because they typically have greater resources in the forms of income and social standing outside the family, and knowledge and expertise that they have acquired from working outside the home. Because of these greater resources, men can display more power and force against their wives than women can display against their husbands. Ironically, the more power and force men are able to display, the less likely they are to resort to actual violence in order to maintain control over their wives. Violence and the threat of violence are used to maintain the husband's dominant position only when he perceives other resources to be depleted (Bersani and Chen, 1988).

Resource theory claims that traditional norms that support asymmetrical power relations in families are a necessary component of men's use of violence against their wives, but these norms are insufficient to explain the violence entirely. Chronic unemployment, low income, or low-status occupations produce high rates of stress and conflict in these families and present a serious threat to the man's attempts to achieve and maintain his status. When he suffers a real or imagined loss of status and power, either at home or in work or social situations, this man may attempt to reinstate his status and power at home through physically dominating his wife (Finkelhor, 1983).

Violence is considered to be the ultimate resource available to husbands to keep their wives in line. Men who subscribe to cultural norms that allow them to dominate women, yet lack the resources that give them higher status, may turn to violence to reestablish their dominance. Violence will be used to compensate for the lack of other resources, such as money, occupational status, or education. Men who suffer stresses associated with unemployment, or who have lower-level jobs or poor social standing, may take out their anger and frustration on their wives. It follows from this theory that because different social classes and ethnic groups have different levels of access to resources, levels of family violence can be expected to vary among social groups.

For large numbers of men, there is a dissonance between cultural ideals about male status and the actual status they achieve through education, income, or occupation. A man who feels his status threatened by a more educated or successful wife may resort to violence to maintain his perceived right to assert his authority over her and to regain a sense of personal power and control. Men who assault their wives may do so because of feelings of failure with respect to cultural ideals about male status, because of anger against someone who is seen as somehow responsible for the loss of power, or simply as a way to regain control by victimizing someone who is less powerful.

Adherents to the resource theory contend that current rates of violence against wives are a result of the confusion surrounding the roles and expectations of men and women in contemporary marriages. As confusion reigns between traditional norms and values and the transition to more egalitarian norms, men may use violence to establish and maintain their authority over their wives, who have traditionally had inferior roles. That is, men may feel the need to assert their authority over women if they are threatened with losing it (Bersani and Chen, 1988). Resource theorists predict that the changing expectations of women and their demands for equality may actually increase violence against them, at least in the short term, until broader agreement is reached about role expectations for women and men. Eventually, equality for women will yield a decline in assaults on wives by decreasing men's perceived rights to punish their wives and increasing women's alternatives and the responses of social institutions (Kalmuss and Straus, 1990).

SOCIAL CONTROL AND GENERAL SYSTEMS THEORIES

Richard Gelles, a well-known family violence researcher, maintains that the approach that best integrates the key elements of the diverse theories used to explain human violence is social control theory (Gelles, 1983). This theory is based on the joint assumptions that people will behave in a socially inappropriate manner unless there are adequate control mechanisms to prevent such behaviour, and that human behaviour is guided by the pursuit of reward and the avoidance of punishment. Extending these assumptions to families, violence is used against family members because the rewards of being violent are greater than the costs, and because social controls against violence are weak at best. Quite simply, people hit and abuse other family members because they can get away with it (Gelles, 1983; Gelles and Straus, 1988).

Many factors reduce social control over the family and reduce the costs of using violence, such as inequality among family members, the privacy of the family unit, and norms that support the image of the powerful man. Inequality is manifested in the fact that men are bigger and stronger than their wives and children, and enjoy higher social status. For the most part, they can use violence without fear of retaliation and without fear of economic or social repercussions. Women do not use violence against men to the same degree because they fear reprisals from their husbands, who are more powerful physically and economically. Witnesses, police, and courts historically have avoided intervening in what they perceive to be private family matters, which limits the social control over the goings-on in the privacy of the household. The "real man" image that continues to be celebrated in North American culture provides rewards for aggressive and violent behaviour.

A related explanation is the general systems theory of family violence. This theory perceives violence to be a product of the family system. Like any system, families have interdependent parts that function to maintain the balance of the system through a process of action and reaction. Gelles (1979) argues that there are certain characteristics of family systems that make them ripe for violence, such as the amount of time family members spend together, the intensity of their involvement, conflicting priorities and needs, and the right to influence others. The role expectations and obligations of members of a family create conflicting demands on members and pressures on the system that may erupt into violence.

Systems regulate themselves through feedback. Batterers who receive positive feedback or perceive positive results from using violence (such as bringing a partner under control, winning an argument, maintaining authority in the family, or commanding respect) will respond with more violence. Negative feedback (such as threats of ending the relationship, or strong negative reactions from outsiders or other family members) serves to suppress the level of violence. If the violent person's goals are satisfied and positive feedback occurs, the possibility of future violence increases and violence may become an established part of the system (Margolin, Sibner, and Gleberman, 1988).

From a systems perspective, a woman who makes a commitment of marriage to a man who has behaved abusively toward her is providing positive feedback that encourages violence in the future. Women who are willing to forgive and forget, or who do not respond to discourage the abuse at the first instance, are providing positive feedback and soon the violence becomes an established pattern (Giles-Sims, 1983). After a certain amount of escalating violence has occurred, negative feedback on the part of the woman will not be effective and she must turn to outsiders for help. Women who are successful in finding support outside the family that helps them to provide negative feedback may be successful in breaking the pattern of violence. If these women then return to the relationship after leaving, they are providing positive feedback to established patterns and the abuse will likely continue.

FEMINIST THEORIES

Feminist theories integrate the principles of several of the theories previously discussed but also incorporates the historical and institutional backdrop in which sex role learning and male status acquisition take place. While several other theories emphasize the role of male status as a causative factor in men's use of violence, feminist theories trace the historical significance of the socio-economic and legal structures and practices that have fostered male privilege and women's dependence on male partners. Men and women learn culturally appropriate sex roles through a process of socialization, but the sex roles do not exist outside of laws and practices that implicitly and explicitly approve of greater power for males. Feminist theory explores the ways in which social relationships and institutions enable male violence against women to occur. A central organizing theme of feminist theories is the patriarchal organization of society.

Rebecca and Russell Dobash (1979:43), prominent feminist researchers, describe two necessary elements of patriarchy: social structures that define and reinforce a superior position for men, and an ideology that serves to reinforce acceptance of this state of affairs by both men and women. The social structures that create and sustain unequal power relations between men and women include laws and legal institutions, religious institutions, educational and health systems, and the family. Ideology is the process by which this hierarchical system is accepted as natural and good by the majority of the population. Male violence against women is permitted to continue because of the unequal status, authority, and power of men and women within the family and the wider society.

Feminist theories view wife battering and sexual assault as natural products of this system of unequal relations between men and women that has existed historically in Western society. The Dobashes assert that "men who assault their wives are actually living up to cultural prescriptions that are cherished in Western society—aggressiveness, male dominance, female subordination—and they use physical force to enforce that domination" (1979:24). The origins of the patriarchal family and the inferior position of women in the family have been documented by many writers (Martin, 1981; Brownmiller, 1975; Dobash and Dobash, 1979; Walker, 1979; Clark and Lewis, 1977; Pleck, 1989). For centuries, men have abused and even killed disobedient wives with the support of the state and the church. Within the last century, the legal system permitted husbands the right to physically chastise their wives, and until just over a decade ago men were entitled to rape their wives with impunity under laws that didn't recognize rape by marital partners and didn't permit women to testify against their spouses.

A result of the unequal status of women is that men occupying powerful positions in the legal, medical, educational, and religious systems have had the authority to define what acts of violence against women would be considered injurious and what actions would be undertaken by these institutions in response (Kelly, 1988:138). Since primarily men have occupied powerful roles (lawyer, judge, police officer, legislator, husband) and women have not, men have had the power to define what is harmful and what is not, and to perpetrate acts of violence against women without great fear of reprisal. For centuries, only the most extreme forms of violence that resulted in severe injury were considered appropriate for criminal justice sanctions. Even very violent assaults, if committed under certain circumstances such as within intimate relationships or against "loose" women, were excused. Because women historically have had minimal access to power positions, they have been unable to change the structures or norms that are biased against them (Kelly, 1988:27).

While the concept of patriarchal power has gained currency in research on violence against women, the important work of theorists such as James Messerschmidt (1993) question the wholesale way in which it has been applied to explain gender relations and men's use of violence to gain power over women. Messerschmidt objects to the one-dimensional way in which masculinity and femininity are commonly defined by both sex role theory and feminist theory, where one type of masculinity—the "typical" male—is endorsed. This approach cannot explain why it is that men who are exposed to the same cultural conditioning do not exhibit the same violent behaviour, except to say that all men are susceptible to prevailing messages about male–female power relations.

Messerschmidt argues that masculinity and violence and the relationship between them is much more complex. He maintains that sex role theory and feminist theory are incapable of explaining the various ways that masculinity and femininity are constructed under different social conditions (1993:47). He argues that a number of different "masculinities" are possible depending on a man's social position, as determined by class and race, and the particular social situation, such as the school, peer group, family, or workplace. The fact that men as a group control the economic, religious, and political institutions in society allows them to impose their interests, authority, and control over women. But all men do not have the same access to resources, which permits some to have greater power over women, and over other groups of men, than others. Masculinities are constructed relative to an individual man's position in society, the resources at hand, and the constraints of specific circumstances.

Hegemony is the dominant conception of reality through which members of a society learn socially appropriate behaviour (Messerschmidt, 1993:81). *Hegemonic masculinity* is defined as the dominant form of masculinity to which most men subscribe, and is characterized by a gendered division of labour and power and male dominance and control over women. Messerschmidt writes, "In contemporary Western industrialized societies, hegemonic masculinity is defined through work in the paid-labour market, the subordination of women, heterosexism, and the driven and uncontrollable sexuality of men" (1993:82). However, Messerschmidt considers the concept of "patriarchy" to be helpful in describing only a certain type of masculinity where men are "patriarchs in the traditional sense," completely controlling women's labour and sexuality.

Men and women both strive to present themselves to others in their social group as "essentially" masculine or feminine, and the way this is accomplished differs depending on the specific situation. Men and women react to unique situations and circumstances to produce a "gendered response." Economically marginal men and women will respond differently from middle-class men and women due to the differences in their position in the social structure and the resources available to them. Lower-income men are denied masculine status in the ways available to middle-income men through education and economic success. What is left for them is physical and sexual demonstrations of power with which to construct their masculinity.

Like traditional feminist theorists, Messerschmidt contends that a man who beats his wife is punishing her for failing to fulfil her obligations as a wife (in the gendered division of labour and power) and for challenging his dominance and his patriarchal rights (1993:145). When his right to assert his authority over her is questioned in the slightest, when she threatens his control and his power over the gendered division of labour through her actions or words, his "essential nature" is threatened. The gendered division of labour and power within the household is so closely tied to the man's sense of his own masculinity and his understanding of the woman's essential femininity, that the slightest threat to this order results in a violent response toward her. "The wife beater attempts to resolve in *his* way what he regards as a conflict over this 'fair' arrangement, even when the wife is not actively or consciously contesting that 'fair' houschold organization" (1993:146).

Rape is explained by Messerschmidt as the product of a specific type of socially constructed masculinity that represents the desire to dominate, control, and humiliate women. An essential component of constructing masculinity is to distance oneself from femininity, to demonstrate one's essential lack of femaleness. The fewer the resources for proving maleness legitimately, the greater the need to dominate women physically. Messerschmidt argues that the function of group rape is to "strengthen the fiction of masculine power" for working-class or racial-minority boys through a "publicly aggressive form of masculinity" (1993:116). Rape by college boys serves many of the same functions but is more likely to involve the use of alcohol in place of overt physical violence.

Sexual harassment in the workplace is also interpreted by Messerschmidt as constructing a particular type of masculinity that differs for working-class and managerial-class men. Working-class men associate manual labour with a certain type of masculinity that celebrates physical strength (1993:126). At the same time, the workplace experience is humiliating to these men because it denies them certain masculine ideals of independence, control, and dominance. When women enter the workplace, two things happen: they are perceived by men as competing for men's jobs and threatening their job security, and they devalue the masculine quality of the work. If women can do the same work, it loses some of its distinctly masculine character. Sexual harassment serves to discourage women from competing with men in the job market, it communicates anger toward them for intruding in a male arena and for invading their economic and social space, it serves to degrade and ridicule women, and it emphasizes their femaleness and the differences between men and women (1993:132).

The type of sexual harassment manual labourers engage in is likely to be publicly humiliating and sexually demeaning. These men are looking to elevate their masculine status in the eyes of their peers through sexual harassment. Managerial-class men, who have greater status and power in the workplace over women and other men, are more likely to make direct sexual advances toward their female subordinates and to threaten them with job action and demotions if they refuse to submit. For these men, sexual harassment of female subordinates is a means of reinforcing their power and their place in the hierarchy (1993:139). Sexual harassment in both cases provides a resource for constructing specific types of masculinity.

Many theorists before Messerschmidt have considered the role of masculinity in men's use of violence against women. The major difference between Messerschmidt's analysis and that of others is that he presumes masculinity *not* to be a fixed entity (1993:xi). Other theories tend to present masculinity as an inherent unchanging trait of the man that is formed early in life and is a cause in his decision to use violence. Messerschmidt turns this around and views masculinity as constructed and reconstructed in everyday interactions with others. Masculinity is something that is constructed with available resources, and various forms of violence against women are resources that are available to all men. The masculinities of the labourer, the middle-class college student, and the middle manager are all constructed with different resources, and different forms of violence against women is the result.

SUMMARY

Our understanding of the complex processes involved in male violence against women has evolved considerably from an early focus on individual character flaws to an appreciation of the relevance of societal and structural factors, and the processes through which men and women learn and display gender-differentiated behaviour. Feminist theories, and offshoots like the reconceptualization of masculinity, lend themselves well to integration with other theories such as resource theory, social learning, sex roles theory, and evolutionary psychology. The theories discussed in this chapter argue for an integrated approach that takes into account a multiplicity of factors associated with acts of violence against women. It will also become clear as we consider the circumstances and dynamics surrounding various types of assault on women that some theories have greater relevance than others. But before considering the applicability of these theoretical approaches, we turn our attention to some of the methods and sources of data available to researchers in this area of study.

Methods of Measurement

In studying violence against women, researchers frequently begin with questions such as "How many women are affected?" "How often?" "Who is affected?" and "What are the consequences?" Answers to these questions are important for determining the seriousness or magnitude of the problem, and to attract the attention of other researchers, policy-makers, and legislators. But the answers are not altogether straightforward.

The most common and longstanding source of statistical information about violent crime is the Uniform Crime Reporting (UCR) Survey, which records criminal incidents that come to the attention of the police (Canadian Centre for Justice Statistics, 1993a). Police statistics are problematic because, for a variety of reasons, a very significant proportion of all types of crimes are not reported to the police, many of which involve serious harm to victims. In order to get around the shortcomings of police statistics, early researchers began using the testimonies of victims in counselling or offenders in treatment to examine the impact of violence on victims and the motives behind these offences. From the testimony of these subjects, researchers began to understand that incidents of sexual assault and wife battering were not rare, sadistic acts of a few psychotic men and were much more prevalent than available statistics or popular belief would suggest. But these approaches also had their limitations. Like police statistics, the samples of women and men used in these studies were extreme cases and not representative of all incidents.

Random sample surveys of the population emerged as a social science tool in the late 1970s, and criminal justice researchers began exploring the "dark figure" of crime that is not reported to the police. One purpose of these surveys was to estimate the prevalence of criminal victimization in the general population. Specialized surveys of family violence and violence against women followed as researchers attempted to address some of the short-comings demonstrated by traditional crime victim surveys in measuring these events. Statistics Canada's national survey on violence against women is one such special survey that is based on the random sample method of surveying. It provides representative data on the nature and the extent of a wide range of violent events reported by women and is referred to extensively throughout this text.

This chapter explores the various methods that have been used to measure the dimensions and the nature of male violence against women, including police statistics, clinical samples, and population surveys, as well as a detailed description of the methodology of the national Violence Against Women Survey. The advantages and limitations of each approach are discussed.

POLICE STATISTICS

For decades, information collected by police and entered into the UCR Survey has formed the basis for official crime rates and criminal justice policies. Yet students of criminology and criminal justice practitioners know that police statistics have certain limitations as a measurement of crime, including the fact that many serious acts of violence are never reported to the police and so will not appear in their records. Another limitation relates to the high degree of discretion that accompanies the police officer's role. While discretion and professional judgment are essential components of effective policing, both can have a profound effect on what is eventually recorded as a crime in police statistics.

Police officers on patrol act as gatekeepers through which complaints from citizens must pass before becoming part of the official crime count. When officers are dispatched to answer calls for assistance, they take with them a personal set of values and beliefs about what constitutes a criminal assault by a man against his wife and what is merely a "domestic dispute." They generally know what kinds of cases Crown prosecutors have set as priorities and which are likely to be dismissed before they get to court; they know from experience what kind of evidence is required to secure a conviction at a criminal trial, and they know before they respond to a call what priorities have been established by their own departments. Dispatchers may be under many of the same directives, and so some calls for assistance may not even be forwarded to a police officer for action (Jaffe et al., 1993).

But the filtering process begins even before a call is made to the police. A labelling process takes place in which the victim defines the incident as a crime and something that is appropriate for the police to know about. A number of factors influence this process and her eventual decision to call the police or not: the seriousness of the event for her; her relationship to the offender; her age, education, and social standing; the circumstances surrounding the incident; her past experiences with the same offender and the same type of incident; and her past experiences with the police. Her relationship to the offender is a critical factor influencing the labelling process and her eventual decision to involve the police or other outsiders. If she or others around her minimize, excuse, or accept a certain amount of violence in the context of marriage, she is unlikely to feel it is appropriate to call the police when her husband assaults her.

All of these factors combine to influence the discretion of both the victim and the individual officer who responds to a complaint. Each can have a significant impact on the official rates of violence recorded by the police, and each may vary among different communities and within the same community over a period of time. Changes in the levels of sexual assault or wife assault over time may reflect real changes in the number of these crimes committed, or they may reflect changes in the willingness of women to report to the police, changes in policies set by individual departments, increases in resources dedicated to responding to certain types of crimes, or even improvements in technology and the ability of the police to detect and record incidents that are reported to them. The way the police record certain crimes, such as wife assault, can also be affected by perceptions of the seriousness of violence among family members and the extent of harm done, perceptions that have undergone dramatic change in recent years. One research study in Newfoundland found that many calls to the police involving violence by men against their wives were recorded by the police as "drunk and disorderly in the home" or "weapons offences" rather than some type of assault, categories that were not even counted as violent crimes (O'Grady, 1991).

When interpreting police statistics, it is also important to note that the UCR Survey covers crimes that have been reported to and *substantiated* by the police. If, after a preliminary investigation, the police officer determines that an offence did not occur, it becomes "unfounded" and is subtracted from the number of reported incidents to produce a figure that represents the "actual" number of incidents. Clark and Lewis (1977), in an examination of rape cases in Toronto police files in 1970, discovered that "unfounding" did not always mean that an incident of rape did not take place. The criteria used by the police in unfounding a case included no injury to the victim; no weapon present; an offender who was known to the victim; a woman who had been drinking; an incident that was not reported immediately; a woman who was separated, divorced, or living common-law, and was unemployed or living on welfare. In many unfounded cases, there was factual evidence that a rape did take place. The reasons for designating a case as "unfounded" seemed more to do with the police officer's perception of the victim's character and the probability that the case would be successfully prosecuted than whether a rape had actually occurred.

THE LAWS ON ASSAULT AND SEXUAL ASSAULT

In the early 1980s, Parliament undertook a review of the Criminal Code provisions related to assault, and in 1983 three offences of assault and three parallel offences of sexual assault came into effect. The definition of assault in Section 265 of the Criminal Code is as follows:

> (1) A person commits an assault when
>
>> (a) without the consent of another person, he applies force intentionally to that other person, directly or indirectly;
>>
>> (b) he attempts or threatens, by an act or gesture, to apply force to another person, if he has, or causes that other person to believe on reasonable grounds that he has, present ability to effect his purpose; or
>>
>> (c) while openly wearing or carrying a weapon or an imitation thereof, he accosts or impedes another person or begs.

Physical violence is not necessary for an assault to occur, but there must be a threatening act or gesture that causes the other person to believe the perpetrator has the ability to carry out an assault.

Assaults are categorized according to the degree of injury or harm done. Simple assault, commonly known as Level I assault, is punishable by a maximum prison term of 5 years. A threatened assault, or an actual assault that did not result in serious physical injury, both would be categorized as Level I assault. Level II assault involves the presence of a weapon or bodily harm to the victim such as broken bones, cuts, or bruises, and is punishable by up to 10 years in prison. Level III, or aggravated assault, results in wounding, maiming, or endangering the victim's life, and can result in a maximum prison term of 14 years.

One important component of these legislative changes, from the perspective of crimes against women, is the manner in which police can now lay assault charges. Under the new law, police officers can lay a charge against someone they suspect of committing an assault if there is "reasonable and probable cause" for believing that an assault has occurred. This is a dramatic and important change from the pre-1983 legislation, which stated that, in the absence of physical evidence such as injuries, there had to be a witness to the assault before a charge could be laid. This was a significant problem in cases of wife assault, where there were seldom witnesses other than the woman herself. Police officers often had to leave the home knowing that further assaults were likely to happen and that they were unable to protect the woman. The new law enables police to offer greater protection to women by laying charges, removing the man from the home, and decreasing the immediate risk of further violence.

Closely following these legal changes, police departments across the country issued directives to police officers to lay charges in cases of domestic violence in which there are reasonable and probable grounds to believe that an assault has occurred. These directives were intended to encourage women to report incidents of wife assault, to demonstrate to the public that these assaults were treated seriously by the criminal justice system, and to change norms and attitudes among many in the justice system who treated assaults on wives as less serious offences. These directives were accompanied by special training for most police officers in the appropriate handling of domestic assaults, and some of the larger police departments have established special units to deal exclusively with these types of calls. Special training, and in some cases special units, have also been developed for Crown prosecutors, to improve the treatment of victims prior to and during court and improve conviction rates.

The legislative changes of 1983 also abolished the offences of rape, attempted rape, sexual intercourse with the feeble-minded, and indecent assault on males and females, and replaced them with three levels of a new offence of sexual assault that parallel the assault provisions. While many of the biases against rape victims that were popular at the time of the Clark and Lewis study have faded substantially over the past 20 years, the new law did nothing to restrict the degree of discretion open to police officers. Sexual assault is undefined by the Criminal Code, except that the general definition of assault described in Section 265(1) (on the previous page) also applies to all forms of sexual assault. This left a great deal of uncertainty among police and discretion as to what differentiated an assault from a *sexual* assault and how these events would be classified in official statistics.

Section 271 simply sets out the penalty for Level I sexual assaults as follows:

(1) Every one who commits a sexual assault is guilty of

    (a) an indictable offence and is liable to imprisonment for a term not exceeding ten years; or

    (b) an offence punishable on summary conviction by 18 months imprisonment and/or a fine of $2,000.

Section 272 describes Level II sexual assaults as follows:

Every one who, in committing a sexual assault,

    (a) carries, uses or threatens to use a weapon or an imitation thereof,

    (b) threatens to cause bodily harm to a person other than the complainant,

    (c) causes bodily harm to the complainant, or

    (d) is a party to the offence with any other person,

is guilty of an indictable offence and liable to imprisonment for a term not exceeding 14 years.

In defining Level III sexual assaults, Section 273 states:

(1) Every one commits an aggravated sexual assault who, in committing a sexual assault, wounds, maims, disfigures or endangers the life of the complainant.

(2) Every one who commits an aggravated sexual assault is guilty of an indictable offence and liable to imprisonment for life.

It wasn't until 1987, in the Supreme Court case of *R. v. Chase,* that the top court provided guidelines as to what constitutes a sexual assault. In this case, a New Brunswick man had been found not guilty of sexual assault after grabbing a 15-year-old girl's breasts. He was originally found guilty after a trial in provincial court, and when he appealed to the New Brunswick Court of Appeal, a conviction for common assault was substituted for the sexual assault conviction. The appeal court argued that "sexual" should be taken to refer to genitalia, and that a broader definition could lead to "absurd results" if it encompassed other parts of the body such as secondary sex characteristics. The Supreme Court rejected this argument, noting that appeal courts in Ontario, Alberta, and British Columbia had also done so. In their judgment, the Justices of the Supreme Court ruled that the test for the sexual nature of an assault does not depend solely on contact with specific areas of the body, but on circumstances of a sexual nature such that the sexual integrity of the victim is violated. The court established certain factors that are relevant in considering whether the conduct is sexual, including the part of the body touched, the nature of the contact, the situation in which the conduct occurred, the words and gestures accompanying the act, and all other circumstances surrounding the conduct, including threats.

TRENDS IN ASSAULT AND SEXUAL ASSAULT STATISTICS

Recent trends in the official rates of sexual and nonsexual assault in Canada paint a picture of rapidly rising rates of violent crime. There have been clear increases in the rates of both sexual and nonsexual assault since the passage of the reform legislation in 1983: in 1993, a total of 34 764 incidents of sexual assault were reported to the police in Canada, a figure that can be calculated as 121 incidents for every 100 000 people in the population, up from 11 932 incidents reported in 1983 (48 per 100 000 population) (Figure 2.1 and Table 2.1). This is an increase of 152 percent in the rate over the 10-year period. In the 5 years prior to 1983 law reform, rates of rape and indecent assault increased only 18 percent, from 38 to 45 per 100 000 (Figure 2.1).

Although the number of nonsexual assaults reported to the police each year is much higher than the number of sexual assaults, they follow a similar pattern. The rate of nonsexual assaults increased only 14 percent in the 5 years prior to 1983, from 427 to 487 per 100 000. Following the enactment of the new legislation, the rate of assaults recorded by the police increased 62 percent, from 498 to 805 per 100 000. Like sexual assaults, rates of nonsexual assault have levelled off in recent years (Figure 2.2).

The historical UCR Survey that dates back to 1962 does not differentiate incidents of wife assaults, and so it is not clear what percentage of the increase in assaults can be traced to increases in reported wife assaults and what percentage are due to other types of assault. Revisions to the UCR Survey began in the 1980s to expand it from a summary survey to a micro-database survey with details about victims, offenders, and incidents that can be cross-tabulated and linked in various ways. Until this revision, the UCR Survey did not contain information about the gender of victims or the relationship between victims and offenders that could identify incidents of violence against women. Although the number of assaults of varying degrees of seriousness were recorded by the police each year, there was no way of telling how many were committed by a man against his wife. A sample of the revised survey indicates that 21 percent of all assaults in 1993 involved assaults against women by their husbands or common-law partners (Canadian Centre for Justice Statistics, 1993a). It also indicates that over half of all sexual assaults (Levels I, II, and

TABLE 2.1

Number and Rate of Incidents of Sexual Assault[1] and Nonsexual[2] Assault Reported to the Police in Canada, 1978–1993

| Year | Sexual Assault | | Nonsexual Assault | |
	Number	Rates per 100 000 Population	Number	Rates per 100 000 Population
1978	8 961	38	100 512	427
1979	9 754	42	107 082	451
1980	10 164	42	110 991	461
1981	10 550	44	114 748	471
1982	10 990	45	119 869	487
1983	11 932	48	123 611	498
1984	14 793	59	129 613	509
1985	18 248	73	137 726	547
1986	20 530	82	149 982	592
1987	22 369	88	163 005	637
1988	24 898	96	171 734	662
1989	26 795	101	183 265	690
1990	27 843	104	199 377	741
1991	30 351	113	218 762	799
1992	34 355	121	226 350	796
1993	34 764	121	231 699	805

[1] Includes rape and indecent assault in the years 1978 to 1982, and sexual assault Levels I, II, and III in the years 1983 to 1993.

[2] Includes wounding, causing bodily harm and other assaults in the years 1978 to 1982, and assault Levels I, II, and III, causing bodily harm, discharging a firearm with intent, and other assaults in the years 1983 to 1993.

Source: Canadian Centre for Justice Statistics, Uniform Crime Reporting Survey (1993).

III) were committed against young people under 18 years of age, an important detail unavailable until recent revisions to this survey.

How can we explain the dramatic increase in rates of sexual and nonsexual assault since 1983? It is unlikely that the passage of the new legislation would have coincided with a real increase in sexual aggression and other acts of violence. It would appear on the surface that the legal reforms, and the publicity surrounding them, have had the desired effect of encouraging victims of sexual and nonsexual assault to come forward to seek redress through the criminal justice system, and that confidence in the justice system continues to rise. On the other hand, increases in rates of these offences could have been caused by gradual increases in the

FIGURE 2.1

Rates of Sexual Assault Reported to the Police per 100 000 Population, 1978–1993

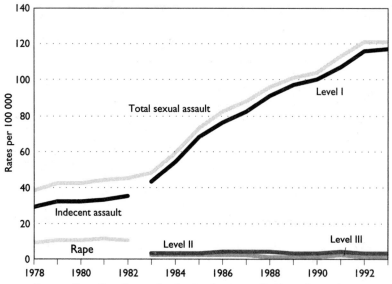

Source: Canadian Centre for Justice Statistics, Uniform Crime Reporting Survey (1993).

Note: Legal reform in 1983 abolished the offences of rape, attempted rape, and indecent assault and replaced them with three levels of a new offence—sexual assault.

numbers of suspects apprehended or charged as police attitudes and charging policies continue to influence the attention these cases are given (recall that these statistics represent cases substantiated by police). An alternative explanation is that both victims and police have interpreted the new laws to include a wider range of behaviours that were not included under the previous offences of assault and sexual assault (Roberts and Gebotys, 1992; Roberts and Grossman, 1994; Johnson, 1996).

Investigations undertaken by the Department of Justice in the evaluation of the reform legislation relating to sexual assault suggest that these factors alone are not sufficient to have caused the sharp increase in reported cases of sexual assault. This research found that incidents now recorded by the police as sexual assault do not differ greatly from the kinds of incidents formerly recorded as rape or indecent assault. Furthermore, legal reform tends not to precede public opinion but to be an expression of it. That is, legal reform generally comes about as a result of widespread dissatisfaction with existing legal codes, intensive lobbying on the part of interest groups, and lengthy public debate. Clark and Hepworth (1994:117) cite a number of historical factors that coincided with or preceded the change in the law on sexual

FIGURE 2.2

Rates of Nonsexual Assault Reported to the Police per 100 000 Population, 1978–1993

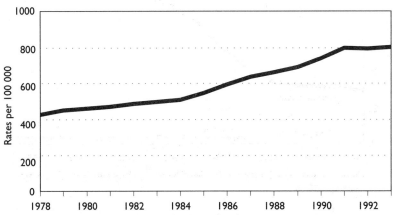

Source: Canadian Centre for Justice Statistics, Uniform Crime Reporting Survey (1993).

assault and that must be taken into account when evaluating the impact of legal reform. These factors apply equally to wife assault:

1. The changing social, economic, and political status of women;

2. Increased media scrutiny on the treatment of women in the courts;

3. Heightened awareness of and focus on victims of crime, particularly female victims, accompanied by government initiatives and services;

4. The growth in specialized investigation units in police departments across the country where expertise has developed regarding the investigation of complaints, the gathering of evidence, and the treatment of victims;

5. The expansion of sexual assault support centres;

6. The growth in specialized treatment teams in hospitals to deal sensitively with victims of sexual assault;

7. The intensive lobbying by women's groups that long preceded the passage of the rape reform legislation.

In view of these important social changes, it would be a mistake to attribute the dramatic and steady increase in the reporting of assaults and sexual assaults entirely to the success of law reform. While important changes were brought about by the law, police statistics cannot be divorced from the context in which the legal reform took place. Significant social changes, of which legal reform was but one, have brought about growing efforts to eradicate the biases that have confronted complaints of sexual assault and wife assault in the justice system and to provide better treatment and services for victims. All of these factors may have had an effect on victims' willingness to report sexual assault, even in the absence of law reform.

In summary, the advantage of police statistics is that they provide a standard measure that can be used with some confidence to track changes in the number of criminal incidents that come to the attention of the police over time. However, increases or decreases in the rates of violent crime must be interpreted within the context of other social factors. Fluctuations in rates of wife assault and sexual assault may be due to changes in reporting practices, changes in legislation, changing social mores, declining tolerance toward these offences on the part of women, and improved response on the part of the justice system.

Police statistics can also be useful for studying the effects of changes in legislation or criminal justice policies, or for studying how the police handle cases of wife assault or sexual assault. If one wants to understand the characteristics and needs of women who seek assistance from the criminal justice system in order to develop training materials for the police, for example, then police statistics are a good place to start. If, on the other hand, the objectives of the research are to develop estimates of the prevalence of violent victimization among women in the general population, or to understand factors that may put women at risk of violent victimization, then police statistics will almost certainly misrepresent the breadth and the nature of violent incidents that women experience.

CLINICAL SAMPLES

The earliest attempts to study rape and wife battering involved case studies of female victims who had been in contact with a helping agency, such as a rape crisis centre or a shelter for battered women, or case studies of men who had been tried and convicted of such offences. These "clinical" or "convenience" samples were drawn primarily from medical or counselling caseloads or jail populations. Clinical caseloads of women and men have the advantage to researchers of being readily available, inexpensive to acquire, and not biased (in the case of female victims) by having to first report to the police. However, they were biased in other important ways. Like women who report wife assault or sexual assault to the police, women who use shelters or other services are unrepresentative of all battered or sexually assaulted women. Most women who seek help from an agency have endured the most severe forms of violence, some for many years, and in the case of shelter users, most are economically destitute with few other options open to them.

The earliest studies of violent men attempted to pinpoint how rapists differ from normal men so that therapies could be developed for them. Most described rapists as having psychological defects that caused uncontrollable violent impulses. The conclusions drawn from this research were largely a function of the sample of men who were studied—very violent men, many psychologically disturbed, who were unable to escape police detection, arrest, and conviction. As few rapes are reported to the police and fewer result in conviction, clinical samples represented only the very extreme examples of men who rape.

The early focus on clinical samples was in part a response to assumptions by therapists and researchers that wife assault and sexual assault were rare and the acts of a few mentally deranged men. And for the most part, the results of these studies helped reinforce these beliefs. But despite significant limitations to clinical samples, some clinicians such as American psychologist Nicholas Groth and his colleagues (1977; 1979), in their work with convicted sex offenders, developed a broader explanation that took into account social factors. Their work was instrumental in dispelling certain myths about rape and increasing our understanding of the motivation of offenders. They identified three components to a rape situation: power, anger, and sexuality (Groth and Birnbaum, 1979:12). These authors argued that feelings of power and anger dominate; sex is merely the weapon through which power and conquest, anger and contempt are expressed.

The growing attention of feminist scholars to issues related to violence against women caused a shift in focus from offenders to victims, and to the study of clinical samples of women using shelters for battered women, rape crisis centres, or hospitals. There are obvious problems of bias associated with this method of selecting samples, and for the most part, the way the sample is selected will determine the characteristics of the women who respond. Women who use shelters, for example, are likely to be poor, to have had their lives or the lives of their children threatened by the most serious types of violence, and to have few other options available to them. These studies seldom include a control group of nonbattered women to indicate how they compare with the clinical sample. As a result, there is no way of knowing from clinical samples how representative these women are of all victims of wife assault, and researchers must be careful not to generalize the characteristics of these women or their experiences to all battered women.

The way in which the clinical or convenience sample is selected can also affect the results of the study and the extent to which the findings can be generalized to other populations. Typically, the researcher has limited funds available and must judiciously select a readily available sample of women to interview about their experiences. Some researchers have attracted subjects through notices posted in magazines or newspapers or on university campuses. This method is called "self-selection" as respondents make the decision to select themselves as subjects. While it may be the least costly method of selecting a sample and does not carry with it the same problems inherent in samples of shelters or police statistics, the biases are clearly unknown as the researcher will not know the criteria the subjects have used to decide to participate in the study. There may be a tendency for women who have already reported their experiences to the police or a crisis centre to come forward, or there may be certain class or education factors at play. The types of magazines or newspapers in which the notice is posted will also have a strong bearing on who responds. For example, subjects recruited from a university will differ in important ways from women responding to an advertisement in a public housing project. The important point is that there is bias in the selection for these studies and the direction of the bias is largely unknown to the researcher.

Despite the limitations of clinical studies, the case study information that has emerged from clinical research has provided much-needed insight into the contexts in which sexual assault and battering occur and the motivations of both victims and offenders. Qualitative information adds richness and meaning to the purely quantitative estimates tallied from police statistics and other sources, and reminds us of the human drama and suffering behind the statistics. Unstructured interviews can capture the nuances of context, meaning, and culture, and the enduring nature of violent relationships, in a way that statistics cannot. Perhaps as importantly, clinical studies were early catalysts for change. In the beginning of the battered women's movement, the real-life accounts of women seeking refuge in shelters caught the attention of the public, governments, and academics. This was instrumental in putting the issue on the public policy agenda and illustrating the need for more services and resources for abused women, as well as for more in-depth research.

POPULATION SURVEYS

In an ideal world, the most accurate and reliable method of measuring the prevalence of violent victimization in the female population would be to interview all women about their experiences. This approach is called a *census survey,* and a prime example is the Census of the Population conducted by Statistics Canada every five years.

It is obviously not feasible, or necessary, to conduct census surveys of the entire Canadian population in order to measure changes in or patterns of various phenomena in society. A sample of the population, so long as the sample is selected randomly from among all eligible subjects, will suffice to produce estimates of social phenomena that are accurate within a measurable range. Sampling essentially involves selecting a segment of the population and attempting to make inferences about the population based on analysis of the sample. Random selection helps ensure that those who respond are statistically representative of everyone in the population and that the results can be generalized to the population at large.

Crime victimization surveys are sample surveys that are based on this model. A number of households are selected at random for these surveys from among all households within a geographic area, and usually one person is selected as the respondent for that household. The first large-scale crime victimization survey undertaken in Canada was the Canadian Urban Victimization Survey (CUVS) in 1982, in which 61 000 people 16 years of age and over were interviewed by telephone about their perceptions of crime and the criminal justice system and about their experiences of victimization (Statistics Canada, 1982). Eight crime types were addressed, including sexual and nonsexual assault, and seven urban centres were included in the sample frame.

Statistics Canada has incorporated a cycle on crime victimization into the General Social Survey (GSS) program (Statistics Canada, 1988; 1993b). This survey interviews approximately 10 000 people 15 years of age and over in the 10 provinces, with each cycle running every 5 years. The first crime victimization component ran in 1988 and the second in 1993. These surveys provide information that is complementary to police statistics as they include incidents that were reported to the police and those that were not reported. They have the added advantage of providing detailed information about victims' experiences with crime and the criminal justice system, the impact of the experience on them, their reasons for contacting or not contacting the police, their perceptions of their personal safety, and other details not available from official police records.

Canada's crime victimization surveys were modelled on the National Crime Victimization Survey (NCVS) conducted every six months by the Bureau of Justice Statistics in the United States (Bachman, 1994; Bachman and Taylor, 1994). The methods used to conduct these surveys have been refined over the past two decades, and the NCVS has served as a prototype for crime victim surveys in many other countries as well as an International Crime Survey that operates in several countries simultaneously. These surveys are not without certain limitations, however. They have been criticized for reducing human suffering to a set of numbers and for failing to account for the context and the meaning of events, particularly in the case of violent interactions. Like the criticisms directed at police statistics, victim surveys are accused of taking single incidents out of the context of what may be ongoing violent relationships.

The accuracy of the information collected in crime victim surveys depends to a greater extent than in clinical studies or police statistics on candid and honest answers from the respondents. In clinical settings and situations in which a victim has called on the police for help, the victim's participation in the interaction is typically initiated by her, whereas in an interview setting, the respondent is selected "out of the blue" and is not prepared for the questions to come. The clinician and the police officer also have physical evidence and witnesses to draw on in their interpretation of the events that are not available to survey researchers. American criminologist Wesley Skogan (1986), who has worked extensively with the NCVS, cites a number of factors that can influence the accuracy of responses provided in crime victim surveys:

1. People may forget about certain things that have happened to them, especially if they seemed unimportant at the time or happened some time ago.

2. They may fail to report incidents that they perceive to be embarrassing or shameful.

3. They may deliberately choose not to tell the interviewer about an incident if they perceive the interview to be an intrusion or a waste of time.

4. They may not perceive certain experiences to be "crimes" worthy of reporting to a crime survey.

5. They may intentionally or unintentionally report incidents that happened outside the reference period of the survey.

6. Questions may be so poorly worded or ambiguous that respondents may be confused about how to interpret them.

MEASURING SENSITIVE EXPERIENCES

The accuracy of reports of very sensitive or personal experiences is of particular concern to survey researchers. Reverse-record checks, in which people who report incidents to police are later interviewed in a telephone survey about the same experiences to test for honesty of disclosure, have found that many of these incidents are withheld. The magnitude of nonreporting increases with the intimacy of the relationship between the victim and the perpetrator. One such study by Statistics Canada found that 71 percent of assaults committed by strangers were recalled to survey interviewers, but only 56 percent of assaults by someone known to the victim, and only 29 percent of those involving someone related to the victim (Catlin and Murray, 1979).

Very often, the willingness of victims to disclose personal or sensitive experiences to interviewers is influenced by the wording of the questions used and the context in which the questions are placed. Omnibus surveys like the CUVS, the GSS, the NCVS, and the British Crime Survey, with a wide-ranging focus on a variety of crimes, were not designed specifically to measure the very sensitive experiences of violence that primarily affect women. As researchers have gained experience and knowledge about the capabilities and shortcomings of crime victim surveys, many have begun to question the ability of these surveys to accurately and reliably measure sexual assault and assault by intimate partners (Skogan, 1984, Hough and Mayhew, 1983; Koss, 1992; 1993). As evidence, crime victim surveys consistently portray wife assault and sexual assault as far less prevalent than other research suggests.

Some of the limitations of these surveys can be addressed by the manner in which the questionnaires are constructed, the order and structure of the questions asked, the training interviewers receive, and how the interview is conducted. For example, respondents typically are not asked directly if they have been assaulted, raped, or sexually assaulted. Rather, they are asked a series of highly explicit questions about acts that have happened to them to avoid having people respond on the basis of preconceived notions of certain offences. How these questions are asked has a significant impact on how people respond to them.

Attempts have been made to address the shortcomings of crime victim surveys in recent years by improving the wording of questions relating to sexual assault and assault by family members. For example, respondents to the 1982 CUVS were first asked if they had been attacked, beaten up, hit or kicked, or had something thrown at them, or if anyone had threatened to beat them up or threatened them with a weapon. In a separate question, they were asked if anyone had attacked or molested them, or tried to attack or molest them, while they were "in a car, in a public place, at home or anywhere else." Those who said they had been attacked, threatened, or molested in some way were then asked how they were attacked, at which point they could reply that the attack was a rape, an attempted rape, a molesting, or an attempted molesting. All respondents were asked a question about the relationship of the attacker to them. As a result of these questions, less than 1 percent of women reported experiencing violence by a spouse in the year preceding the survey, and a similar percentage reported a sexual assault (Solicitor General Canada, 1985).

The 1988 GSS, which was modelled on the CUVS, attempted to clarify the wording of questions concerning sexual assault and assaults by spouses. The phrase "including members of your own household" was added to questions about attacks and threats. Respondents who said they had been attacked or threatened were then asked how they were attacked, at which point they could reply that the attack was a rape, an attempted rape, a molesting, or an attempted molesting (all one category). The number of women assaulted by a partner was 1 percent. There were too few cases of sexual assault reported to produce statistically reliable estimates (Sacco and Johnson, 1990).

The 1993 GSS attempted to clarify questions about family attacks even further, and completely changed the questions relating to sexual assaults. The initial question about attacks asks respondents to "please remember to include acts committed by family and non-family." Two questions about sexual assault were included. The first reads as follows: "Has anyone forced you or attempted to force you into any sexual activity when you did not want to, by threatening you, holding you down or hurting you in some way? Remember this includes acts by family and non-family and that all information provided is strictly confidential." The second sexual assault question reads: "Has anyone touched you against your will in any sexual way? By this I mean anything from unwanted touching or grabbing to kissing or fondling." Those who said they had been sexually assaulted in these ways were later asked how they were attacked, at which point responses were categorized as sexually assaulted, molested, or attempted sexual assault or molesting (one combined category). These questions had the effect of raising the overall rate of violence against women to be higher than that of men; the rate of violent victimization in 1993 (including robbery, assault, and sexual assault) was 84 per 1000 women (C. Wright, 1995). The wording of the questions had relatively little effect on the rate of wife assault (from 15 to 19), but sexual assaults increased from a negligible number to a rate of 29 per 1000 women. In all three of these surveys, too few spousal assaults and sexual assaults were reported by men to permit statistically reliable estimates to be made.

The NCVS in the United States has also undergone major revisions to the wording of questions concerning rape and domestic assault (Bachman and Taylor, 1994). Prior to 1993, the NCVS did not ask specific questions about attacks involving relatives or other offenders known to the respondents, nor did it specifically ask about rape or sexual assault. Like the Canadian surveys, questions simply asked about attacks, attempted attacks, and threats. If respondents volunteered information about attacks by known offenders, rape, or attempted rape, they were categorized as such. Respondents were not asked directly whether they had been victims of attempted or completed rape, and no definition of rape was ever given. In 1993, questions were added that broadened the type of attack or threat that could be chosen, and that encouraged respondents to include events they were not certain would be considered crimes. In addition, respondents were told that "incidents involving forced or unwanted sexual acts are often difficult to talk about," and were specifically asked about such incidents involving strangers, acquaintances, and well-known offenders. Respondents who replied that they had experienced forced or unwanted sexual acts were then asked to clarify what type of sexual activity had occurred. Incidents could be categorized as completed or attempted rape, verbal threat of rape, sexual attack (grabbing, fondling, etc.), verbal threat of sexual attack, unwanted sexual contact, and verbal harassment (such as abusive language) (see Bachman and Taylor, 1994).

One-year incident rates of sexual assault and wife assault produced by Canadian and American crime victimization surveys are presented in Table 2.2. It is evident from the increases in rates of these crimes with improvements to the wording of questions how important this wording can be to the results. Questions must be very specific in order to orient respondents toward thinking about these acts as crimes, and they must be sensitively worded in order for victims to feel comfortable reporting their experiences.

The differences in the rates presented in Table 2.2 also indicate the problems in comparing rates of violence produced by seemingly similar surveys. One must be cautious in making comparisons about the level of violence against women in Canada and the United States and over different time periods, even though the methodologies are similar. Comparability among surveys is affected by a number of factors, in addition to the wording of questions, including:

1. Definitions of violence (strict definitions of rape were used in the CUVS and in the 1972–92 version of the NCVS);

2. Precise question wording and placement of these questions relative to others in the questionnaire;

3. How the purpose of the survey was explained to respondents;

4. The definition of "spouse" (whether it includes ex-spouses and common-law partners);

5. The method of counting, i.e., whether victims or individual incidents are counted;

6. Whether incidents over one year or the woman's lifetime are counted;

7. Whether rates are based on all women or only those who have ever been married or lived with a man in a common-law relationship; and

8. Characteristics of the sample, for instance, age cutoffs and geographic area.

All of these factors are important to interpreting the findings of different surveys and trends over time.

TABLE 2.2

One-Year Victimization Rates of Sexual Assault and Wife Assault per 1000 Adult Female Population, Produced by Crime Victim Surveys

Survey	Year	Sexual assault	Wife assault
		Rate per 1000 female population	
Canadian Urban Victimization Survey	1982	6[1]	4
General Social Survey	1988	—[2]	15
General Social Survey	1993	29[3]	19
U.S. National Crime Victimization Survey	1987–92	1[4]	5
U.S. National Crime Victimization Survey	1992–93	5[5]	9

— not statistically reliable

[1] Includes rape, molesting, and attempts against women age 16 and older.

[2] Includes, rape, molesting, and attempts against women age 15 and older.

[3] Includes sexual assault, molesting, and attempts against women age 15 and older.

[4] Includes rape and attempts against women age 12 and older.

[5] Includes rape, attempted rape, sexual attacks, and unwanted sexual acts against women age 12 and older.

Sources: Solicitor General Canada, *Female Victims of Crime*, Canadian Urban Victimization Survey, Bulletin 4 (1985); Canadian Centre for Justice Statistics, "Conjugal Violence Against Women," *Juristat Service Bulletin* 10(7) (1990); Statistics Canada, *General Social Survey*, Microdata File, Ottawa (1993). Ronet Bachman, *Violence Against Women: A National Crime Victimization Survey Report*, Washington, D.C.: Bureau of Justice Statistics (1994); Ronet Bachman and Linda Saltzman, *Violence Against Women: Estimates from the Redesigned Survey*, Washington, D.C.: Bureau of Justice Statistics (1995).

The Violence Against Women Survey

Despite gradual improvements to national crime victim surveys, it became evident to policymakers that a large-scale survey dedicated entirely to women's experiences of male violence was needed in order to obtain the kind of detailed data required to understand the issue more fully. Canada's federal Department of Health responded to this need by commissioning a national population survey on male violence against women. This survey was conducted by Statistics Canada in 1993, and interviewed 12 300 women by telephone about their adult experiences with sexual and physical assault by marital partners, dates and boyfriends, other men known to them, and strangers. The survey also included questions about noncriminal forms of sexual harassment and detailed questions about women's fear of violence in public places. The technique used for the VAWS was the crime victim survey approach of interviewing people about their experiences as crime victims.

An entire survey dedicated to asking women about their experiences of violence over their adult lifetime has several advantages (Johnson and Sacco, 1995). First, a great many women are not comfortable relating these occurrences on traditional crime victim surveys, perhaps because of the lack of sensitive lead-in questions, lack of special training for interviewers, and the use, in some cases, of male interviewers. Second, in their attempt to measure a wide variety of both personal and property crimes, victim surveys cannot address the issue of violence against women in its complexity or in the detail necessary to test theories or devise prevention strategies. Traditional crime victim surveys typically orient respondents to think about crime in their own neighbourhood, which may dissuade some women from reporting certain types of violence.

The third advantage to a focused survey is the added information about threats, intimidation, and sexual harassment that can help to place women's experiences of sexual assault and wife battering into a broader social context and can significantly enhance discussions about the correlates of women's fear. It is more common for women to be threatened and intimidated through acts of sexual harassment, but because these acts are not considered "criminal" in the legal sense, they typically are not considered in victim surveys or analyses of women's fear. The effect of these experiences is to remind women that they are targets for sexual violence and to undermine their feelings of security. The importance of considering these experiences in analyses of women's fear will be discussed in Chapter 3. Finally, the one-year reference period used by most crime victim surveys is problematic. It draws an artificial boundary around certain experiences while discounting others. This practice may avoid problems of memory recall and may be useful for tracking trends over time, but it can undercount the rate of victimization in the population and obscure the scope of the problem. The need to rethink this practice is underscored by the fact that *80 percent* of violent incidents reported to Statistics Canada's VAWS occurred *before* the 12 months leading up to the survey (Statistics Canada, 1994a). The analytical benefits of this type of expanded information about women's experiences of violence and harassment will be demonstrated in later chapters.

CONSTRUCTING DEFINITIONS OF VIOLENCE

Definitions of violence against women in the research literature vary widely. Some include psychological and emotional abuse, financial abuse, and sexual coercion, as well as physical and sexual assault as legally defined (see DeKeseredy and Kelly, 1993c; Koss and Gidycz, 1985). The prevalence of "violence" was restricted in the Violence Against Women Survey to legal definitions of physical and sexual assault as contained in the Canadian Criminal Code in view of the fact that respondents would be asked questions about the actions they took to get help, including reporting to the police, whether the incident resulted in an offender appearing in court, and satisfaction with actions taken by the police and the courts. However, the scope of the questions extended beyond those contained in traditional crime victim surveys that yielded very low rates of disclosure.

Questions inquiring about sexual assaults by men other than spouses are shown in Box 2.1. These are the same questions used in the 1993 GSS, although in the VAWS, the questions were repeated for different categories of relationships. Physical violence outside marriage was measured through responses to the two questions shown in Box 2.2. Incidents that had both a sexual and a physical component were counted only once as sexual assaults.

An important distinction was made when questioning women about sexual violence involving intimate partners. With respect to dating and marital relationships, women were asked about violent sexual attacks but not about unwanted sexual touching. While unwanted sexual touching does technically fall under the legal definition of sexual assault, when the questionnaire was tested the majority of respondents found the concept of unwanted sexual touching by intimate partners to be ambiguous and confusing. They were excluded because of a concern among the survey

Box 2.1   Sexual Assault Outside Marriage

designers that the results of these questions would not be reliable or valid.

The method used by the VAWS to derive estimates of wife assault differs substantially from the single-question methods used in crime victim surveys. Ten specific questions were used to measure violence by a spouse ranging from threats of physical harm to use of a gun or knife. This method is intended to take account of the advice of Smith (1994) and others to offer many opportunities for disclosure in order to counteract a reluctance to disclose painful or embarrassing experiences. Obtaining details about specific types of violent acts also adds important information about the dimensions and the nature of wife assaults. These 10 items, in the order in which they were asked, appear in Box 2.3.

THE PREVALENCE OF VIOLENCE AGAINST WOMEN

An advantage of random sample surveys such as the VAWS and crime victim surveys is that, by interviewing a relatively small sample, the responses can be weighted to represent all women in the general population. The responses of the 12 300 women who participated in this survey were each given a weighting factor that represents all other women in the geographic region of the

Box 2.2   Physical Assault Outside Marriage

respondent who were not interviewed. Responses total the approximately 10.5 million women (18 years of age and over) in the Canadian population in 1993. National estimates are expected to be within 1.2 percent of the true population at the 95.0 percent confidence interval. Estimates of subgroups of the population have wider confidence intervals.

According to the Violence Against Women Survey, 51 percent of Canadian women have experienced at least one incident of physical or sexual assault since the age of 16 and 10 percent had been victims of violence in the 12-month period preceding the survey (Table 2.3). Sixteen percent have been assaulted by a date or boyfriend, 23 percent by a stranger or other nonintimate, and 29 percent of ever-married women have been assaulted by a spouse (this includes common-law marriages). As other research has suggested, women reported higher rates of violence by men they know than by strangers. Grouping together all known men and comparing them with strangers, almost half of all women (45 percent) have been victimized by men known to them (spouses, dates, boyfriends, friends, neighbours, acquaintances, etc.) compared with 23 percent who reported violence by a stranger.

Sexual assault was somewhat more common than physical assault, with 4 out of 10 (39 percent) women reporting this type of experience (Figure 2.3). The less serious forms of unwanted sexual touching and violent sexual attacks occurred with almost equal frequency (25 percent and 24 percent, respectively). A smaller proportion of women reported sexual attacks by spouses (8 percent). Approximately 34 percent of women have experienced a nonsexual assault, and the majority of these involved spouses. Less common were physical assaults by men other than spouses.

The VAWS estimates that a total of 572 000 women experienced at least one incident of sexual assault in the one-year period preceding the survey, and 201 000 women experienced violence by a spouse. Figures 2.4 and 2.5 illustrate the differences in the number of women who reported these experiences to the VAWS, the GSS, and the police in 1993. The VAWS captures almost twice as many incidents as the GSS, 3 times as many cases of wife

---

Violence by Spouses

Violence by husbands and common-law partners was measured by response to the following:

We are particularly interested in learning more about women's experiences of violence in their homes. I would like you to tell me if your husband / partner has every done any of the following to you. This includes incidents that may have occurred while you were dating.

- *Threatened to hit you with his fist or anything else that could hurt you*
- *Threw something at you that could hurt you*
- *Pushed, grabbed or shoved you*
- *Slapped you*
- *Kicked, bit or hit you with his fist*
- *Hit you with something that could hurt you*
- *Beat you up*
- *Choked you*
- *Threatened to or used a gun or knife on you*
- *Forced you into any sexual activity when you did not want to, by threatening you, holding you down, or hurting you in some way*

Source: Statistics Canada (1994b), pp. 35–43.

Box 2.3   Violence by Spouses

TABLE 2.3

Number and Percentage of Women 18 Years of Age and Over Who Have Experienced Violence, by Relationship of Perpetrator

Relationship	Number in Millions	Percent adult lifetime	Percent 12 months
Total women victimized	5.38	51	10
Spouse or ex-spouse	2.65	29[1]	3[1]
Date/boyfriend	1.72	16	2
Other known man	2.46	23	4
Stranger	2.46	23	4

Figures do not add to totals because of multiple responses.

[1] Based on the number of women who have ever been married or lived with a man in a common-law relationship.

Source: Holly Johnson and Vincent Sacco, "Researching Violence Against Women: Statistics Canada's National Survey," *Canadian Journal of Criminology* 37(3): 294 (1995). Reprinted with permission.

assault as are reported to the police, and about *38 times* as many cases of sexual assault as police statistics. This graphically illustrates the extent to which victim surveys more completely represent the population of assaulted women than police records. Equally important, these surveys provide information about victims' perceptions of these experiences, how they were affected, what the consequences were for them, and how they reacted. These surveys are founded on the belief that, in may ways, victims are the best source of information about their own experiences, and that they are experts on what has happened to them, how it has affected them, and the decisions they made in response to the experiences.

FIGURE 2.3

Types of Violence Reported by Canadian Women

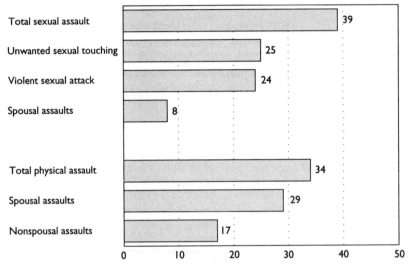

Figures do not add to totals because of multiple responses.

Source: Statistics Canada, *Violence Against Women Survey,* Microdata file (1994).

ETHICAL CONSIDERATIONS IN SURVEY RESEARCH

The sensitivity of the subject matter of the VAWS presented a number of complex methodological and ethical issues in the survey design. A survey of this nature asks the respondents to disclose the most intimate and perhaps the most troubling details of their lives to a stranger over the telephone. Survey designers must be cognizant of the fact that questions asking respondents to relive these very troubling memories have the potential to cause serious emotional trauma. Perhaps even more importantly, from an ethical point of view, researchers must never lose sight of the possibility that with every telephone call the respondent could be living with an abusive man and that her safety could be jeopardized should he learn of the content of the survey (Johnson and Sacco, 1995).

In the design phase of the Violence Against Women Survey, solutions to these issues were found through an extensive consultation process with a wide variety of experts, including academics,

FIGURE   2 . 4

Number of Sexual Assaults Against Adult Women in 1993 Recorded by Police, the General Social Survey, and the Violence Against Women Survey

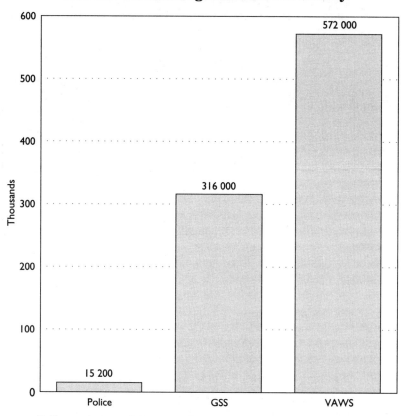

Police statistics and the General Social Survey count the number of incidents of sexual assault. The Violence Against Women Survey counts the number of women who have been sexually assaulted.

Sources: Canadian Centre for Justice Statistics, Revised Uniform Crime Reporting Survey, Unpublished data, Statistics Canada (1994a); *1993 General Social Survey*, Microdata File, Statistics Canada, *Violence Against Women Survey*, Microdata File.

federal and provincial government representatives, a police advisory group, shelter workers, crisis counsellors, as well as victims of violence seeking support from these agencies. These groups offered suggestions about the content of the questionnaire, the wording of the questions, and innovative approaches that would

FIGURE 2.5

Number of Wife Assaults in 1993 Recorded by Police, the General Social Survey, and the Violence Against Women Survey

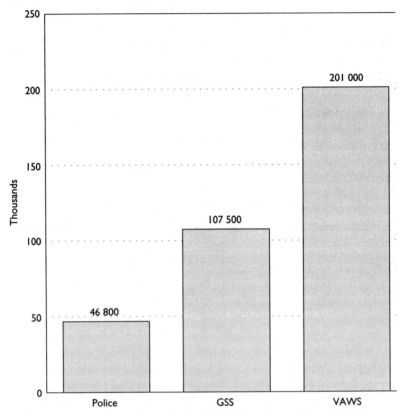

Police statistics and the General Social Survey count the number of incidents of assault. The Violence Against Women Survey counts the number of women who have been assaulted.

Sources: Canadian Centre for Justice Statistics, Revised Uniform Crime Reporting Survey, Unpublished data, Statistics Canada (1994a); *1993 General Social Survey*, Microdata File, Statistics Canada, *Violence Against Women Survey*, Microdata File.

give respondents options as to when and where they would participate. At the outset of the interview, every respondent was provided with a toll-free telephone number that she could use to call back to resume the interview in the event that she had to hang up suddenly. No callbacks were made to respondents' households, which gave them control over their participation. Many women took advantage of the callback option. A total of 1000 calls were received on the toll-free line over the 5-month period of interviewing; 150 of these were from women who wanted to continue an uncompleted interview that they had had to interrupt or who were calling to add additional information to a completed interview. Over half of all calls were from women wanting to verify the legitimacy of the survey, many at the point of sensitive questions about violence in their lives. This response signals the level of emotional commitment that this line of questioning can provoke and to which survey researchers must respond.

A common concern among survey researchers is that results will be biased if a large proportion of respondents refuse to participate in the survey or refuse to answer specific questions. A number of reasons why a woman may not wish to reveal her experiences to an interviewer over the telephone were articulated by Smith (1994): she may feel they are too personal or painful to discuss, she may be embarrassed or ashamed about them, she may fear further violence from her abuser should he find out, or she may have forgotten about them if they were minor or happened a long time ago. The selection and training of interviewers were critical factors in fostering a relationship of trust between interviewers and respondents, a climate in which respondents would feel comfortable discussing their experiences. Knowledge and sensitivity about the issue of violence against women were central criteria in selecting interviewers for this survey, in addition to standard interviewing skills, interviewing experience, and keyboard skills, as the survey would be conducted using Computer Assisted Telephone Interviewing (CATI). Only women were considered for the job of interviewing because of the concern that many respondents would refuse to discuss their personal experiences with male interviewers. Through training and experience, interviewers became skilled at detecting whether respondents had privacy and were able to speak freely. Women who disclosed abuse in a current relationship were asked if they were able to continue the conversation freely, and interviews were rescheduled if they were unable to proceed at that time.

In a survey of this sensitivity, survey managers have a responsibility to respond to emotional trauma. This applies to respondents, but it also applies to interviewers who may be distressed by the personal stories they hear. Distress can occur as a result of a particular interview, or it can be cumulative, building up over the course of many weeks or months of hearing about experiences of violence and feeling powerless to help.

A clinical psychologist became part of the survey team for the purpose of providing support to interviewers. It was her responsibility to help in selecting appropriate interviewers by assessing each candidate's level of knowledge and sensitivity toward the issue of violence against women, as well as the ability of each to handle the kinds of stress anticipated through participation in the survey. The psychologist took part in training sessions, and conducted regular debriefing sessions with interviewers where they could discuss stress management techniques and other issues that arose as a result of their work on the survey.

To enable them to react effectively to respondents' emotional trauma, interviewers had available to them an automated list of shelters and other services for abused and sexually assaulted women across the country. When the interviewer activated a special computer key, services in the respondent's geographic area appeared on the screen, linked to the area code and prefix of her telephone number (this was facilitated by the CATI system). Using this system, interviewers were able to offer support to respondents who either reported current or recent cases of abuse, or who appeared to be in distress. It was emphasized throughout the training sessions that interviewers must not undertake to counsel respondents, no matter how upset a respondent might be. Referring respondents to support services in the community addressed the need to respond to their distress without compromising the role of the interviewer or the collection of objective statistical data.

A WORD ON THE CONFLICT TACTICS SCALE

The Conflict Tactics Scale (CTS) is the most commonly used instrument in family violence surveys (Straus, 1990a). Using the "family conflict" approach, the CTS consists of 18 items intended to measure ways of handling interpersonal conflict in family relationships. The items range from "verbal reasoning" (from discussing the issue calmly to bringing in someone to help settle things) to "verbal aggression" (ranging from insults and swearing to throwing, smashing, hitting, or kicking something) and "physical aggression" (from throwing something at the other person to using a knife or gun). Respondents are asked how frequently they had perpetrated each act in the course of settling a disagreement with a spouse, a child, or a sibling, and how frequently they had been the victim of these acts. Estimates of rates of violence and victimization for both men and women are tallied from these self-reports. Sexual assault is absent from the scale.

Studies using the Conflict Tactics Scale consistently produce equivalent rates of wife battering and husband battering on both minor and severe types of violence (Brinkerhoff and Lupri, 1988; Lupri, 1990; Kennedy and Dutton, 1989; Steinmetz, 1981; Stets, 1990; Szinovacz, 1983). However, research that is designed to test the reliability of responses given to the CTS has established large discrepancies in the reports of violence given by men and women as to the occurrence and frequency of violence committed between them (Dobash et al., 1992; Brush, 1990; Szinovacz, 1983; Edleson and Brygger, 1986). In clinical studies of counselling groups for violent men using the CTS to assess violent behaviour, the female partners of these men reported higher levels of violence committed by their husbands than the men reported themselves (Browning and Dutton, 1986; Edleson and Brygger, 1986), and men frequently ignored the fact that their actions caused severe injury to or hospitalization of their wives (Browning and Dutton, 1986; Brush, 1990; Makepeace, 1986).

This discrepancy in reporting is not surprising, since many men who inflict violence and injury on their wives will feel remorseful and guilty and will deny their actions. Others may rationalize their actions as a way of maintaining an image of themselves as good people. Many therapists working with abusive men have found denial to be a typical response of those confronted about their behaviour. In other cases, batterers may honestly have difficulty recalling events or not realize the consequences of their actions for their female partners if they were intoxicated at the time. And some victims may conceal their injuries from their partners in an attempt to smooth over the incident (Makepeace, 1986). Further qualitative work is needed to more fully understand the differences between men's and women's perceptions and responses to questions about their own use of violence and their partners' use of violence against them.

The way the CTS is traditionally applied has been criticized on the grounds that it ignores the gendered power imbalances that exist within marriage and society and excludes crucial details about motives, intentions, and consequences (Dobash et al., 1992; Brush, 1990; Browning and Dutton, 1986; Saunders, 1988; DeKeseredy and MacLean, 1990). This scale rests on the assumption that a level playing field exists in families and society whereby men and women enjoy equal power, authority, and resources. The CTS overlooks the unique social roles of men and women within marriage that cause them to assign different meanings to similar acts and to suffer different consequences of acts that appear similar when measured without context. Treating a slap by a man and the same act by a woman as equivalent ignores the damage that can be inflicted, as well as victims' ability to restrain assailants or to retaliate. The meaning of a violent act also differs significantly for male and female victims. Men begin as the dominant partners in marriage, and one episode of violence, or even the threat of violence, has the potential to change the dynamics of the relationship, reinforcing his dominance and her passivity (Walker, 1984). A woman's violence against her husband seldom has such an effect.

Murray Straus, the architect of the CTS, acknowledges the need to give primary attention to wife battering as the more pressing social policy issue on the basis that men tend to underreport their own violence, men are more likely to use very dangerous and injurious forms of violence (such as beating and using a knife or gun), men use more repetitive violence against their wives, women very often must endure beatings by their husbands because of economic and social constraints to terminating the relationship, and much of women's violence is committed in defence against their husbands' assaults (Straus, 1990a:200; Gelles and Straus, 1988; see also Browne, 1987; Saunders, 1988; Dobash and Dobash, 1988; Makepeace, 1986). Straus concedes that it is "advisable to base analyses of violence by men on data provided by women" (Stets and Straus, 1990a:162).

The manner in which the CTS is typically introduced to respondents, as a list of ways of "settling differences," is also problematic. It reads as follows:

> No matter how well a couple get along, there are times when they disagree, get annoyed with the other person or just have spats or fights because they're in a bad mood or tired or for some other reason. They also use many different ways of trying to settle their differences. I'm going to read some things that you and your spouse might do when you have an argument. I would like you to tell me how many times in the past 12 months you have (done any of the following). Thinking back over the last 12 months you've been together, was there ever an occasion when your spouse (did the following)? Tell me how often. (Straus, 1990a:33)

Introductions are crucial components of sample surveys. They establish the context of the survey at the outset and ensure that respondents have a common understanding of the focus of the questions to follow. One reason that traditional crime victimization surveys have had difficulty eliciting responses about sexual assault and wife assault is that respondents are told that the survey is interested in experiences of crime, and the wording leading up to questions about victimization reinforce this. Reliability of sample surveys will be badly affected if there is ambiguity in the wording of the questions and if respondents are likely to attach significantly different meaning to the same questions. Validity is affected by questions that poorly represent what the researcher is attempting to measure.

Both of these problems are present in the above introduction. The wording is potentially ambiguous and is inappropriate for orienting respondents toward thinking about violence they have suffered at the hands of their partners. While some respondents may think about experiences of violence as ways of settling differences, a great many may not. This brings into question the reliability and validity of a scale to measure violence that is, in fact, designed to address ways of settling differences. There can be little doubt that most violent relationships are conflict-ridden; however, there is substantial evidence that many acts of aggression by men against their wives are not precipitated by an argument or disagreement between them, and it is questionable whether respondents would think these acts appropriate to include (Dobash and Dobash, 1984; Browne, 1987).

The Violence Against Women Survey departs from the conflict tactics approach in the extensive lead-up it has to questions about spousal violence, through detailed questions about fear of violence in public places and precautions taken to protect oneself, sexual harassment, and sexual and physical violence by strangers, dates and boyfriends, and other known men. The VAWS does not use the "verbal reasoning" scale or the "verbal aggression" scale to ease respondents into questions about violence. Moreover, the introduction to the section inquiring about wife assault states very directly that "We are particularly interested in learning more about women's experiences of *violence* in their homes. I'd like to ask you to tell me if your husband/partner has ever done any of the following to you" (Statistics Canada, 1994b:35). This survey is concerned not with ways of settling differences but with violence against women, and this context is established at this point.

The 10 items of the VAWS used to measure acts of wife assault are similar to those used in the CTS; however, a number of modifications were made to the original items during the testing phase in order to correct ambiguity in the question wording. The CTS item "threatened to hit or throw something at you" was altered to read "threatened to hit you *with his fist or anything else that could hurt you.*" Similarly, the item "threw something at you" has been clarified to read "thrown anything at you *that could hurt you.*" The item "hit you with something" now reads "hit you with something *that could hurt you.*" These modifications were made following focus-group testing and field-testing, in which some respondents were clearly confused about whether to include incidents in which they were threatened or hit in a playful way with harmless objects that could not possibly hurt them. The addition of an item on sexual attacks takes into account sexual violence in marriage and the links between wife battering and marital rape.

SUMMARY

The growing awareness of sexual violence and wife battering over the past two decades has been accompanied by significant improvements to the methods used to study these issues. Researchers have moved from an early reliance on police records and clinical samples, which tap only a small proportion of cases, to wide-scale sample surveys that are capable of capturing the broad range of experiences, the consequences for the woman involved, her reactions to the incident, the reactions of others around her, her decisions to involve the police or other services, and the way she is treated by the police and the court process.

While sample surveys offer the best hope for the most comprehensive information about violence against women, the estimates produced almost certainly undercount the true prevalence of violence. Survey researchers can do their best to ensure a sensitive approach with valid measures of violence, but it is almost certain that some women will refuse to reveal their experiences to an interviewer. The issue of underreporting or nonresponse can be addressed by special attention to the difficult situation many abused women find themselves in when responding to survey questions. However, it is clear that victim surveys, like other data sources, are imperfect tools, and that researchers must continue to strive for better and improved methods of measuring the physical and sexual abuse of women. In the next chapter, we will learn that even the knowledge that such abuse exists creates fear in women who do not experience abuse directly and affects the choices they make.

Women's Fear of Public Violence

THE SUBJECTIVE MEANING OF WOMEN'S FEAR

One of the reactions women have to the threat of crime and violence is fear. Fear of crime is generally understood by researchers as encompassing a "diffuse sense of danger about being physically harmed by criminal violence. It is associated with concern about being outside the home, probably in an urban area, alone and potentially vulnerable to personal harm" (Stanko, 1995:48). In small, infrequent doses, fear can enhance a sense of prudence in unfamiliar and potentially dangerous situations and help avert danger. But for many women, concerns about safety affect mundane decisions about where to live, what jobs to accept, what to wear, and which places and people to avoid. Concerns about their safety may lead women to turn down certain jobs that require them to take public transportation into unsafe areas, avoid night classes, or avoid going out in the evening if it means having to walk or travel a distance alone. Women's concerns about safety can thus limit their possibilities and prevent them from taking full advantage of the opportunities available in their communities.

In a survey of American women and men, Gordon and Riger (1989) found that not only do women frequently restrict their leisure activities outside their homes, very high proportions also avoid common everyday situations, such as shopping and other errands, because of fear for their safety: 34 percent of women in their sample said they "fairly often" or "most of the time" avoid such ordinary tasks as shopping or errands, 36 percent often avoid going to movies or visiting friends, and 42 percent stay at home all or most of the time to avoid attack (1989:121).

Some men, too, feel threatened or fearful in certain situations. Certain groups, such as men in prison and gay men, can be particularly vulnerable targets of attack. However, women's experiences of violence are unique because of their unique vulnerability to sexual violence. And because their personal experiences are qualitatively different from men's experiences, women's perceptions of their safety are significantly different as well (Stanko, 1990a). Women grow up with an awareness of their vulnerability to sexual violence, a vulnerability that shapes their perceptions of their safety, the strategies they use to protect themselves, the ways in which they manage their lives, and the decisions they make. Following in-depth interviews with women and men about their anxieties related to crime, Elizabeth Stanko concludes that rather than a fleeting reaction to specific situations, women's fear is a direct result of the condition of growing up female. The reverse is also true: the condition of women's lives is a direct result of their fear of sexual violence.

Researchers who have attempted to explain the source of women's fear have found that women's concerns about their personal safety in almost any situation are intrinsically tied to concerns about sexual violence. Most women perceive rape to be extremely serious but, unlike most other serious offences such as homicide, which they perceive to be rare, they judge rape to be very likely to happen. Mark Warr (1985) found that women perceive rape to be equal in seriousness to murder, and that women under 35 years of age fear rape more than any other crime. When asked how likely they think they are to become victims of a range of crimes, rape is viewed as the most probable of all violent crimes (Warr, 1985; Wolfgang, 1978, as quoted in Skogan and Maxfield, 1981; Gordon and Riger, 1989). Women also perceive their risk of most other crimes, a break-in into their homes for example, to involve the potential for sexual violence.

The topic of public perceptions of crime has been a focus of sociological research since the genesis of crime victim surveys two decades ago. This chapter presents some of the methodological challenges presented by this area of study, and describes what the various sources tell us about the nature of women's fear. It explores in some detail the extent to which Canadian women worry about their personal safety in common everyday situations, factors that affect women's sense of security, and the precautions they take to defend themselves against a violent attack.

How Has Women's Fear Been Studied?

The objective of crime victim surveys, beginning in the 1970s, to get at the dark figure of crime not captured in official police statistics also included efforts to quantify public perceptions of the risk of crime and the extent to which people harbour fears about their safety in public (the format of these surveys was discussed in Chapter 2). For many years, fear of crime has been measured on national victimization surveys, such as Statistics Canada's General Social Survey, the National Crime Survey in the United States, and the British Crime Survey, by responses to a two-part hypothetical question about how safe one feels (or would feel) walking alone in one's neighbourhood alone after dark and during the day. The results of these questions have consistently shown that women score higher than men on feelings of "unsafety." In the 1993 General Social Survey, 42 percent of Canadian women said they felt "very" or "somewhat" unsafe walking alone in their area after dark compared with just 10 percent of men. Urban dwellers, older people, and the poor are also more fearful than residents of rural areas, younger people, and the middle class, and fear for both men and women varies according to these sociodemographic characteristics (Sacco and Johnson, 1990; Miethe, 1995; Skogan and Maxfield, 1981). However, the strongest factor in predicting fear of crime is gender: women are more fearful than men regardless of place of residence, age, income, or any other factor.

Some have argued that the question is a better measure of perceptions of risk than feelings of fear ("How *safe* do you feel?" rather than "How *afraid* do you feel?") (LaGrange, Ferraro, and Supancic, 1992:315). There are also problems with the way the question measures *women's* fear in particular on a number of counts. First, this hypothetical question mixes the responses of those who feel unsafe and threatened when they must walk alone in their neighbourhoods with those who, for whatever reason, rarely or never walk alone and can only imagine how they would feel. Many women seldom, if ever, walk alone at night for a number of reasons, some unrelated to fear—some women have full-time responsibility for young children, some are infirm or have a disability that makes it difficult to get around in the dark, some routinely walk the dog at night but always with a companion, others have no occasion to go out at night. Asking these women to say how they think they would feel if they had to walk alone at night is asking them how they think it would feel to do something they never do. In effect, it is like asking some women how they would feel if they went sky-diving; it is not likely something they would ever do. In the absence of direct knowledge, many women who never go out at night may report that they fear the worst.

A second problem with the way traditional crime surveys have attempted to explain women's fear relates to the way crimes of violence were measured. Those surveys that produced high levels of fear among women consistently estimated the risk of violence against women to be lower than the risk to men for all but sexual offences. According to Statistics Canada's 1988 General Social Survey, rates of victimization against men were 90 per 1000 men in the preceding year, compared with 77 per 1000 women; however, 39 percent of women reported feeling unsafe walking alone in their neighbourhoods after dark compared with only 11 percent of men (Sacco and Johnson, 1990). This pattern has been repeated in surveys conducted in Canada, the United States, and Great Britain. Chapter 2 discusses how improvements to the wording of questions on the 1993 GSS resulted in a shift to higher rates of violence for women than for men. For many years, the inverse relationship between women's low rates of victimization and high rate of fear was considered "ironic" and a "paradox" (Skogan and Maxfield, 1981:78).

It was also considered a paradox that women reported relatively low rates of victimization despite their frequent use of precautions to protect themselves. This apparent anomaly was explained as follows: because women have higher levels of fear than men, they are so much more cautious in where they go and with whom, in installing extra locks, and in not going out alone, that they have effectively reduced their chances of violent victimization. Because men put themselves at risk of encountering violence more often than women, they have higher rates of violence to report to victim surveys. According to routine activities theory, certain segments of the population, like men and young people, have higher rates of victimization because their occupational and leisure activities expose them to a higher risk of violence (Cohen and Felson, 1979). To the extent that lifestyle puts men in dangerous situations or out on the street late at night, their risk of victimization will increase. Women are socialized to take fewer chances that would put them at risk of victimization, and because men are conditioned to take risks, the probability that they will be victimized is higher (Sacco, 1990).

Since women's fear could not be explained by their objective risk of attack as determined by police statistics and victimization surveys (sources we now know undercount women's experiences of violence), this fear was assumed to "reflect concerns of a symbolic or emotive nature, rather than concrete possibilities" (Skogan and Maxfield, 1981:78). In other words, women's perceptions were thought to be influenced more by what they hear happening to other people, by feelings of vulnerability to attack by a much bigger and stronger man, by the specific concern about sexual assault, and by concerns about how they might be injured or about the emotional effects of an attack. These factors were assumed to play a more important role in shaping women's perceptions than personal experiences, which were thought to be rare.

DISORDER AND HARASSMENT

More recently, American sociologist Wesley Skogan (1990) has expanded on this concept of symbolic or emotive concerns. Drawing on extensive research conducted in cities throughout the United States, Skogan maintains that the higher levels of fear among certain groups is fostered by signs of disorder or incivility in local communities that cause people to feel uneasy (Skogan, 1990; LaGrange, Ferraro, and Supancic, 1992). Many neighbourhoods throughout North America have witnessed a gradual erosion in community standards that adversely affects residents' perceptions of their personal safety. Skogan identifies two types of social disorder that negatively affect communities: *social disorder,* which encompasses such behaviour as public drinking, prostitution, graffiti, vandalism, loitering, catcalls, and sexual harassment; and *physical disorder,* which refers to visual signs of neglect and decay, such as abandoned or ill-kept buildings, broken streetlights, and garbage. Social disorder tends to occur in a series of episodes, while physical disorder represents ongoing conditions. Some activities, such as public drinking, prostitution, and vandalism, are illegal while others are not, but their ongoing presence may be perceived by citizens as signifying unmanageable law enforcement problems.

Residents who witness the continuing presence of these problems and a steady decline in the social and physical order may feel that they and the police have lost control over the neighbourhood. If residents then retreat from public places, certain disorders can generate more disorder and some may flourish into criminal activity. Some groups, such as poor inner-city dwellers, are more likely to be exposed on a regular basis to these signs of urban decay, and this creates anxiety and fear. According to Skogan (1990:10), disorder in neighbourhoods is closely related to crime rates, fear of crime, and a belief that crime in the neighbourhood is a problem. He concludes that disorder and crime have separate, independent effects on the morale and cohesion of communities. So even if crime statistics don't show an increase in criminal acts, fear levels may be a reflection of the public's belief in a less safe society as decline and disorder become more evident.

Disorder and decline in some American and Canadian communities do seem to affect levels of concern about crime, despite statistical evidence of stable or declining crime rates. A feeling of loss of control over one's environment will affect both men and women, and may raise the anxieties of women about sexual violence. However, the "concrete possibilities" are also much more numerous than initially imagined or than crime victim surveys were able to measure. These surveys found that direct personal experience plays a relatively limited role in explaining fear because the surveys were able to capture only a limited range of women's experiences. They counted only events that occurred in a one-year reference period, and emphasized "crime" as the phenomenon of interest. No special effort was made to capture the very personal experiences of sexual violence or violence by intimate partners, and as a result, relatively few of these experiences were reported to interviewers. Traditional crime victimization surveys are geared toward orienting respondents to think about the level of crime in their neighbourhood and whether it has increased or decreased recently. Respondents are primed to think about crime in the traditional manner of something that happens outside the home, primarily committed by strangers. Respondents who are unsure about whether to consider physical abuse by a husband or boyfriend, or a sexual assault by a date or cousin, as a "crime" very likely will not think that these experiences are what the interviewer wants to hear about. If a woman does consider her experience a crime and it happened outside the one-year reference period, it will not be counted.

Victim surveys then assign "victim" status to women who have been sexually or physically assaulted in the previous year and "nonvictim" status to those not victimized very recently. This confounds our analysis of the correlates of women's fear, since many women classified as nonvictims in reality have been victims of very serious violence that has fundamentally altered their perceptions of their vulnerability to further violence. Admittedly, there are problems associated with measuring lifetime experiences of violence, particularly with respect to forgetting incidents that happened a long time ago, as discussed in Chapter 2. But it is unlikely that serious incidents causing physical and emotional trauma will be quickly forgotten. Serious incidents, no matter when they happened, as well as an accumulation of minor incidents whose results are not so traumatic, and any type of incident that occurred recently, are all likely to have an effect on the way women feel about their safety and vulnerability.

The restricted focus of traditional victim surveys on acts of criminal violence also present problems for understanding women's fear. A wide range of acts that are not considered criminal in the legal sense but that are nonetheless threatening and intimidating are typically omitted in victimization surveys or analyses of women's fear. These are experiences that serve to remind women that they are potential targets for sexual violence and to undermine their feelings of security. The suggestive comments and looks women receive from strange men on the street and from men in the office and in bars, curb crawling, jokes and comments that are designed to degrade and humiliate—it is because these experiences are so common and have been considered acceptable and perceived (by the offender and some bystanders) as harmless or even flattering attention that men bestow upon women, that they have been overlooked in efforts to understand women's fear. Young (1988:175) makes the point that "women do not only suffer crime per se but also an undertow of incivilities and harassment which men do not."

Sexual harassment figures prominently in women's understanding of their personal safety because of the frequency and the uncertainty of these encounters and the fear they cause. Acts that are classified as sexual harassment may be considered to be less harmful because they fall outside the Criminal Code, but they hold the potential for something worse, in reality as well as in the mind of the female victim. The eventual outcome of the act is usually unknown to the woman at the time—she cannot predict, for instance, whether the man exposing himself to her will silently back off, or whether his actions are a prelude to sexual assault; she doesn't know beforehand if the sexual comments made to her as she passes a group of men on the street will be of the everyday variety or whether they will evolve into something worse. She cannot know what kind of response from her will deter and what kind will aggravate the situation. Depending on the eventual outcome, the encounter will be classified later by police or on a survey as flashing, jeering, being followed, a physical attack, or a sexual attack. Something that ends in "just" flashing or harassment or being followed may look minor in retrospect, but at the time of the incident the woman may fear the worst: that she will be grabbed and won't be able to defend herself, and that she will be sexually assaulted. The most terrifying situations involve more than one man, in which case the woman knows she won't be able to ward off an attack. Naturally fearing the worst that could happen, women are terrified, and then relieved in retrospect that "nothing happened" or "they were lucky this time." In their mind is what could have happened; every woman fears the worst because she knows what is possible.

An assault confirms and exacerbates women's fear, but a direct assault is not always necessary to keep them feeling threatened and victimized. In interviews with British women about their feelings of safety, researchers Hanmer and Saunders found that the greater the uncertainty about the outcome of a situation, the more terrifying the encounter will be (Hanmer and Saunders, 1984:33). In actual fact, women are unable to predict when a male harasser's behaviour might lead to a violent assault. Hanmer and Saunders conclude that "women define violence by how frightened or out of control of the situation they are. The more uncertainty about the outcome, the more terrifying the encounter" (1984:70). In many of what are regarded as routine or minor incidents of sexual harassment, where "nothing happened," the level of uncertainty and fear is considerable.

The original concept of feeling safe walking alone in one's neighbourhood at night intentionally does not specify the object of the fear, but is assumed to be asking people about a personal attack from someone outside the household in the immediate vicinity (Skogan and Maxfield, 1981:50). This measurement of fear was designed with the express intention of measuring anxiety about strangers, assuming that is the source of greatest danger. It was reasoned that most people fear strangers because of the unpredictability and the apparent randomness of violence committed by them. While it may be true that most people perceive the threat of violence by strangers to be a source of danger, there is growing evidence that a great deal of violence, particularly against women, is committed by people who are well known to their victims. Public concern about crime and violence may be focused on sudden, violent attacks by strangers, but the more hidden acts of violence by known offenders can have a negative effect on women's overall sense of vulnerability, ultimately affecting their responses to questions about fear. These experiences and non-criminal threats of violence need to be better accounted for in order to more fully understand the factors that contribute to women's fear.

THE NATURE OF WOMEN'S FEAR

Women responding to Statistics Canada's national survey on violence against women were asked a series of questions intended to measure the extent to which they worry about their personal safety in a number of situations, and how frequently they are involved in these situations. To estimate the extent to which fear restricts women's behaviour, those who expressed worry were asked whether they would engage in these situations more frequently if they felt safer doing so. They were then asked a number of questions about actions they might take to make themselves feel safer. This combination of questions was designed to explore more deeply the level of concern women feel for their safety in common everyday situations, the extent to which fear imposes limits on their freedom of movement, and how they manage threats to their safety in their everyday lives.

Unlike the traditional approach that implicitly orients respondents to think about crime in their neighbourhoods, questions about fear were introduced in the Violence Against Women Survey by the following introduction:

> I would like to start by asking you some questions about your personal safety. Most of us worry, from time to time, about the threat that violence poses to our personal safety. I am going to ask you about some everyday situations, and I would like you to tell me how you feel in each of them. (Statistics Canada, 1994b:1)

Women were asked to think about how worried they feel (not how "safe" they feel) and the object of the worry was clearly specified as the threat of violence.

Very different results are possible from this series of questions, depending on whether all women are considered or only those who are ever involved in particular situations. Recall that the traditional approach treats these questions as hypothetical for those never involved the situations, essentially asking some people to imagine how they would feel. Depending on the situation, this can be a majority of the population. For example, when asked how worried they are when waiting for or using public transit, 69 percent of women said they never use public transit, leaving only 7 percent who said they are "very worried" doing so. Removing those women for whom this is a hypothetical question (the 69 percent), the percentage who are "very worried" jumps to 22 percent. The percentage who are "very" or "somewhat" worried climbs to 76 percent.

As Table 3.1 indicates, a majority of women who have to walk alone after dark, use public transportation alone after dark, or use parking garages worry about their safety while doing so: 60 percent of women who walk alone in their own areas after dark, 76 percent who use public transportation alone after dark, and 83 percent who use parking garages report being "very" or "somewhat" worried about their personal safety in these situations. Forty percent of those who are ever home alone in the evenings also feel worried to some degree. Significant proportions of women, approximately one in four, feel "very" afraid using public transportation and parking garages.

For most women, concerns they have about their safety are not irrational. What they are expressing is a realistic appraisal of the cues in their environment that tell them they are vulnerable

TABLE 3.1

Percentage of Women Who Worry about Their Personal Safety in Certain Situations

Situation	Very Worried	Somewhat Worried	Not at All Worried
		percentage	
Walking alone in her area after dark	8	52	40
Waiting for/using public transportation alone after dark	22	54	24
Walking alone to her car in a parking garage	27	56	17
When home alone in the evening	6	34	61

Excludes women who are never in these situations.

Source: Statistics Canada, *Violence Against Women Survey*, Microdata File, Ottawa (1994a).

to sexual attack. Fully 89 percent of women were either sexually harassed or assaulted or threatened in any way mentioned in the Violence Against Women Survey (see Box 3.1 for questions used to define sexual harassment); a mere 11 percent reported none of these experiences. There is therefore no paradox that 60 percent of women who walk alone in their neighbourhoods alone after dark express worry about doing so, and that even greater proportions express concern about using public transportation after dark or walking alone in parking garages. When only 1 in 10 women says she has not been followed by a man, had an obscene telephone call, been flashed at, been sexually harassed in other ways on the street or by some known man, sexually assaulted, or physically threatened or attacked in any way, it should not be surprising that levels of fear are this high. A majority of women know either through first-hand experience, or through friends and

VAWS Survey Questions on Sexual Harassment

Sexual harassment was measured by responses to the following:

- *Have you ever received an obscene phone call?*
- *Has a man ever indecently exposed himself to you?*
- *Have you ever received unwanted attention from a male stranger (anything that does not include touching such as catcalls, whistling, leering, or blowing kisses)?*
- *Have you ever been followed by a man in a way that frightened you?*

The next few questions refer to unwanted attention you may have received from men you knew, such as someone at work or at school, a doctor, a landlord or a relative.

- *Has a man you knew ever made you uncomfortable by making inappropriate comments about your body or sex life?*
- *Has a man you knew ever made you uncomfortable by repeatedly asking you for a date and would not take "no" for an answer?*
- *Leaned over you unnecessarily, got too close or cornered you?*
- *Hinted that you could lose your job, or that your job situation might be hurt, if you did not have a sexual relationship with him?*

Source: Statistics Canada, *Violence Against Women Survey, Questionnaire Package* (1994b), 5–8.

Box 3.1   Sexual Harassment

family, the potentially devastating physical and emotional consequences of a sexual attack and fear the same consequences for themselves.

A great many women cannot avoid spending time in activities that cause them to worry about their safety. It is impossible for large proportions of women to avoid walking alone in their own neighbourhood when they hold jobs or attend classes that require them to be out after dark, considering how early night falls during the winter months in most parts of Canada. Women who can't afford to own a car, or for whom driving to and from work is not feasible, cannot help but be in a position where they must use public transportation alone after dark, whether this causes them to be fearful. And many women who own cars must regularly park in public garages, either at work or at home. Forty-two percent of women who fear for their safety while walking alone in their areas must walk alone at least once a week and sometimes daily (Table 3.2). One-third of women who are fearful of using public transportation or parking garages also must do these things at least once a week. For many women, fear is a part of their everyday reality, and fearful situations are an unavoidable aspect of their lives. Altogether, 24 percent of women say they are worried at some level for their safety in every one of these situations (Statistics Canada, 1994a).

For many women, fear inhibits them from doing many things they might otherwise do. A majority of women (66 percent) who

T A B L E   3 . 2

Percentage of Women Who are Very or Somewhat Worried about Their Personal Safety in Certain Situations by Frequency of Doing So

Situation	Total	Daily	At Least Once a Week	At Least Once a Month	Less than Once a Month
			percentage		
Walking alone in her area after dark	100	10	32	24	33
Waiting for/using public transportation alone after dark	100	9	23	22	46
Walking alone to her car in a parking garage[1]	100	13	18	24	45

Excludes women who are never in these situations.

[1] Based on women who drive.

Source: Statistics Canada, *Violence Against Women Survey*, Microdata File, Ottawa (1994a).

express fear for their personal safety walking alone in their own area say that they would walk alone more often if they felt safer (Statistics Canada, 1994a). The percentage of women who say fear prevents them from using public transportation or parking garages is close to one-half. What is perhaps even more important is that a great many women who *never* engage in these activities say the reason is because they are too fearful. Approximately half of all women who say they never walk alone after dark never use public transportation, or never use parking garages say that if they didn't feel so fearful, they would do these things. This excludes women for whom public transportation and parking garages are not available in their communities. The use of such services as public transportation and parking garages is obviously influenced by other factors in addition to fear, such as cost, convenience, and availability. It may seem unbelievable to some that of all the women who have buses, streetcars, and subways available to them and who never take them alone after dark, a primary reason is that they are worried about personal safety. In addition, half of all women who have parking garages available to them never use them because of fear.

FACTORS THAT AFFECT WOMEN'S SENSE OF SECURITY

Levels of worry and anxiety about violence vary across the female population depending on such factors as age, living situation, health, income, and direct experience with threats and violence. We might expect, for example, that women with the financial resources to live in safer neighbourhoods would have different perceptions about safety resulting from different life experiences than women without the same resources. What we find, however, is that women living in lower-income households (and presumably lower-income neighbourhoods) are no more likely to say they are very or somewhat worried than middle-income women when walking alone in their neighbourhoods, and only slightly more worried than upper-income women (Table 3.3). The percentage who are worried while using public transit or parking garages increases with income. It is middle-income women who feel slightly more worried about being home alone in the evening.

The effect of income is strongest in extreme levels of worry, however: 14 percent of those in the lowest income group compared with 5 percent of those with the highest incomes stated that they are "very" worried walking alone. The reverse is true for public transit and parking garages: in these situations, women from

TABLE 3.3

Percentage of Women Who Are Very or Somewhat Worried about Their Safety, by Personal Characteristics

Characteristics	Walking Alone	Public Transit	Parking Garages	Home Alone
		percentage		
Total fearful	60	76	83	40
Household Income				
< $15 000	62	70	78	39
$15 000–$39 999	63	74	81	38
$40 000–$59 999	61	80	84	44
> $60 000	57	84	87	40
Educational Attainment				
Less than high-school diploma	58	65	76	41
High-school diploma	59	76	83	40
Some post-secondary	62	80	85	39
University degree	61	78	85	37
Residence				
Urban area	66	77	84	40
Small town/rural area	44	68	78	39
Age Group				
18–24	69	81	83	44
25–34	67	80	88	47
35–44	60	79	86	41
45–64	52	71	81	38
65 and over	52	51	62	26
Health				
Excellent	56	73	82	34
Very good	62	78	84	40
Good	62	76	82	42
Fair	64	72	83	45
Poor	62	70	83	45
Disabling health problem	65	74	85	44

Excludes women who are never in these situation.

[1] Employed at a paid job or business for 6 months or more during the year.

Source: Statistics Canada, *Violence Against Women Survey*, Microdata File, Ottawa (1994a).

higher-income households are more likely to express concern about their safety. The reason for this may lie in the contrast between the relative safety of these women's neighbourhoods and other parts of the city. Women from higher-income neighbourhoods may feel more threatened outside their own areas while using public transit and parking garages where they feel they have less control over unfamiliar situations.

Generally speaking, women with higher education also worry more about their safety in public situations. However, at the extreme levels of fear, women with the lowest levels of education are those most likely to say they are very worried about walking alone, using public transit, and being home alone.

For many women, poverty is tied to single parenthood. And for the majority of women raising children on their own, single parenthood brings a life of economic stress, neighbourhoods in states of decline, and few extra resources for taxis, car phones, or extra locks on the door. A full 60 percent of women raising children on their own in Canada are living below the poverty line (Statistics Canada, 1995). Single parenthood also increases the responsibility of women, not only for their own safety but for the safety of their children. Women raising children on their own are among those who express the highest levels of concern for their safety in all situations.

The daily experiences of women in large cities are also different from those of women living in small towns and rural areas. Women living in urban areas, where anonymity and threats from strangers are more prevalent, report higher rates of violence and sexual harassment from strangers than women in small towns and rural areas. The Violence Against Women Survey found that in a one-year period, 5 percent of urban women were assaulted by strangers compared with 3 percent of women living in small towns and rural areas; 42 percent of urban dwellers had at least one experience of sexual harassment during the one-year period compared with 30 percent of small-town and rural residents. Consequently, urban women have higher rates of fear in public situations (Table 3.3).

A woman's overall perception of herself as physically capable of protecting herself may affect her sense of vulnerability when out alone in potentially threatening situations. Health status, a proxy measure of physical health, at first glance does not appear to have a strong effect on feelings of safety (Table 3.3); however, there is a striking effect on the highest level of fear, those feeling very worried. The proportion of women feeling very worried while walking alone increases from 6 percent for women who describe their health as excellent to 17 percent for those who describe their health as poor. This higher fear for women with poor health exists for all situations: women feeling very worried using public transit doubles from 17 percent of those in excellent health to 38 percent of those with poor health, those feeling very worried using parking garages increases dramatically from 26 percent to 46 percent, and there is a threefold increase from 4 percent to 14 percent in those who are very worried when home alone. Similarly, women who have a disability appear not to be much more fearful than the average woman; however, they are much more likely than others to report being very worried: 14 percent compared with 7 percent with no disability when walking alone, 33 percent compared with 20 percent when using public transit, and 33 percent compared with 26 percent when using parking garages.

THE AGE–FEAR DEBATE

One of the strongest links to women's fear is age, but it is not in the direction indicated by earlier research that used the hypothetical question "How safe do you feel, *or would you feel*, walking alone in your neighbourhood after dark?" Results of this question show that fear *increases* as a function of age: people over 65 years of age consistently report higher levels of "unsafety" than younger people (Sacco and Johnson, 1990; Skogan and Maxfield, 1981). When women who never engage in these activities are factored out, however, the extent to which women worry about their personal safety actually *declines* with age: 69 percent of women 18–24 years of age who walk alone in their areas after dark are worried doing so, compared with 52 percent of women over the age of 45 (Table 3.3). The proportion who worry about their safety also declines for using public transit and being home alone, while for those who use parking garages, the most fearful women are those aged 25–44.

Nor do elderly women predominate in the group at the extreme end of fearfulness. The proportion of women who are very worried using public transit or parking garages actually increases up to age 64, and then drops off sharply. In the case of walking alone, similar proportions of women in all age groups are very worried.

The relatively low rates of fear among elderly women might lead those who have grown accustomed to the idea that the elderly are prisoners of fear in their homes to assume that older women simply do these things less often because they are too fearful, and that the few remaining women courageous enough to do them are naturally those who score low on fear. While it is true that the proportion of women who never walk alone, use public transit, or use parking garages increases quite dramatically with age, their reasons, for the most part, are unrelated to fear. When asked if they would walk alone or use public transit or parking garages if they felt safer about doing so, older women were less likely to say that they would. In the case of walking alone after dark, for example, 72 percent of 18–24-year-old women who never do so said fear was a factor for them, and this percentage declined with age to 42 percent of women 65 years of age and over. Older women are less likely than younger women to engage in these activities, and less likely to feel fearful doing so, and their decision not to do these things is not as likely to be attributed to fear.

It is interesting to note that the negative relationship between fear and age remains even when the entire population of women is considered and not just those who are ever in these situations. When respondents are given the option of saying they don't engage in these activities, the percentage who worry about their personal safety declines with age as the percentage who never do these activities increases.

It is interesting to note that the negative relationship between fear and age remains even when the entire population of women is considered and not just those who are ever in these situations. When respondents are given the option of saying they don't engage in these activities, the percentage eho worry about their personal safety declines with age as the percentage who never do these activities increases.

In his study of community disorder, Skogan (1990:55) reports that older people perceived less physical and social disorder than younger people living in the same areas. He attributes this to the fact that younger people more frequently come into contact with more diverse elements in the community. It seems the greater concern younger women have for their safety is a common-sense reflection of the threats in their environment and their feelings of vulnerability to violence. The lessons of vulnerability are learned at a young age, and for young women, the possibility of violence is a lived reality. In all cases of sexual harassment, intimidation, threats, sexual assault, and even wife battering, young women aged 18–24 reported by far the highest rates, while women 45 and over reported the lowest rates (see also Chapters 4 through 6). Young women are involved much more frequently in dating, parties, social activity in bars, high-risk jobs, and travelling to evening jobs and night classes. In short, they have higher-risk lives. They accurately assess their environment to hold the threat of violence. This is not the perception, nor is it the reality, for older women.

Despite the differences in perceptions of personal safety among women of different socioeconomic statuses and living situations, there are also many commonalities. Women with cars, for example, may not have daily first-hand experience of the dangers of public transportation, but they know the fear that accompanies a late-night walk through a parking lot or parking garage. Women who live with other people may feel secure in their homes most of the time, but on evenings when they are alone, they might feel quite insecure. In fact, the survey data show this: feelings of fear when staying home alone in the evening are more prevalent among women from larger households because women who are accustomed to having other people around are more fearful when left on their own. Those who have chosen to live alone and who spend most evenings alone cannot afford to worry about their safety; these women express lower levels of fear.

FEAR AND EXPERIENCES OF VIOLENCE

How do women's experiences of violence influence their feelings of safety? Are women who have been victimized more likely to fear for their safety in these situations? If early researchers were correct in their assumption that violent victimization by strangers is the type of situation that has the greatest impact on perceptions of personal safety, we would expect fear levels to be highest for women who have had these experiences. On the other hand, some writers have suggested that violence by someone close to the victim will have a stronger effect on future feelings of vulnerability because of the violation of trust that accompanies such an event (Smith, 1988; Junger, 1987). It is argued that being violated by someone who is defined as "safe" makes it more difficult to rationalize the experience and predict dangerous situations in the future.

Table 3.4 does not support either of these hypotheses. Nor does it show that sexual assault victimization, which is the crime women fear most, has a greater effect on perceptions of safety. It seems that violent victimization, no matter what sort or by whom, has similar effects on women's feelings of safety and that women who did not report a violent experience have lower levels of fear. The problem with Table 3.4 is that more than half of all women who reported a violent incident reported more than one experience to report to this survey. A woman who was a victim of dating violence, for example, might also have been attacked by a stranger or a spouse, and her response would be tallied in all three columns. If any of these experiences involved sexual assault, she would also be counted in the sexual assault column. This presents a problem of sorting out the causal factors and what can be said with confidence about the impact of different kinds of violence on women's fear.

An important point with respect to the usefulness of victim-type surveys to illuminate our understanding of women's fear is that, generally speaking, recent experiences of violence do not have a stronger effect on feelings of safety than others that happened a longer time ago. Women who reported experiencing violence in the 12 months prior to the survey were not significantly more likely to report feeling fearful than women victimized prior to that. In some situations, there was no difference at all in the levels of fear reported by these two groups, and in the case of women who are fearful using parking garages, those who were victimized prior to one year ago actually express higher levels of fear. This shows how fear-inducing parking garages are for the majority of women. It also illustrates how essential it is to include in calculations of victims or abused women those who experienced violence some time ago but for whom the effects continue to be felt. Violent victimization can have long-term consequences for a woman's emotional well-being; the experience confirms for her that she is an easy target, a feeling that carries over to all situations in which she feels the slightest bit apprehensive.

FEAR AND SEXUAL HARASSMENT

Situations that are considered noncriminal occur with greater frequency than those typically considered violent and can have an even greater effect on women's feelings of safety. As Table 3.5 shows, experience with any type of sexual harassment results in increased concern about personal safety, and the few women who did not report sexual harassment of any type reported feeling significantly less worried than women who had. The type of harassment that is most likely to affect women's sense of vulnerability is being followed by a man in a way that was frightening to them. Women who have had this experience are more likely to feel worried walking alone after dark and being home alone in the evening. Any type of harassment has the effect of making women feel insecure about using public transportation alone after dark or using parking garages, situations that heighten concerns about attack any time for the majority of women.

Combining the responses of women who had experiences of sexual harassment with those who had experiences of physical or sexual assault (a sum total of those harassed, threatened, or assaulted in any way), overall levels of fear are similar to levels of fear for these two types of experiences separately (Figure 3.1). One perplexing feature of Figure 3.1 is how to account for the very high proportions of women who did not report either violence or sexual harassment but who are worried about their safety. Sixty-six percent of women who had no experiences of violence or

Percentage of Women Who Are Very or Somewhat Worried about Their Personal Safety in Certain Situations by Type of Victimization Experience

Situation	Any Violent Victimization	Sexual Assault	Stranger Violence	Dating Violence	Wife Assault[1]	Acquaintance Violence	No Violent Victimization
				percentage			
Walking alone in her area after dark	65	64	65	68	66	64	55
Waiting for/using public transportation alone after dark	79	80	81	82	78	80	70
Walking alone to her car in a parking garage[2]	86	88	88	90	87	87	79
When home alone in the evening	44	45	45	46	46	47	34

Excludes women who are never in these situations.
[1] Based on women who have ever been married or lived in a common-law relationship.
[2] Based on women who drive.

Source: Statistics Canada, *Violence Against Women Survey*, Microdata File, Ottawa (1994a).

TABLE 3.5

Percentage of Women Who Are Very or Somewhat Worried about Their Personal Safety in Certain Situations, by Experiences of Sexual Harassment

Situation	Any Sexual Harassment	Obscene Phone Call	Indecent Exposure	Being Followed	Known Men	Street Harassment	No Harassment
				percentage			
Walking alone in her area after dark	63	64	66	69	65	65	41
Waiting for/using public transportation alone after dark	78	79	78	81	81	81	52
Walking alone to her car in a parking garage[1]	85	86	88	89	87	87	65
When home alone in the evening	42	42	43	47	44	44	26

Excludes women who are never in these situations.
[1] Based on women who drive.

Source: Statistics Canada, *Violence Against Women Survey*, Microdata File, Ottawa (1994a).

harassment to report nevertheless were worried about their safety when using parking garages, 48 percent when using public transportation alone after dark, and 40 percent when walking alone in their areas alone after dark. Even in the situation least likely to cause women to worry, being home alone in the evening, 25 percent of women who had never been victimized reported being worried. One possible explanation is that the few women who did not report any experiences of violence or harassment to this survey (only 11 percent of all women) had some of these experiences at some point in their lives that they either forgot about, or felt were too trivial or too traumatic or embarrassing to mention. A second possibility is that women fortunate to have avoided all forms of harassment or assault covered in this survey cannot escape the effects. Women are affected by the experiences of other women that they learn about through second-hand tales of harassment and assault, and worry about the consequences of similar acts against themselves. Women know of the experiences of their sisters, friends, and colleagues, they hear about violence through the media, and they are warned about it by the police, their parents, and other people. Very few women can escape the conditioning effects of violence around them.

Just as "old" experiences of violence can continue to have a negative effect on perceptions of safety, the effects of sexual harassment can linger long past the actual incident to remind women of their vulnerability to assault. While fear levels were higher in most situations for those who reported harassment in the most recent 12 months, those who reported harassment prior to the usual 12-month cutoff also experienced substantial levels of fear. Again, this suggests a need for researchers to include fear-provoking events that may have occurred some time ago and may not qualify as crimes under the legal code. These episodes can have a major effect on women's understanding and perception of their vulnerability to sexual attack.

In trying to come to terms with the paradox of women's high levels of fear and low levels of victimization, fear-of-crime researchers have claimed that while levels of fear are affected by violent victimization, most of those who are fearful have not been victimized during the survey reference period. Early theorists claimed that "recent personal victimization is simply too infrequent to explain why most people report being afraid" (Skogan and Maxfield, 1981:66). Contrary to this assertion, most women who are fearful have been threatened or attacked in one way or another. When all experiences of violence are counted, not just those that occurred during the previous year, 60 percent of women who are worried walking alone in their area after dark have been victims of assault. A full 90 percent of women who are worried

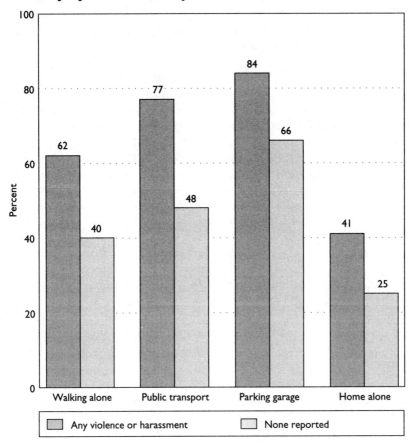

FIGURE 3.1

Percentage of Women Who Worry about Their Personal Safety by Whether They Were Assaulted or Harassed

Source: *Violence Against Women Survey*, 1993.

walking alone reported at least one incident of sexual harassment. These figures reaffirm the need to look beyond a narrow focus on recent criminal victimization to the entire range of threatening experiences that women are subjected to throughout their lifetimes to begin to understand the significance of these experiences in women's lives.

WOMEN'S USE OF SAFETY PRECAUTIONS

Just as violence and concern about violence are common occurrences in women's lives, precautions women take to avoid victimization and reduce this concern are also numerous. Two types of behaviour were addressed in the Violence Against Women Survey, techniques aimed at avoidance and those that are geared toward self-protection. Avoidance involves changing one's behaviour to limit exposure to dangerous people and situations, whereas self-protection involves actions that could be taken to defend oneself in the event of a confrontation. The Violence Against Women Survey asked women directly about three types of avoidance behaviours: checking the back seat of a parked car for intruders before getting in, trying to avoid walking past teenage boys or young men, for example, by crossing the street and locking the doors when alone in the car. It also addressed two types of self-protection measures: taking a self-defence course and carrying something to defend oneself or to alert other people. All respondents also had an opportunity to add to this list with the open question "Is there anything else you do to increase your personal safety that I have not already mentioned?" Women had a great deal to say about how they try to protect themselves: 57 percent said they do something else to increase their personal safety. These responses were recoded into the categories that appear in Figure 3.2.

Again, these data show that Canadian women find using cars to be fear-inducing. Being alone in a car makes women vulnerable targets in the event of engine failure, an accident, or a flat tire, or in the more remote chance of a car-jacking. Over one-half of all women who drive say they always lock the car doors when they are driving alone, and a similar proportion say they check for the possibility of someone hiding in the back seat before they get in (Table 3.6).

Walking down the street is also worrisome to many women. Not only are a large percentage of women worried about walking alone, but the number of women who always or usually try to avoid walking past teenage boys or young men stands at almost one-third, and 17 percent routinely carry something to defend themselves or alert other people. The most common thing that women carry with them is keys (between the knuckles, points out), whistles or other noise-makers, and knives or other sharp objects (Figure 3.2). Less common are mace and other sprays, blunt or heavy objects, and a purse heavy enough to use as a weapon. One in 10 women have taken a self-defence course in an attempt to improve their ability to defend themselves from an attack.

The majority of other protective behaviours that women volunteered to survey interviewers focused on safety on the street: staying home if the alternative was going out alone, avoiding going out at certain times or to certain places, walking in well-lit areas, walking assertively, telling others where or when they were

FIGURE 3.2

What Women Carry to Defend Themselves and Other Precautions

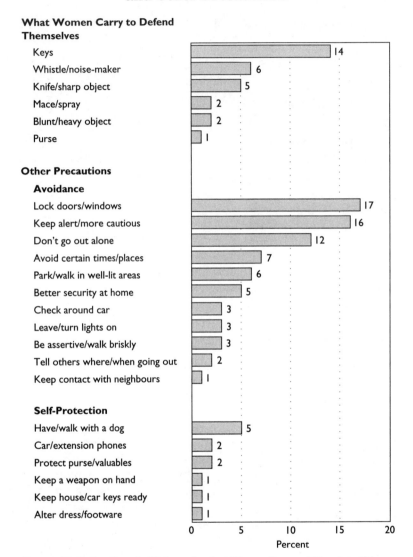

What Women Carry to Defend Themselves

- Keys — 14
- Whistle/noise-maker — 6
- Knife/sharp object — 5
- Mace/spray — 2
- Blunt/heavy object — 2
- Purse — 1

Other Precautions

Avoidance

- Lock doors/windows — 17
- Keep alert/more cautious — 16
- Don't go out alone — 12
- Avoid certain times/places — 7
- Park/walk in well-lit areas — 6
- Better security at home — 5
- Check around car — 3
- Leave/turn lights on — 3
- Be assertive/walk briskly — 3
- Tell others where/when going out — 2
- Keep contact with neighbours — 1

Self-Protection

- Have/walk with a dog — 5
- Car/extension phones — 2
- Protect purse/valuables — 2
- Keep a weapon on hand — 1
- Keep house/car keys ready — 1
- Alter dress/footware — 1

Percent (0, 5, 10, 15, 20)

Source: Statistics Canada *Violence Against Women Survey, Microdata File,* Ottawa (1994a).

TABLE 3.6

Percentage of Women Who Take Safety Precautions

Safety Precautions	Total	Always	Usually	Sometimes	Never
			percentage		
Avoidance					
Check the back seat of the car[1]	100	51	9	15	25
Try to avoid walking past teenage boys or young men	100	17	14	32	36
Lock the doors while alone in the car[1]	100	56	11	20	12
Self-protection					
Carry something to defend herself or alert other people	100	13	4	9	74

[1] Based on women who drive.

Source: Statistics Canada, *Violence Against Women Survey*, Microdata File, Ottawa (1994a).

going, keeping contact with neighbours, keeping alert and more cautious while on the street, having or walking with a dog, protecting purse or valuables, carrying a weapon, keeping house or car keys ready, and altering the way of dressing to make running easier if necessary. Others relate to safety around the home: leaving lights on, routinely locking doors and windows, improving security at home; and others are precautions taken while operating the car: parking in well-lit areas, and checking around the car—not just in the back seat—before getting in, and installing a car phone.

How do these differ from the actions men take to protect themselves? The 1993 General Social Survey makes some comparisons between men and women on actions they *routinely* take to make themselves safer from crime, and whether or not they have ever taken certain other measures to protect themselves or their property from crime. The results of this comparison are shown in Table 3.7.

Although the question wording differs somewhat, with the GSS inquiring about actions routinely taken and the VAWS asking how often certain actions are followed (always, usually,

TABLE 3.7

Percentage of Men and Women Who Undertake Measures to Protect Themselves from Crime

Precautionary Measures	Women	Men
	percentage	
"Do you routinely ...?"		
Lock the doors when alone in a car	68	40
Check the back seat for intruders before getting into a car	58	33
Plan your route with safety in mind	58	33
Stay home at night because afraid to go out alone	24	3
Carry something for self-defence	17	7
"Have you ever done any of the following to protect yourself or your property from crime?"		
Changed your routine/avoided certain places	44	32
Got a dog	14	11
Changed your telephone number	11	7
Took a self-defence course	9	11
Got a gun	1	3

Source: Statistics Canada, *General Social Survey*, Microdata File, Ottawa (1993b).

sometimes, and never), the combined "always/usually" responses listed in Table 3.6 are remarkably similar to responses given by women regarding actions routinely taken (Table 3.7). For example, 67 percent of women said they always or usually lock the car doors when alone in the car; 68 percent in the GSS said they routinely do so. The comparison between men and women shows that women are much more likely than men to do certain things to protect themselves as a matter of course. Women routinely take precautions when driving, like locking the doors when they are alone and checking the back seat before getting in, and they practise these behaviours more frequently than men. Safety also plays a bigger role for women than for men when it comes to deciding when and where to go out. More than half of all women take safety into account when planning how they will get somewhere, and they are more likely than men to change their daily routine in an attempt to protect themselves from crime. They are 8 times as likely as men to forego an evening activity because of concerns about their safety (24 percent of women compared with 3 percent of men). Women are also twice as likely as men to routinely carry something to defend themselves against an attack (17 percent of women compared with 7 percent of men). Smaller and more even proportions of women and men obtained a dog for protection, changed their telephone number to protect themselves against unwanted and obscene telephone calls, and have taken self-defence courses.

Most women alter their behaviour in some way as a safeguard against violence, and women who have been assaulted are even more likely to do so. Those who are worried about their personal safety are also more likely to take safety precautions, and in some cases they are twice as likely to do these things as women who are not at all worried. Women who are worried while walking alone in their area after dark, using public transportation alone after dark, or walking alone to a car in a parking garage are at least twice as likely as women who are not worried in these situations to say that they carry something to defend themselves and that they go out of their way to avoid walking past teenage boys or young men. Very high proportions of women take preventive action around cars, even those who say they are not worried: more than half of all women who are not worried nevertheless lock the car doors while driving, and about half also check the back seat before getting in.

SUMMARY

The potential for violence creeps into the daily consciousness of a significant proportion of women and causes them to worry about their safety when going about their daily lives. For most women, precautions are a matter of routine, built into their acquired knowledge of what is common sense and what every woman does unless she is very foolish. Often this means restricting their activities in some way. Concerns about safety affect the choices women *make* make about the time of day they will go out, the areas of the city they will travel through, and the way they dress. Fear prevents many from going out at all if the only choice is going out alone, and it makes women guarded in their interactions with strangers, especially young men. These feelings of vulnerability make women nervous about the possibility of intruders in their own homes and fearful of attack while alone on the street at night, and makes them feel dependent on the presence of others for their safety. Fear exacts a psychological burden on women in addition to the financial burden of installing extra locks or burglar alarms in their homes and telephones in their cars.

Direct experience with threats and sexual violence confirms for women that they are available targets for intimidation and harassment. These experiences have a direct effect on women's perceptions of their safety and the precautions they take to try to reduce their exposure to violence by strangers. The effects can be the result of a single incident, or they can be cumulative over time. Women who are subjected to frequent threats of sexual violence may develop a "tough" exterior that allows them to carry on with their daily lives without becoming paralyzed with fear. These women cannot afford to let fear control their lives because they have few alternatives, either in the type of neighbourhood they live in, the type of jobs they accept, or the fact that they must use public transportation. Agnew (1985) calls these "techniques of neutralization" that allow victims to deny the impact or the seriousness of the experience and to continue functioning in a normal manner.

Early fear-of-crime researchers maintained that the widespread tendency for women to engage in precautionary behaviour actually has the desired effect of reducing their risk, and that it is because of their prudence that women suffer lower rates of violence than men. More recent research causes us to question this assertion. It seems that women take these precautions because they regularly feel threatened and vulnerable in many everyday situations, and the source of their fear is well documented by studies like the Violence Against Women Survey. Women who haven't had first-hand experience of violence have either had a frightening experience of sexual harassment that fell short of actual assault or have heard about such an experience second-hand from a sister, friend, or neighbour. But many women know from experience that taking precautions against attack is no guarantee against victimization. When a woman is attacked despite her best efforts to be cautious, she may feel that she is helpless to prevent it from happening again, and she may feel guilty if she believes that it is a woman's responsibility to avoid attack and that those who are attacked must have been careless in some way. In the next few chapters, we will discuss the prevalence of such attacks on women by strangers, dates or boyfriends, and spouses.

C H A P T E R 4

Violence by Male Strangers

The previous chapter examined the dimensions of women's fear of attack by strangers in public places. For the most part, women's feelings of vulnerability stem from a ubiquitous concern about sexual violence that is heightened when they are out alone after dark. Crime prevention programs routinely advise women to take practical steps to avoid being alone and vulnerable, to stay away from certain areas of town, and to learn self-defence techniques. The catalyst for much of this advice were surveys that documented women's fear of danger, along with statistics that described the source of that fear as stranger violence.

Chapter 3 also highlighted the significance of noncriminal acts of harassment and intimidation on women's perceptions of their vulnerability to attack. What can survey research tell us about the incidence of assaults, threats, and intimidation involving male strangers? In what context do these incidents most often occur? This chapter begins with an assessment of the frequency with which women report both criminal assaults and threatening acts of harassment by male strangers, and concludes with a discussion of factors associated with the risk of stranger violence and explanations that have been offered to interpret these risk patterns.

THE PREVALENCE OF STRANGER VIOLENCE

The Violence Against Women Survey was specially designed to address women's victimization. It provides evidence on a national scale that physical and sexual violence is not an uncommon experience for Canadian women over the course of their lifetimes. But, contrary to popular conceptions of the stranger rapist, the primary threat to women's safety does not come from strangers.

As of 1993, 51 percent of all women had experienced at least one incident of physical or sexual violence since turning the age of 16 (see Table 2.3). Twenty-nine percent of ever-married women have been sexually or physically assaulted by spouses. Twenty-three percent have been assaulted by strangers, the same proportion by acquaintances and other known nonintimates, and 16 percent by dates and boyfriends. Overall, almost half (45 percent) of all women have been victims of violence by men known to them, twice as many as were assaulted by strangers.

Although they do not happen as frequently as assaults by acquaintances or intimate partners, this is not meant to suggest that women don't have good reason to fear violence from male strangers. Two and a half million women have suffered a physical or sexual attack by a stranger that would have been actionable by the police—not an insignificant number by any means. An assault or even a threat involving a stranger can have devastating physical and social consequences. It can be sudden and brutal, leaving the victim physically and psychologically traumatized, and leaving her feeling vulnerable, frightened, and unable to protect herself from further danger.

The biggest threat by far that women experience from strangers is the threat of sexual violence. As shown in Table 4.1, 19 percent of all Canadian women aged 18 years and over have been sexually assaulted by a stranger since turning the age of 16. The definition of sexual assault used in this survey, which is consistent with Canadian criminal law, ranges from unwanted sexual touching to violent attacks resulting in serious injury to the victim. Seven percent of Canadian women have been violently sexually attacked by a stranger in their adult lifetimes, and over twice as many have been victims of unwanted sexual touching. Less common were physical assaults that didn't involve a sexual component (8 percent). Boxes 2.1 and 2.2 contain the exact questions used in this survey to measure frequency of sexual and physical assaults.

The number of women who have been victims of various forms of sexual and physical assault by strangers exceeds the total number of women with any stranger assaults. This is due to the very high incidence of repeat victimization. The 2.5 million victims of stranger violence reported 8.1 million actual incidents. Two million women experienced 6.3 million incidents of sexual assault, and 800 000 women reported 1.8 million incidents of physical assault.

It seems that when a woman has been assaulted once by a stranger, she has a significant risk of being assaulted again and even a third or fourth time. This is true for sexual assault in particular: the majority of women who have been sexually

Number and Percentage of Women 18 Years and Over Who Have Experienced Violence by Strangers[1] by Number of Incidents

Type of Assault	Number of Women in Millions	Percent of All Women	Number of Incidents in Millions	Percent of All Incidents
Total women assaulted by a stranger	2.5	23	8.1	100
Total sexual assault	2.0	19	6.3	78
Unwanted sexual touching	1.6	15	4.6	57
Sexual attack	0.7	7	1.7	21
Physical assault	0.8	8	1.8	22

Figures do not add to totals because of multiple responses.

[1] A stranger is someone the victim did not see or recognize, or someone she knew only by sight or hearsay.

Source: Statistics Canada, *Violence Against Women Survey*, Microdata File, Ottawa (1994a).

assaulted by a stranger have been victimized on more than one occasion. As Table 4.2 shows, 55 percent of women who have been violently victimized by a stranger reported more than one incident, and 26 percent have been assaulted *four or more times*. One-third of women who have been violently sexually attacked, and 58 percent who reported unwanted sexual touching, said it happened to them more than once (Table 4.2).

There may have been more than one man involved in some of these attacks (for example, gang rape), but not the same man more than once. These are separate incidents, each time involving a man (or men) who was unknown to the victim. It is unwanted sexual touching that happens most frequently of all. As we see later in this chapter, young single women are at greatest risk of stranger violence overall and of multiple incidents of stranger violence (Rodgers and Roberts, 1995).

TABLE 4.2

Percentage of Women 18 Years and Over Who Have Been Assaulted by a Stranger, by Number of Occurrences

Number of Occurrences	Total Women Assaulted	Sexual Attack	Unwanted Sexual Touching	Total Sexual Assault	Physical Assault
Total	100	100	100	100	100
One	45	68	43	46	66
Two	19	18	20	19	13
Three	10	7	12	11	66
Four or more	26	7	26	23	14

Figures do not add to totals because of rounding.

Source: Statistics Canada, *Violence Against Women Survey*, Microdata File, Ottawa (1994a).

WOMEN TAKE ACTION

Women's groups have taken collective action over the years in response to what they perceive to be the inability of police to protect women from sexual attacks in public places. Beginning in the 1970s, sexual assault centres have organized annual Take Back the Night marches in major cities across the country. These night-time marches involve large groups of women and men parading through the city streets demanding recognition of women's right to walk alone without fear of attack. Through these marches, women's groups have attempted to raise public awareness of not only the dangers women face in public places but also the restrictions placed on their lives by the fact that they cannot walk the streets alone without fear of assault.

More recently, other groups have been working to make communities safer places through the use of safety audits. Safety audits are an initiative of Toronto's Metro Action Committee on Violence Against Women and Children (METRAC), which has been expanded to university campuses across the country and to other public spaces, such as housing complexes and shopping centres. The basic principle behind the safety audit is that women's safety can be improved through very simple measures, such as improved lighting, clearing bushes away from walkways, and situating bus stops near well-travelled areas and away from remote ones. Safety audits have demonstrated that once planners and administrators are made aware of the kinds of situations that serve to isolate women and increase their chances of attack, these risks can be reduced through fairly simple and inexpensive means.

SEXUAL HARASSMENT

A number of writers have described the broad range of violent acts committed against women as existing on a continuum, with violent rape at one extreme and noncriminal threats of sexual violence at the other (Kelly, 1987; 1988; Stanko, 1990a; Koss and Oros, 1982). However, violence, to many people, typically conjures up images of rape and battery involving blows of some kind that result in serious injury to the victim. But for women, covert threats of male violence can also have long-term social and emotional consequences. Various types of sexual harassment, for example, even though they may not result in an actual attack, can hold the threat of violence. And some incidents of sexual harassment in which women feel threatened and intimidated by men are so commonplace that the fear and harm they cause often goes unnoticed. For some women, such incidents are a routine part of their lives. These situations and the harm they cause to women's sense of well-being were discussed in Chapter 3. They almost always contain a sexual undercurrent that warns women of their vulnerability to attack. Such behaviours may or may not evolve into something that qualifies as violence under the legal code.

British researcher Liz Kelly (1988) delineates the similarities in the dynamics of various types of violence along the continuum—the intrusion, the uncertainty, the feelings of powerlessness, the fear, and the vulnerability. Quoting from the *Oxford English Dictionary*, Kelly (1988:48) defines a continuum as "a basic common characteristic that underlies many different events, and a continuous series of elements or events that pass into one another and cannot readily be distinguished." She identifies the basic common characteristic underlying these experiences as the implicit or explicit threat of unwanted sexual contact or sexual assault over which the victim has no control. The continuous series of elements or events aspect of the definition indicates that the range of intimidation, coercion, and abuse is not easily classified into analytic categories for research.

Kelly and many others have underscored the potential for violence that lies behind sexual harassment, and point out that women don't experience flashing, obscene phone calls, or being followed as minor incidents (Kelly, 1988; McNeill, 1987; Stanko, 1990a; Smith, 1993a and 1993b; Sheffield, 1989). In fact, women are often very frightened and upset by these experiences despite the fact that they may be encouraged by others to define them as minor or harmless. The perpetrators usually have the intention of frightening or intimidating their victims, and that tends to be the effect. A woman receiving an obscene telephone call might be afraid that the man knows her, knows where she lives, and might be watching her, all of which increase her fear both at home and when she is out. It is not only that the recipient of these calls feels frightened by whatever threats the man might make; researchers have found that women feel equally threatened and disturbed by silent calls (Kelly, 1988; Smith, 1993a).

Indecent exposure by men with the intent to shock female passersby is another activity that has rarely been perceived to be harmful because, statistically, it is unlikely to evolve into an actual assault. While it may be true that most women who have been flashed at can look back and agree that they were not physically harmed or attacked, it is not true that most were not harmed in any way. As with an obscene telephone call or any other situation in which a man makes sexual advances or threats of sexual contact, there is no way the woman can know for sure if he intends to go further. In a study of women who had been flashed at, McNeill (1987), describes the predominant reactions of fear, panic, shock, disgust, anger, outrage, guilt, humiliation, and shame. The women's initial reactions were based on the threat of violence they perceived and the possible outcome. What was most striking was that while many women linked the experience with a fear of being raped, at the time of the incident women feared death, not rape. For the majority of women, the reason for their fear was "What is he going to do next?" and at the back of their minds was death.

The experience of being flashed at had a negative effect on the lives of these women. McNeill (1987:105) found that half of the women reported restricting some aspect of their lives, a particular area or activity connected to how or where the flashing occurred, and that 40 percent said the flashing added to their existing fears about going out alone. McNeill makes the important observation that if women are already restricting their lives because of a generalized fear of male violence, the direct effects of flashing will be unexceptional. She found that for some the experience meant a serious restriction on their freedom of movement, while for others, it was a reminder of the necessity to be vigilant about their safety.

THE PREVALENCE OF SEXUAL HARASSMENT

Sexual harassment is a more frequent occurrence for Canadian women than are actual assaults. According to the Violence Against Women Survey, 87 percent of Canadian women have experienced sexual harassment in a form that was memorable enough to respond to at least one of the questions included in this survey. These acts range from obscene telephone calls and indecent exposure to threatening job action for refusing to comply with a sexual request (the complete list of sexual harassment items is included in Table 4.3). Virtually all (85 percent of women) have been sexually harassed by a stranger: they either had an obscene phone call, catcalls, and other types of harassment from strangers on the street; have been followed by a man in a way that frightened them; or had a man indecently expose himself to them. The most common of these were obscene phone calls and street harassment. More than seven million and six million Canadian women, respectively, have had these experiences. Three and a half million women have had the frightening experience of being followed by a man, and two million have been flashed at. Although some obscene phone calls may be made by a man who knows the woman, in most cases, she doesn't know who it is, so these calls were considered here as incidents involving strangers.

About half (51 percent) of all women have also been sexually harassed by men they know. The survey asked about four types of harassment: making inappropriate sexual comments; leaning over a woman unnecessarily, getting too close, or cornering her; repeatedly asking her for a date and refusing to take "no" for an answer; and hinting that her job situation might be hurt if she did not have a sexual relationship with the man. Over five million women have had at least one of these experiences, the most common of which were making inappropriate sexual comments, leaning over a woman unnecessarily, and getting too close or cornering her. In almost half of all these situations in which women were sexually harassed by someone they know, the offender was described as an acquaintance or a friend (Figure 4.1). A large proportion of these situations were also work-related: 25 percent involved a co-worker, 18 percent a boss or supervisor, and 6 percent a client, customer, or patient. Relatives (fathers, brothers, in-laws) were responsible for 11 percent of cases, doctors for 4 percent, and other men (such as landlords, teachers, students, repairmen) for 7 percent.

TABLE 4.3

Number and Percentage of Women Who Have Experienced Sexual Harassment, by Type of Harassment

Type of Sexual Harassment	Number in Millions	Percent
Total women sexually harassed	9.2	87
• *Strangers*	8.9	85
Obscene phone call	7.2	69
Unwanted attention from male stranger	6.3	60
Followed in a frightening way	3.5	33
Indecent exposure	2.0	19
• *Known men*	5.3	51
Made inappropriate comments about her body or sex life	3.8	36
Leaned over unnecessarily, got too close, cornered her	3.6	34
Repeatedly asked for a date and wouldn't take "no" for an answer	2.6	25
Hinted her job situation might be hurt if she didn't have a sexual relationship	0.5	5

Figures do not add to totals because of multiple responses.

Source: Holly Johnson and Vincent Sacco, "Researching Violence Against Women: Statistics Canada's National Survey," *Canadian Journal of Criminology* 37(3): 294 (1995). Reprinted with permission.

These data suggest that sexual harassment is not a rare event for the majority of women and in many cases it is not considered minor. It is evident from the very high numbers relative to the totals in Table 4.3 that most women have experienced a variety of

FIGURE 4.1

Sexual Harassment from Known Men, by Relationship to the Woman

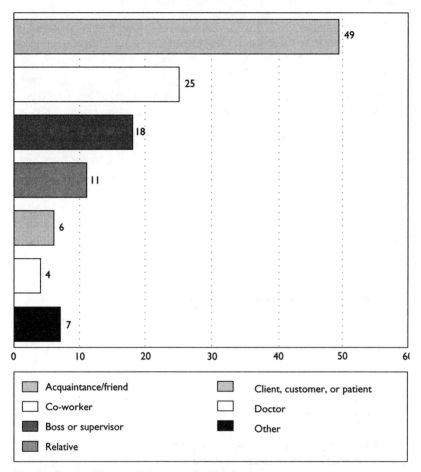

Figures do not add to totals because of multiple responses.

Source: Statistics Canada, *Violence Against Women Survey*, Microdata File, Ottawa (1994a).

different types of harassment. And, although the survey doesn't say so, many women likely have experienced some of these categories of harassment more than once. The only thing that separates some of these experiences from those classified by this survey or by the police as assaults is that in the case of assaults the threat is carried out. In some cases, it is only a matter of time before cornering a woman turns into unwanted sexual touching. In other cases, only a matter of happenstance such as someone passing by that prevents an incident of being followed from becoming a sexual attack. Regardless of whether a threat is actually carried out, the effect on the woman is often similar to an actual attack: she feels frightened, vulnerable, and powerless. There is no way for her to know how the situation will turn out, whether it will evolve into something more serious, or whether the man will suddenly turn around and move on. These types of experiences are widely understood to be a minor part of life, something every woman should expect to encounter at some point. However, some of these encounters are not so easily dismissed or quickly forgotten by the woman on the receiving end.

In a national survey of sexual harassment of working women, Smith (1993b:70) found that 90 percent of his sample had been subjected to at least one incident of unwanted sexual attention by a man in a public place. Although these women were not injured or assaulted in the legal sense, most were shaken emotionally. As Smith makes clear, it is not necessarily what happens during these episodes that produces these feelings, but rather the "lack of control over how such episodes will end, and the nagging, gnawing sense that something horrible *could* happen."

FACTORS ASSOCIATED WITH RISK OF VIOLENCE BY STRANGERS

Random sample surveys of the population have the advantage of being able to compare the lifestyles and characteristics of women who have been victims of violence with those who have not. This allows researchers to establish which segments of the population are at highest risk of victimization and thereby to suggest interventions that might reduce rates of violence for particular groups and for the population as a whole. Figure 4.2 and Table 4.4 present a snapshot of women's reports of assault and sexual harassment by strangers according to the sociodemographic characteristics of age, marital status, household income, education, and urban/rural residence.

TABLE 4.4

One-Year Rates of Sexual Harassment by Sociodemographic Characteristics of Women

Sociodemographic Characteristics	Any Harassment	Obscene Phone Call	Street Harassment	Followed	Indecent Exposure	Known Men
			percentage			
Total in past 12 months	**39**	**13**	**27**	**7**	**2**	**14**
Age Group						
18–24	79	26	69	22	5	37
25–34	57	17	44	9	2	21
35–44	38	11	26	5	2	13
45 and over	19	9	7	2	1	5
Marital Status						
Married	29	10	18	3	1	8
Common-law	56	14	46	8	2	21
Separated/divorced	50	17	33	8	2	23
Single	68	22	57	18	4	31
Widowed	14	10	4	—	—	4

(Table continues on next page.)

Sociodemographic Characteristics	Any Harassment	Obscene Phone Call	Street Harassment	Followed	Indecent Exposure	Known Men
			percentage			
Household Income						
less than $15 000	36	15	23	7	2	13
$15 000–$29 999	37	14	24	7	2	14
$30 000–$59 999	42	14	29	7	1	15
$60 000 or more	43	11	33	6	1	15
Education						
Less than high-school diploma	27	11	15	4	1	9
High-school diploma	38	14	26	6	1	14
Some post-secondary	48	14	36	8	2	19
University degree	44	13	34	8	2	14
Place of Residence						
Urban area	42	14	29	7	2	15
Small town/rural area	30	10	20	4	1	11

— not statistically reliable

Source: Statistics Canada, *Violence Against Women Survey*, Microdata File, Ottawa (1994b).

One-Year Rates of Stranger Violence, by Sociodemographic Characteristics of Women

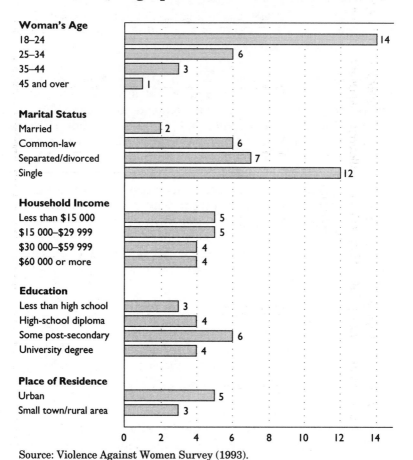

Source: Violence Against Women Survey (1993).

What emerges from this risk analysis is that certain groups of Canadian women have an elevated risk of assault and harassment by strangers either because of where they live or where they work, or simply because their youth makes them appealing and acceptable targets for men motivated to commit assault or harassment. The strongest correlates of stranger violence, how it occurs and against whom, are being young and unmarried. Threats of violence from strangers shape women's perceptions of their personal safety and their relationships with men at an early age. Young women 18–24 years of age reported a one-year rate of stranger violence that was more than three times the national average (which stands at 4 percent of all women), and more than twice the rate for women in the next age group (see Figure 4.3). Rates of sexual harassment follow the same pattern (Table 4.4). For women who were victimized as children, an important group omitted from this survey, an awareness of sexual violence comes even earlier.

Single women (the largest proportion of whom are in the youngest age group) also report rates of stranger assaults that are twice as high as women living in common-law relationships and separated or divorced women, and six times as high as women who are married (Figure 4.3). As well, this group reports considerably higher rates of sexual harassment than married or formerly married women (Table 4.4). In some cases, such as being followed, rates for young and unmarried women are several times higher than for other women. With respect to other types of harassment, the rates are very high for almost all women but astonishingly high for young and unmarried women. Overall, 79 percent of young women have experienced some type of sexual harassment, and 69 percent have been harassed on the street by strangers *in a 12-month period alone.*

The significant difference in rates of stranger violence for women living in common-law relationships and for married women warrants some discussion. At first glance, one might expect rates of violence reported by these two groups to be more similar because of the apparent similarities in lifestyle. For many couples, living common-law is a "trial" marriage with all the rights and responsibilities of a legal union. Very often the couple has children. Many are stable relationships that continue for many years and closely approximate legal marriages. In the province of Quebec, men and women are more likely to choose cohabitation over state-sanctioned unions, and many are raising children within these unions (Statistics Canada, 1995).

Overall, however, common-law unions are significantly different from legal unions in important ways that may help to explain the very different rates of stranger violence reported by these two groups. For example, both men and women in common-law unions tend to be quite a bit younger, on average, than couples in legal marriages (Stout, 1991). The period of time in which they live together is considerably shorter, and they tend to have a greater number of consecutive unions (Dumas and Péron, 1992). Fewer common-law couples share children (Barr, 1993). Children in common-law households are more likely than in legal marriages to have originated from the woman's previous union. In some cases, there is a much looser commitment to the relationship by one or both partners, and to the obligations of a marital union, than is expected in a legal marriage. All of these factors—the couples' youth, their freedom from responsibilities related to caring for children, and often an unwillingness to accept the obligations of a legal marriage—permit a lifestyle that is more similar to single, separated, or divorced people than to married couples. As a result, rates of stranger violence against women living in common-law relationships bear a greater resemblance to those of unmarried women.

Contrary to common stereotypes of violent victimization as predominantly a lower-income phenomenon, a woman's household income is not related to her risk of attack by strangers. But overall rates of sexual harassment, and street harassment in particular, do show a positive relationship to household income, with women from higher-income families reporting the highest rates. With respect to educational achievement, women who have only some postsecondary education (predominantly young women again) reported the highest rates of harassment and assault, while women with less than a high-school education (who are disproportionately older) had the lowest rates.

EXPLANATIONS FOR STRANGER VIOLENCE

Lifestyle/routine activities theory is a common explanation for the higher rates of violence experienced by young single people and those living in large cities (Hindelang, Gottfredson, and Garofalo, 1978; Cohen and Felson, 1979). As discussed in Chapter 1, the central propositions of this theory are that age, gender, income, marital status, and place of residence are determinants of the type of lifestyle one leads, and that these lifestyle factors, in turn, can affect vulnerability to criminal victimization. Lifestyle factors associated with increased risk of victimization include the amount of time spent in public places after dark, the riskiness of the activities undertaken in these public places, the proximity to potential offenders, and one's ability to guard against attack. The risk of violence by strangers is expected to increase to the extent that one's paid work or recreational pursuits puts one in dangerous places or out on the street late at night.

Consistent with routine activities theory, the majority of incidents of stranger assaults took place in outside locations or in what might be described as risky situations. With respect to violent sexual attacks, 26 percent took place on the street or in a parking lot, and 20 percent happened in a car, possibly hitchhiking related (see Table 4.5). Unwanted sexual touching by strangers also happens frequently on the street (20 percent), but it is also an occupational hazard for some women as 11 percent happened in the women's workplace. Unwanted sexual touching is also a risk women face in using public transit and certain public buildings or going to bars or dances. Nonsexual physical assault is predominantly a street crime, but it also happens frequently in public buildings and in the women's workplace.

T A B L E   4 . 5

Location of Stranger Assaults

Location	All Stranger Assaults	Sexual Attack	Unwanted Sexual Touching	Total Sexual Assault	Physical Assault
		perc	entage		
Total	100	100	100	100	100
Street/parking lot	27	26	20	22	47
Bar/dance	13	—	20	15	6
Public building	14	8	15	13	15
Public transit	6	—	10	8	—
Car	8	20	6	10	—
Her home	7	13	5	7	6
His home	4	11	3	5	—
Someone else's home	6	11	5	7	—
Her workplace	10	—	11	8	14
Other	5	7	4	5	—

— not statistically reliable
Note: Some columns do not add to 100 because of rounding.

Source: Statistics Canada, *Violence Against Women Survey*, Microdata File, Ottawa (1994a).

It is difficult to know from this survey how these assaults occurred without important details about the context of the incidents. However, it seems that a significant proportion of stranger assaults occur in places frequented by young single people that also attract young men who are looking for raucous interactions, which then may escalate into violence. Many assaults occur within the context of drinking, parties, and other social events. According to responses to the Violence Against Women Survey, it is quite common for attackers to be intoxicated in incidents of stranger assault: altogether, in about 40 percent of incidents, the man had been drinking at the time. Not surprisingly, fully 90 percent of assaults that took place in bars involved an intoxicated offender.

Contrary to the assumptions of routine activities theory, a significant proportion of women were attacked by strangers in a private home. One might assume that a certain level of safety from stranger violence is assured while spending time in one's own home or in someone else's home. More than 1 in 10 violent sexual attacks happened in the woman's home, possibly through a break-in where the intruder found the woman home alone and sexually attacked her. It is knowing that this is a possibility that causes women to fear sexual violence as a component of almost any crime (see Chapter 3). Similar proportions of sexual attacks occurred in someone else's home, such as at a mutual friend's or acquaintance's or at a house party, and at the attacker's home. Altogether, 35 percent of violent sexual attacks took place in someone's home, either the woman's, the man's, or someone else's, in almost equal proportions. While little is known about the situations that preceded these assaults, drinking was involved in about half of the incidents (54 percent) that took place in a private home (Statistics Canada, 1994a). This was less likely to be the case when the assault took place in the woman's home (36 percent) than when it happened in the assailant's home (56 percent) or in someone else's home (73 percent). It seems plausible that a majority of stranger assaults that occurred in private homes took place during parties or other activities that involved drinking, prior to which the man and woman did not know each other.

It can also be anticipated from routine activities theory that the lifestyles of urban dwellers differ significantly from residents of rural areas or small towns in their contact and interactions with strangers and therefore their risk of assault by strangers. Women who live in cities had higher one-year rates of stranger violence than women living in rural areas or small towns (5 percent compared with 3 percent, respectively, in one year). An obvious point is that there are fewer true "strangers" in rural areas or small towns where residents are more likely to know, or at least recognize, almost everyone else. This may put rural and small-town women at lower risk of strangers simply because there are fewer of them. There also tend to be more effective networks of informal social control in small communities than in large urban areas that can respond to and control aggression and violence. By contrast, family and community ties generally tend to be weaker in urban areas, where people can act with greater anonymity without fear of apprehension or social censure. Given this fact, one might expect an even bigger difference in the rates of stranger violence among urban and rural women. However, neither formal nor informal social controls can effectively discourage behaviours that are kept secret and not brought to public attention. Sexual violence is something that many women keep hidden and private, even if committed by strangers, because of the associated humiliation and social stigma (women's decisions to use the criminal justice system are discussed in Chapter 8).

Although the routine activities theory is not aimed primarily at acts of crime by strangers, one might assume this theory would have greater explanatory power in the case of stranger assaults because of its focus on public interactions. In a test of this assumption, Rodgers and Roberts (1995) used the Canadian Violence Against Women Survey to assess women's risk of repeated victimization by men other than spouses. They hypothesized that, because the theory was developed and tested using surveys that focus primarily on public violence, it would have greater applicability to incidents involving strangers than to incidents of violence by boyfriends and acquaintances. Surprisingly, they did not find the difference they were expecting. Measures of lifestyle—including age, income, main activity, and marital status—had strong effects on rates of multiple victimization by both strangers and known men. Exposure, assessed by the frequency of walking alone or using public transportation alone after dark, also increased the risk of both stranger and acquaintance violence. Measures of proximity to offenders, including perceptions of one's neighbourhood as a threatening or dangerous place (worry about walking alone or using public transportation alone after dark, and urban residency), were associated with higher rates of multiple victimization. Indicators of guardianship, on the other hand, such as household size and self-protection activities, were generally insignificant or were associated with lower rates of multiple victimization.

When the effects of the individual measures were combined, the lifestyle variables (age, income, main activity, marital status) were the only measures to remain significant across the different types of multiple victimization. The effects of age and marital status on risk of multiple assaults were similar to the effects shown for overall stranger violence in Figure 4.3, with young women and single women reporting the highest rates of multiple assaults. Lower-income women also had an increased risk of multiple victimization, as did women who were attending school while also working at paid jobs. These authors conclude that there is something about being a young, unmarried woman who is working at a low-paid job that is untapped by survey research and that elevates the risk of victimization by both strangers and known men. In a test of the applicability of the routine activities theory to experiences of rape, Beknap (1987) suggested that disparities in power between men and women foster a situation conducive to assaults on women, and that women's risk of sexual violence has little to do with extraneous factors.

Rodgers and Roberts (1995) attribute the high rates of multiple victimization reported by working students to the fact that many employment opportunities for students are in high-risk occupations, such as waiting tables at bars, where unwanted sexual touching occurs with greater frequency. Women living in lower-income households are also at greater risk of repeat victimization, which may occur while working in lower-paid service industry occupations or while walking to work or using public transportation. Although the Violence Against Women Survey offers no details about the types of evening activities in which young women are involved, crime victim surveys like the GSS question people about their frequency of going out in the evenings and about the types of nighttime activities involved. These surveys show that not only frequency of going out increases the risk of violent victimization but also that certain types of activities, such as going to bars and parties, increases that risk even more (Sacco, Johnson, and Arnold, 1993).

SUMMARY

The lifestyle/routine activities perspective offers a partial explanation for the differences in the rates of stranger violence faced by some demographic groups of women. Certainly, the pattern demonstrated by victim surveys, that young unmarried women face an increased risk of assault and harassment from unknown men, is confirmed by the data presented in this chapter. It is not difficult to see how the lifestyles and responsibilities of young single women are very different from those of older married women, which allows single women greater freedom and opportunities to socialize, especially in the evenings. Their chances of interacting with strangers are significantly greater, and very often these encounters involve alcohol and potentially volatile situations. A significant number of stranger assaults take place on the street or in bars, and many happen in the context of drinking and parties, situations in which younger women and unmarried women are more likely to be involved.

Yet, frequency of contact with strangers cannot fully explain the high rates of sexual violence by unknown men against young unmarried women in particular. It cannot explain why women are harassed and assaulted in such high numbers, or why young women are seen as legitimate targets for humiliation, intimidation, and assault. If applied too liberally, the lifestyle/routine activities theory can help perpetuate negative stereotypes about women who "ask for it" by their appearance, their style of dress, or simply their decision to frequent certain nightspots. Focusing on the prudence that a person did or didn't take in certain situations may be more appropriate to understanding bar fights, robberies, or purse-snatching. What is needed for a clearer understanding of public forms of male sexual violence toward women is a wider range of theories that focus on the actions and cognitive processes of offenders and on societal factors that result in the harm caused by these actions to be overlooked. Rodgers and Roberts (1995) recommend reconciling theories of criminality and victimization and incorporating theories that focus on the broader social context in which threats and assaults on women occur. It is important to understand, for example, the assumptions men make about the "availability" of young women in particular as acceptable targets for sexual violence, and why in certain contexts sexual harassment and intimidation of women are accepted as normal life events. Equally important, we need to understand the implications for the emotional and physical well-being of young women whose initiation into adulthood involves threats of sexual violence. The next chapter will examine dating violence, to which young women are especially vulnerable.

C H A P T E R 5

Dating Violence

Young adulthood is a time of transition when young people are forging an identity independent of their parents, taking on new rights and responsibilities, and enjoying new freedom from the restrictions of family and high school. Beginning full-time work, going off to university, often in a new city, or moving out of the parental home represents a break with family rules and an opportunity for independence. Adulthood brings the rights and obligations associated with driving a car, drinking alcohol, and choosing a future. For most young people, it is also the time in which they begin thinking about the qualities they want in a mate.

As they develop relationships with the opposite sex, young women and men are experimenting with adult roles they have been learning and rehearsing since childhood. By adolescence, young women have specific ideas about what it means to be female, and about attracting a boyfriend and eventually a husband. Young men also have developed ideas about what it means to be male, and about confirming one's masculinity through displays of daring, power, and sexual prowess. Both women and men are concerned about being sexually attractive to the opposite sex. In fact, a great deal of adolescent anxiety and confusion is tied to the transition to adult roles and anxiety about sexual attractiveness.

During adolescence and young adulthood, fragile identities and egos are evolving, and both young women and men are looking for acceptance from their peers and from the opposite sex. For many young people, having a dating partner signifies acceptance, sexual attractiveness, and status in the eyes of one's peer group. But the intimacy that accompanies dating invariably involves conflict as the young couple negotiates time spent alone and with others, and makes decisions about joint activities. The ways in which problems are negotiated and resolved will depend on the experience the young people have had in solving conflicts with their siblings, parents, peers, and other dating partners, the image they have of themselves, and the ideas they hold about the proper roles of women and men in intimate relationships.

This chapter explores the nature of sexual and physical violence committed against young women within the context of dating relationships. It will become apparent that many situational and societal factors come into play to elevate the risk of violence by dating partners.

THE PREVALENCE OF DATING VIOLENCE

The Violence Against Women Survey estimates that 1.7 million Canadian women have been involved in at least one incident of sexual or physical assault by a date or boyfriend since the age of 16, a figure that represents about 16 percent of all women. The many young women who began dating at an earlier age and who were subjected to violence by these dates are not counted in this figure. Nor are those who were subjected to unwanted sexual contact that did not involve outright violence or threats of violence. These less overtly violent acts are considered to be illegal under Canadian law but were not included in the definition of dating violence used in this survey. (See Boxes 2.1 and 2.2 for the definitions of sexual and physical assault used in the VAWS.)

"Dates and boyfriends" in this survey range from "pick-ups" or "one-night stands" to first dates to long-term boyfriends and committed relationships. Unmarried couples living in common-law relationships are classified as spouses and are discussed in Chapter 6. But not all women are at equal risk of assault by a date or boyfriend. Some women would not have been at risk of dating violence at the time of the interview because they were married or for whatever reason considered themselves to be out of the "dating game." (An unknown number of women responding to the survey were homosexual and therefore not involved in intimate relationships with men.) Older women may also forget or underreport experiences of dating violence that happened long ago. If we narrow our focus to those women who are at greatest risk of being assaulted by dates or boyfriends, we see the rates of violence rise. Half of all women who reported an incident of dating violence were between the ages of 18–34. For single women in the 18–24 age group, the group with the shortest time at risk but the highest proportion of women who are unmarried and dating, the rate of women ever assaulted by dates is 24 percent (Table 5.1). This figure is 50 percent higher than the national figure of 16 percent.

TABLE 5.1

Number and Percentage of Women 18 Years and Over Who Have Experienced Violence by a Date or Boyfriend

Type of Assault	Number in Millions	Percent
All women 18 and over	**1.7**	**16**
Sexual assault	1.3	12
Physical assault	.8	7
Single women 18–24	**0.2**	**24**
Sexual assault	0.1	15
Physical assault	0.1	14
Single women 25–34	**0.2**	**29**
Sexual assault	0.1	19
Physical assault	0.1	18
Students	**0.6**	**25**
Sexual assault	0.4	17
Physical assault	0.3	12

Figures do not add to totals because of multiple responses.

Source: Statistics Canada, *Violence Against Women Survey*, Microdata File, Ottawa (1994a).

For single women 25–34 years of age, most of whom have been dating for longer periods of time, the percentage ever assaulted by a date is 29 percent.

Overall, women reported higher rates of sexual violence than of nonsexual assaults. Twelve percent of all women aged 18 and over have been sexually assaulted (an estimated 1.3 million women), and 7 percent have been physically assaulted (800 000 women). The type of sexual violence counted here closely resembles popular notions of date rape, although rape is no longer a legal category under Canadian law. These are acts in which a date or boyfriend forced or attempted to force the woman into any sexual activity by threatening her, holding her down, or hurting her in some way. They are acts of sexual activity of any kind that were committed or attempted through the use of violence or threats. Physical (nonsexual) assaults include hitting, slapping, kicking, or grabbing, or being beaten, knifed, or shot. Some would resemble what are considered to be battering relationships. The Criminal Code definition of physical assault also includes face-to-face threats of physical harm, so long as the woman expected that the threat could or would be carried out. Incidents that involved both a sexual component and physical injury were counted only once in this tally as sexual assaults; however, a substantial proportion of sexual assault victims (40 percent) also reported being physically assaulted in a separate incident by either the same or another boyfriend, and a smaller proportion of physical assault victims (20 percent) reported being sexually assaulted in a separate incident (Statistics Canada, 1994a).

A very high number of women who have been assaulted by a date or boyfriend have been the targets of such assaults by more than one man. As shown in Table 5.1, the numbers of women who reported sexual and physical violence exceeds the total number of women with any dating violence. This is due to the fact that a very large proportion of women have had more than one violent dating partner. Table 5.2 presents the number of individual violent partners reported by all victims of dating violence: about 40 percent of these women said acts of violence were committed by more than one date or boyfriend, and 12 percent had been assaulted by four or more violent partners. Sexual assaults were more likely to be committed by multiple partners than were nonsexual assaults.

VIOLENCE IN UNIVERSITY AND COLLEGE DATING RELATIONSHIPS

Concern has been growing over the past decade about dating violence on university and college campuses across the country. In the wake of growing publicity about sexual violence, women's groups on campus have organized "No Means No" campaigns designed to increase awareness about the prevalence of sexual violence and to promote better understanding among students about the issue of consent. These groups have also been instrumental in organizing escort services for female students to enable them to move safely among campus buildings after dark.

T A B L E 5 . 2

Percentage of Women 18 Years and Over Who Have Been Assaulted by a Date or Boyfriend by Number of Violent Dating Partners

Number of Violent Dating Partners	Total Women Assaulted	Sexual Attack	Physical Assault
Total	100	100	100
One	61	66	74
Two	20	18	14
Three	7	6	5
Four or more	12	10	7

Source: Statistics Canada, *Violence Against Women Survey*, Microdata File, Ottawa (1994a).

The Violence Against Women Survey estimates that 25 percent of all women who were attending school at the time of the interview in 1993 had been sexually or physically assaulted by a male date or boyfriend (Table 5.1). Dating violence among university and college students has received widespread attention among other survey researchers in both Canada and the United States. Mary Koss of the University of Arizona has developed the Sexual Experiences Scale to investigate women's experiences of sexual aggression (Koss and Oros, 1982). This scale consists of a gradual progression of 10 acts, with coercion to engage in sexual activity at one end and rape at the other. Women are asked to report on whether they have had any of these experiences, and men are asked whether they have committed any of these acts against a woman. The scale includes criminal assaults as well as acts that are not normally considered to be violent, with the intention of capturing the broader range of unwanted sexual contact that women experience. For example, the first few items ask the female respondent about giving in to sex play when she didn't want to because she was overwhelmed by a man's continual arguments and pressure, or because a man used his position of authority (boss, teacher, camp counsellor, supervisor) over her, or because a man had given her alcohol or drugs. The final item asks about forced sexual intercourse.

In a national survey by Koss and her colleagues of 6159 women and men enrolled in 32 colleges and universities across the United States, 54 percent of the women reported at least one form of sexual aggression since reaching the age of 14, while half as many men (25 percent) reported involvement in at least one of these types of sexual aggression (Koss, Gidycz, and Wisniewski, 1987). Twenty-seven percent of college women reported experiencing an act that meets the legal definition of rape in the United States (including attempts), and 8 percent of college men reported perpetrating such an act.

Canadian sociologists Walter DeKeseredy and Katharine Kelly (1993c) replicated Koss's Sexual Experiences Scale in a 1992 national survey of Canadian college and university students. A total of 3142 students in 44 colleges and universities completed the questionnaires for this survey. Female students reported overall rates of sexual abuse of 45 percent since leaving high school (which includes the entire range of sexual coercion and legally defined assaults); by contrast, only 20 percent of male students said they had committed such acts. The percentage of women who reported acts of forced sexual intercourse in dating situations was four times higher than the percentage of men who said they had committed a similar act (6.6 percent compared with 1.5 percent).

DeKeseredy and Kelly also included a slightly modified form of the Conflict Tactics Scale in order to measure physical violence among Canadian students. Physical violence was measured through nine questions ranging in seriousness from "throwing something at her" to "using a gun or knife on her." A total of 35 percent of female students said they had been physically assaulted in a dating relationship, and 17 percent of male students said they had been physically violent toward a date since leaving high school.

How do survey researchers account for the wildly different responses given by female students about the amount of sexual and physical violence they have had inflicted on them compared with the number of incidents male students say they have committed? Female students in Koss's study were twice as likely as the male students to report an incident of sexual aggression, and three times as likely to report a violent sexual assault. Women in DeKeseredy and Kelly's study reported rates of both sexual and physical violence against women that were twice as high as those reported by men. A seven-college study in the United States by Makepeace (1986) also uncovered a striking difference in the perceptions of women and men as to whether forced sex had occurred, with affirmative responses by women outnumbering those by men eight to one.

One possible explanation for the disparity in responses provided by women and men is that both sets of responses are accurate and the problem lies with the method used to select the sample of students to be interviewed. The classes of students selected for participation in the surveys were chosen randomly, and all students within each class were asked to take part. The students who responded were not matched with dating partners, so it is possible that large numbers of women were dating men outside the class (or even outside the university) and that the men, in their responses, were also referring to women who were not participating in the survey. If large numbers of college and university students are involved in dating people other than their classmates, this explanation would seem plausible.

However, the assumption routinely made by researchers faced with these data is that the reports by women are more accurate than those given by men. This seems a reasonable assumption to make considering that the actions men are being asked to admit to are morally and, in most cases, legally wrong. Many men who hurt their dating partners will not want to admit to doing so. Others may have rationalized their behaviour to themselves as justifiable under the circumstances and don't consider it relevant to report. If heavy alcohol use was a factor in the assault, a man may not be able to recall the details of the event. Many reasons like these might cause men to under-report the fact that they were responsible for harming a girlfriend.

Koss suggests from these results that men do not admit enough sexual aggression to account for the number of victimizations reported by women because they do not perceive or conceptualize sexual experiences in the same way that women do (Koss et al., 1987:169). She interprets this to mean that "some men fail to perceive accurately the degree of force and coerciveness that was involved in a particular sexual encounter or to interpret correctly a woman's nonconsent and resistance" (Koss et al., 1987:169). Koss also asserts that some men fail to perceive a little force or coercion as wrong, and refuse to recognize their actions as violent. Others, knowing that they had used force to overcome a woman's objections, may either rationalize it to themselves that the woman needed a little persuasion to overcome her own inhibitions, or simply deny it to an interviewer for fear of social disapproval. In fact, many of the perpetrators of rape in Koss's survey felt proud of what they had done and believed that the woman was equally or more responsible. Half said that they expected to engage in similar acts again, and the vast majority who reported committing rape were adamant that their behaviour was definitely not rape (Koss, 1989). Victims in this survey saw their expressions of nonconsent to be more clear and the violence more serious than did the perpetrators.

Young men and women in the Canadian dating violence survey also differed in the extent to which they reported that physical violence was used against female dating partners. These situations should be less ambiguous than sexual assaults but could be rationalized by men if they felt the woman "had it coming" or somehow provoked the attack. Large discrepancies in the reports of wife battering given by wives and husbands are not uncommon (Dobash et al., 1992; Brush, 1990; Szinovacz, 1983; Edleson and Brygger, 1986; Browning and Dutton, 1986; Makepeace, 1986). Men who see their behaviour as justified under the circumstances will not perceive it to be wrong and will respond to survey questions differently than the women who were assaulted.

We now turn to a discussion of the issue of consent and the central role it plays in understanding sexual violence.

THE ISSUE OF CONSENT

The essence of sexual violence is lack of consent. What separates sexual assault from other forms of sexual activity between adults under the law is whether or not both parties agreed to their participation. Upon reaching the age of 18, any type of consenting sexual activity (so long as it is performed in private), is legal. Anything else is sexual assault.

The specific Criminal Code sections and case law governing sexual assault offences were set out in Chapter 2. When someone, usually a woman, reports a sexual assault (although the law on sexual assault is gender-neutral), the primary issue to be decided in a court of law is generally that of consent. And it is generally the word of the victim against the word of the accused. Why is there such confusion in the perceptions of women and men regarding a woman's consent to sexual activity? In some cases of dating violence (about half, according to the research cited above), the man admits to using force to overcome the woman's resistance, but even then he often does not see this as socially or legally wrong. Many young men will brag to their peers about using force and look for and receive approval for their success (Sanday, 1990). But in many cases, the man either is reckless about finding out whether the woman consents, or carries on with force despite her protests. Very few of these cases land in court, but if they did, the issue would undoubtedly be one of consent.

In 1992, Parliament established a definition of the concept of consent as it applies to sexual assault in an effort to assist judges, lawyers, and juries in determining guilt in sexual assault trials. Section 273.1 of the Criminal Code specifies that no consent is obtained in the following situations:

- Consent is given by someone other than the victim.

- The victim is incapable of consenting due to intoxication or other condition.

- Consent is induced by abusing a position of trust, power, or authority.

- The victim indicates by word or conduct her lack of consent.

- The victim indicates by word or conduct that she has withdrawn her consent.

The last two conditions above, specifying either *word* or *conduct*, were included in recognition of the unique vulnerability of disabled women to sexual assault and the fact that some physical and mental disabilities prevent a person from articulating lack of consent.

The Code also says that "Nothing in (the above) shall be construed as limiting the circumstances in which no consent is obtained." In other words, this list is not exhaustive, and the prosecution may present other conditions as indicative of absence of consent. This change to the law represents a shift away from a focus on whether the perpetrator used force or caused injury to a focus on the complainant's articulated consent to engage in sexual activity.

The legislation also restricted the conditions under which the accused could say he "mistakenly believed" that the victim was consenting. The issue of "mistaken belief" in consent arose in a case in 1980 (*R. v. Pappajohn*) when the Supreme Court of Canada decided that a person accused of sexual assault may claim as a defence that he honestly believed the woman consented, even if she did not. As a consequence of this decision, men who used the defence of honest mistaken belief in cases involving passive, sick, or unconscious women were acquitted. This defence gave priority to the perception of the accused over the perception of the victim in sexual assault cases, and the door was open to any interpretation an accused person wanted to give to the situation—consent was in the eye of the beholder. Just as passivity could be perceived as consent by some people, so too could resistance. Some men may interpret a woman's physical resistance to sexual advances as feigning protest to preserve her reputation or as an invitation for "rough sex" (Boyle, 1994). Men who were reckless about obtaining consent could attach almost any meaning to the struggles of the woman objecting to their advances.

Limits to the mistaken belief defence were codified in law in the 1992 changes to the Criminal Code. They were intended to shift the onus to the accused to ensure that the woman was, in fact, consenting. According to Section 273.2, the accused cannot now use the defence that he mistakenly believed the victim was consenting if the belief stems from his drunkenness, recklessness, or willful blindness, or if the accused did not take adequate steps to determine whether the victim was in fact consenting. In other words, the accused cannot use the excuse that he thought the woman was consenting if he was too intoxicated to know, or if he didn't take the time or care to find out—to simply say he thought she was consenting is not enough.

Shortly afterward, in the 1994 case of *R. v. Daviault*, the Supreme Court altered the law with respect to the culpability of an accused person in an extreme state of intoxication. The court in this decision allowed the defence of severe drunkenness and overthrew the conviction of a man who had been found guilty of sexually assaulting an elderly woman. One of the court's justifications in granting this defence was that the degree of intoxication required is so extreme that the situation would rarely arise again. Yet in the months that followed, the same defence was successful in several acquittals of intoxicated men who had assaulted women. In 1995, Parliament passed amendments to the Criminal Code that allow the drunkenness defence in violent offences such as murder that require a "specific intent," but not in offences such as assault and sexual assault that require only a "general intent."

The law clearly states that a woman cannot be considered to be consenting to sexual activity if someone else consents for her, if she is drunk or high on drugs so that her judgment is impaired, if she complies by reason of a person's position of trust or authority over her, or if she indicates by words or gestures that she does not consent. Yet some young men believe that a lack of vigorous resistance can be interpreted as willingness and that force is acceptable under certain conditions (Sanday, 1990; Muehlenhard, 1989; Benson, Charlton, and Goodhart, 1992). In a sample of 1547 Canadian high-school students, 1 in 5 male students said that forced intercourse was all right "if he spends money on her," "if he is stoned or drunk," or "if they had been dating for a long time" (Sudermann and Jaffe in Wolfe et al., 1995:257).

Researcher Eugene Kanin (1985) interviewed 71 self-identified date rapists on American university campuses to test the hypothesis that these men committed rape because they had difficulties obtaining consensual sex. Kanin found that, on the contrary, these men had considerably more sexual experiences than other men as they engaged in "a more persistent quest" for sexual encounters. He describes these men as "sexual predators" for whom "scoring" is of paramount importance in the maintenance of self-esteem and their vision of their masculinity. The date rapists used techniques of intoxication, deception, and false promises to ensure success in sexual encounters, and received strong support from friends for their use of aggression in sexual relationships. Their approach to male–female relations was driven by the goals of sexual exploitation and dominance. Violence ensued when the woman resisted.

Young men interviewed in college fraternities in the United States by researcher Peggy Sanday had a restricted definition of rape that encompassed only overt demonstrations of force. Everything else was considered "seduction," or what the respondents called "working a yes out" (1990:118). Working on the belief that "no" never means "no," that a woman can always be persuaded to have sex, these young men encouraged one another to push as far as they liked (1990:134). This often involved getting the woman drunk so that she couldn't physically resist. These young men were adamant that what happened after the woman got drunk was her own responsibility and that they could not be held accountable for their behaviour under those circumstances. The young men did not see that they had a responsibility not to exploit a woman who had been made vulnerable, either through her own doing or through theirs. In Canada, the law on consent has shifted the obligation from the complainant having to prove that force was used and that it was countered by physical resistance, to the defendant having to ensure that consent, and not just lack of active resistance, was obtained.

EXPLANATIONS FOR DATING VIOLENCE

SOCIAL LEARNING THEORY

Today, young people live in an environment in which it is difficult to avoid images of violence. They face violent images in video games, music videos, movies, and television programs. Violence is glorified to a large extent, and much of it glorifies violence against women. Through these messages, some young people may come to approve of violence as an acceptable and effective way to solve problems and to advance one's interests, and they may come to view women as legitimate targets for aggression.

According to social learning theory, regular exposure to violence and violent images can influence some people to model that behaviour. Media depictions can contribute to the formation of attitudes and can be a contributing factor to learning violent behaviour (Malamuth, 1989). The chances that violence will be imitated will increase if the viewer identifies strongly with the violent actor or shares important characteristics in common (Bandura, 1977). Young people who emulate rock stars, for example, may be strongly influenced by the misogynous lyrics in the latest music video. A desensitization effect can occur in some youth as a result of repeated exposure over time: the more often violent behaviour is observed or violent language is heard, the less likely the viewer is to regard such behaviour or language as wrong. Media violence is commonplace in the culture of young people, and those who receive a great deal of exposure to these images may become unsure about what constitutes normative dating behaviour (Wolfe et al., 1995). Increasing numbers of young people are growing up in environments where the factors that normally mediate the effects of violent media—such as stable, caring relationships with extended-family members—are weak or absent.

Young people who have had direct experience with violence in childhood may be at even greater risk of using violence against dating partners (Laner and Thompson, 1982; Gwartney-Gibbs, Stockard, and Bohmer, 1987). Children who grow up in homes where violence is routinely used by parents as a disciplinary tool, or where wife battering occurs, do not have normal opportunities to develop positive ways of responding to conflict in their interpersonal relationships. Clinical psychologists have found that children from violent homes are more likely than other children to condone violence as a means of resolving conflict, and are more likely to misinterpret the intentions, thoughts, and feelings of other people (Jaffe, Wilson, and Wolfe, 1988). These children often suffer a disruption in their emotional attachments to their parents and therefore lack parental support in times of conflict or crisis (Jaffe, Wolfe, and Wilson, 1990). The added effect of violent media images on these young people may make them especially prone to responding violently when they encounter stressful or upsetting events in dating situations.

SEX ROLE THEORY

Sex role theory points to the differences in how boys and girls are socialized to explain men's use of aggression toward female dating partners. As set out in Chapter 1, this theory asserts that, through a process of socialization, boys learn to value competitiveness, strength, daring, and the use of control as appropriate masculine behaviour. Girls are more likely to learn to be submissive, nonassertive, and nurturing and to believe that women, not men, are responsible for maintaining emotional relationships. These stereotypes of masculine and feminine behaviour become especially striking during adolescence as young people struggle to develop their own identities and values (Wolfe et al., 1995). If young men worry about their ability to live up to these masculine ideals, they may overcompensate for feelings of inadequacy through extreme displays of strength and power that may involve physical or sexual violence toward their intimate partners.

In interviews with young men in college fraternities, Sanday (1990) describes how acts of sexual aggression and demeaning behaviour toward women were central to the bonding process and the cohesion of the all-male group. Fraternity brothers in her study rationalized the use of coercion and aggression in their sexual relationships with women through a belief in the explosive, uncontrollable nature of male sexuality.

According to Sanday, gangs and fraternities serve a function for young men: they help them to make the transition from a state of relative dependency in adolescence to the power and authority required of manhood. Gangs confer status to young men who cannot yet stand on their own (1990:139). Young men who come to expect power and prestige in their social relationships, but who in fact feel powerless and inadequate, may look to gangs to compensate for these feelings. Sexual attacks on women serve a similar purpose—through these attacks, young men acquire an all-powerful image of themselves, moulding their identity to fit what Sanday refers to as the "mythologies of masculinity" (1990:175). In a similar vein, Diana Russell (1984:118) refers to the "masculinity mystique" that centres on extreme acting-out of the qualities of aggression, force, power, strength, toughness, dominance, and competitiveness that are regarded as masculine. These authors argue that, although there are vast differences among individual men and women, cultural messages that endorse a certain amount of male privilege over women has particular appeal to some males.

On the flip side are the romantic images about love and marriage aimed at girls and women. From very early on, little girls absorb varying degrees of the romantic ideal of finding a prince and living happily ever after. Many young women enter into early dating relationships with these ideals firmly intact. Fantasies of being rescued by a prince that seem harmless in young girls are cultural messages that may condition young women to be passive in their relationships with men, and that can interfere with their ability to assert their own needs and identify issues of importance to them in dating relationships. When jealousy, possessiveness, and control enter into dating relationships, some young women may mistake them for love and commitment. Mercer (1988) surveyed 304 secondary students in Toronto and found that 20 percent of the young women had experienced at least one form of abuse in a dating relationship and 13 percent of the young men reported committing abuse against a dating partner. She concludes that

> The young woman who has internalized the restrictions of traditional femininity is at risk as she enters into caring relationships with young men. If her dating partner has spent his formative years learning traditional masculine behaviour and attitudes, he very likely views women as somehow inferior, defined by their domestic role and their deference to males. He may expect passive and submissive behaviour from a woman. He may also regard her as a sexual adversary. Holding these views, he presents a very real danger to the young woman who has been taught to have similar role expectations for herself. Already there exists a very distinct imbalance of power and rights in favour of the young man. The stage is set for the male abusive tactics in order to maintain and enforce this imbalance (Mercer, 1988:16).

Young women who share the romantic images of male dominance and female passivity and who are looking for acceptance from their peers through having a dating partner, and from the young man himself, may continue to tolerate or excuse increasingly violent behaviour in exchange for the security and status of an ongoing relationship. In situations like this, the young woman's needs for acceptance and dating partners may overshadow her needs for safety and autonomy.

Over the past two decades, the career and family aspirations of young women have changed dramatically, and women have broken down many barriers to inequality. There is much greater awareness and discussion about the damaging effects of gender stereotypes, which have been incorporated into many dating violence prevention programs. According to some psychologists, however, strong differences remain in the formative development of girls and boys that relate to the formation of gender identity. Chapter 1 discusses Nancy Chodorow's (1974) description of the process through which girls form their gender identity in an ongoing relationship with someone of their own gender, and as a result see the world as composed of relationships and connections to others. Boys also begin with a strong attachment to their mothers as the primary caregiver, but at a young age they absorb strong cultural messages that they must reject femininity in order to develop a masculine identity. For men who are insecure in their masculine identity, assaults on women represent assaults on femininity and confirmation of their masculinity.

ROUTINE ACTIVITIES THEORY

According to this perspective, risk of victimization is influenced, to a large extent, by the routine activities people engage in as they go about their work, social, and recreational activities. The extent to which these activities put people at risk of being the victim of a crime depends on a number of demographic characteristics, including their marital status, age, employment status, and income. The higher rates of dating violence reported by young, unmarried women are explained by this theory as the result of the lifestyle of this group of women, which is likely to put them in close proximity to young men (the demographic group most likely to use violence) in locations where violence is likely to occur.

Sacco and Kennedy (1994) offer a variation of the routine activities theory that enhances its relevance to dating violence. These authors explain criminal events in the context of interactions among players: crimes are the outcome of social exchanges between people who find themselves in specific circumstances. How they interact and react to one another determines the outcome. A sexual assault does not occur merely because there is an offender who is motivated to commit a sexual assault and there is an opportunity to do so. The potential victim may react in certain ways to escape harm, such as by fighting back or physically fleeing the situation, so that it becomes an attempted or lower-level sexual assault rather than an aggravated attack. Or, her attempts to protect herself may antagonize the aggressor into inflicting more severe injury. Victims are seen as neither passive objects in the interplay nor active contributors to their own victimization; rather, they are viewed as key participants whose actions help to shape the outcome of events (1994:107).

Criminal events from this perspective are described as social events that cannot be separated from the physical and social settings in which they occur. They are intricately linked to the lifestyles and the routine activities of both victims and offenders and to the places where these activities occur (Sacco and Kennedy, 1994:114). Violence committed by a man against a woman in a dating situation, for example, is likely to evolve under certain circumstances and to involve people with certain characteristics. Interaction among participants shapes the course of events and determines how it will progress and how it will eventually turn out. Because young people spend more of their time and energy in leisure and dating activities, they run the greatest risk of encountering violence in those situations. To the extent that campus life exerts pressures to engage in dating, college and university students will have higher rates of involvement in dating violence.

Within this "event" analysis, the dynamics of modern dating rituals play an important role. These include patterned interactions between men and women that reflect traditional assumptions about their appropriate social roles and about male power and privilege in dating situations (Sacco and Kennedy, 1994; Muehlenhard, 1989; Muehlenhard and Linton, 1987). The traditional dating interaction awards greater control and decision-making power to males in the dating process—men typically initiate the date, choose the dating activity, assume responsibility for any expenses, and maintain control over the mode of transportation. The man not only controls the circumstances of dating, he is also the person who may or may not be motivated to commit sexual assault and who controls the opportunities for offending. For instance, if the man controls the mode of transportation, he can control the sequence of events, which may turn out to be driving to a secluded spot where "parking" can take place. He is able to orchestrate the situation to his advantage, and to restrict the woman's options for escape.

Particular locations and activities have been shown to be associated with dating violence. Driving in a private car, for example, provides freedom of movement for the couple as well as privacy, both of which can work against a woman's attempts to extricate herself from unwanted advances from a male date. A substantial proportion of assaults by dating partners reported to the Violence Against Women Survey (1 in 5) took place in a car (Figure 5.1). Similar proportions occurred in the privacy of the woman's home (28 percent) or the man's home (22 percent) and 10 percent in someone else's house. A minority of all incidents (1 in 5) took place on the street or in some other public place. Sexual violence was more likely than physical violence to take place in a car, while physical assaults more commonly occurred in the home of the man or the woman.

Traditional dating "scripts," in which men are scripted to initiate and control the situation, may lead to situations where a woman's willingness to engage in sexual activity is misinterpreted. When a woman asks a man out or indicates a willingness to go to certain places or to spend the evening drinking with him, this may be interpreted by some men to mean that she is interested in sex, even if she indicates otherwise (Muehlenhard, 1989; Harney and Muehlenhard, 1991; White and Humphrey, 1991). In studies of college and university students, both women and men associated certain dating sites with a readiness to engage in sexual activity on the part of the woman, but men were more likely to perceive this to be the case on all counts. The probability that the man will misinterpret the woman's expectations about

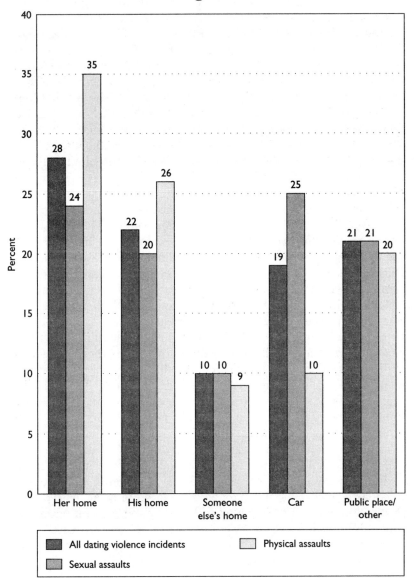

FIGURE 5.1

Location of Dating Violence Incidents

Source: Statistics Canada, *Violence Against Women Survey*, Microdata File, Ottawa (1994a).

sex is highest in situations with a greater sexual connotation, such as "parking" or accompanying the man to his home.

The ambiguity of the dating situation, in which consensual sex is a possibility, adds to the probability that misinterpretation of the woman's level of interest in sex, and sexual assault, will occur (Sacco and Kennedy, 1994:227). This has led to a tendency to attribute blame to the victim for putting herself in the situation in the first place and to dismiss the injury and trauma she experiences as a result of the assault. Her resistance in these situations might be perceived by the aggressor as token resistance. If her resistance is perceived as real and the man feels she has led him on, he might feel that rape is justified. Students who hold traditional attitudes about sex roles and the adversarial nature of male–female relationships were found to be more likely to believe that rape is justifiable in certain situations (Muehlenhard and Linton, 1978).

Many of the social settings frequented by young people in the course of a date, such as bars, restaurants, and house parties, involve the use of alcohol. In fact, in 51 percent of all incidents of dating violence reported by Canadian women, the offender had been drinking at the time of the incident (Statistics Canada, 1994a). Alcohol itself cannot be said to be a direct cause of sexual aggression because of the many other social and personality factors that precede the drinking occasion. But alcohol can contribute directly to dating violence in several ways: alcohol acts as a disinhibitor to violence in some people and can alter their emotional reactions to social slights against them; there is a social willingness to excuse certain unacceptable behaviour that occurs while drinking; and some people may drink knowing it will give them a socially approved excuse for violent behaviour. At the same time, intoxication may cause a blurring of perceptions and communication skills that may increase the possibility that expectations about sexual activity will be misinterpreted and forced sex will result. If the woman is intoxicated, she may appear more sexually available and easier to seduce (Benson, Charlton, and Goodhart, 1992). She also may be considered to be at least partly responsible for what happened to her if she was drinking at the time of the assault. In a practical sense, being intoxicated also decreases the woman's control over the situation and impairs her ability to flee or to defend herself.

POWER AND CONTROL

For young men whose self-image and sense of identity depend on maintaining a dominant position in relationships with women, attempts on the part of female dating partners to assert their autonomy will be a major source of anxiety. They may react by endeavouring to limit the amount of time the women spend with other people, particularly other males, in an attempt to ensure that they will be the sole recipients of the women's attention and affection. These demonstrations of control over dating partners may also win the approval and admiration of male peers.

This need for control is exacerbated by the inherently competitive nature of the dating process, where young people actively compete with members of their own gender for the attentions of the opposite sex. There is the ever-present awareness that other competitors are available, which makes for jealousy and sometimes vigilance in the young man lest the young woman be wooed away by another admirer. Researchers have found that jealousy over the real or perceived involvement of the other person with someone else, and disagreements over drinking, are prominent factors leading to violence in dating relationships (Makepeace, 1981; 1989; Roscoe and Benaske, 1985; Sugarman and Hotaling, 1989).

DeKeseredy and Kelly (1993b) tested the contention that men who hold certain beliefs and attitudes about men's right to dominate women in intimate relationships have higher rates of violence against intimate female partners than men who hold more egalitarian beliefs. These beliefs are those governing a man's rights to obedience, respect, loyalty, dependency, and sexual fidelity from his partner. Based on a representative sample survey of 1835 female and 1307 male college and university students, DeKeseredy and Kelly (1993b:33) assessed the existence of patriarchal beliefs among the male students through the following four statements:

1. A man has the right to decide whether or not his wife/ partner should work outside the home (6.1 percent agree or strongly agree).

2. A man has the right to decide whether or not his wife/ partner should go out in the evening with her friends (9.5 percent agree or strongly agree).

3. Sometimes it is important for a man to show his wife/ partner that he is the head of the house (18.1 percent agree or strongly agree).

4. A man has the right to have sex with his wife/partner when he wants, even though she may not want to (2.4 percent agree or strongly agree).

Attitudes supportive of physical violence against girlfriends were measured (Dekeseredy and Kelly, 1993b:33) via responses to six conditions under which the man would approve of a man slapping his girlfriend, including:

1. She won't do what he tells her to do (1.5 percent said yes).
2. She insults him when they are at home alone (1.0 percent said yes).
3. She insults him in public (1.5 percent said yes).
4. She comes home drunk (1.3 percent said yes).
5. She is sobbing hysterically (1.3 percent said yes).
6. She won't have sex with him (0.9 percent said yes).
7. He learns she is dating another man (6.2 percent said yes).
8. She hits him first when they are having an argument (7.1 percent said yes).

This research shows that, overall, most students do not hold attitudes or beliefs supportive of male dominance in intimate relationships. However, male students who do hold these attitudes and beliefs were most likely to sexually assault their dating partners, and men who hold these attitudes were most likely to physically assault their partners (through a similar test, Smith, 1990a, demonstrates a relationship between patriarchal beliefs and attitudes and assaults on wives—see Chapter 6).

These researchers also found a link between the time spent in male peer groups and the probability of using violence against dating partners (DeKeseredy, 1990a; DeKeseredy and Kelly, 1995). Social support networks are critical reference points in the lives of both young men and young women that provide feedback through which young people gauge their own behaviour. For some men, these networks take the form of attachments to male peers who abuse their own partners and who provide guidance and advice that abuse of girlfriends is all right (DeKeseredy, 1990a). Sexually aggressive behaviour against women is strongly correlated with having peers who are sexually aggressive and who hold attitudes that approve of violence (Alder, 1985; Kanin, 1985; DeKeseredy, 1988; DeKeseredy and Kelly, 1995). Learned norms about a dominant role for men in dating relationships are reinforced by like-minded peers who provide important support for abusive men. These peers can provide abusive men with justification for their actions, which enables them to continue to view themselves as normal and respectable males despite their abuse of dating partners (Kanin, 1985).

A number of authors have noted that the seriousness and frequency of dating violence actually increases with the seriousness of the dating relationship (DeKeseredy, 1989; Makepeace, 1981; Cate et al., 1982; Laner and Thompson, 1982; Stets and Straus, 1989). Once the violence begins, after intimacy is established and the relationship increases in intensity, it is often not viewed as grounds for dissolution of the relationship (Cate et al., 1982). As a couple become more committed to each other and to the relationship, their involvement with each other becomes more intense, and they have greater privacy and more time alone. Rather than contributing to feelings of security, increased intensity often isolates the couple from outsiders and may increase feelings of insecurity. Greater commitment and intensity also may have the effect of increasing the male partner's perceived right to exert control over the woman, which may involve displays of aggression (Stets and Straus, 1989).

Emotional dependency of the woman on the man is often cited as an explanation for why women stay with partners and husbands who abuse them, even when the abuse is serious and frequent. DeKeseredy applies the notion of dependency in the male partner to explain why men abuse their dating partners and why rates of abuse increase in more serious relationships. He states: "Men in dating relationships which involve a high degree of intimacy may be more emotionally dependent on their partners than males in casual dating relationships. A highly dependent man may abuse a woman in an attempt to establish or maintain the dependency or commitment of the woman on him ..." (1989:59). Despite increased levels of emotional attachment, commitment may seem tenuous to either person at stages of the relationship. The potential for loss of the relationship may contribute to feelings of vulnerability that the young man responds to through physical assaults (Laner and Thompson, 1982:232).

For young couples who accept the "ideal of romantic love with its emphasis on intensity, isolation and total mental and physical possession and obsession" (MacLeod, 1987:5), attempts by young men to control their dating partners through the use of violence is a real possibility. Some young women may believe that "he did it because he loved her so much" and "he couldn't stand seeing her with another man" as a way of explaining or rationalizing the violence to themselves and their decision to tolerate or forgive the abuse (Messerschmidt, 1993; Sugarman and Hotaling, 1989; Henton et al., 1983). The young man's violence against her, when he suspects her of being unfaithful or flirting with other men, may be interpreted by her as evidence of his commitment to her, not of control or jealousy.

SUMMARY

Risk of dating violence stems from a number of interrelated factors that, taken together, increase a woman's chances of being victimized. Dating violence occurs in a variety of situations, but it seems to follow from societal factors and particular situations that give men control over when and how dates will proceed. These factors that enhance the degree of male control work to increase women's vulnerability to assault and to decrease their chances of avoiding assault.

Children who grow up with a deficit of positive role models for ways to handle conflicts constructively, and an abundance of role models that endorse the use of violence and aggression, may be at particularly high risk of using violence in dating relationships. Some young men are particularly susceptible to cultural norms that endorse a position of dominance over women in dating relationships, especially if these norms are supported by their peers. Adolescents who, because of conflicts in their families, are isolated from their parents and other adults, may not have the social supports they need when they are confronted with conflicts they cannot resolve peacefully. Many young women and men feel pressure from their peer groups to be accepted, and this acceptance may depend on having a dating partner. In some situations, the need for acceptance may overshadow the young woman's need for safety, causing her to minimize or rationalize violence committed against her. Through the formation of gender identity, some women tend to view their role in intimate relationships as one of "emotional fixer," which may cause them to overlook or suppress their own needs.

Young people growing up with certain expectations about the appropriateness of using violence to settle conflicts, and the proper roles for men and women in intimate relationships, may be at risk of forming abusive relationships with marital partners. In the following chapter, it will become apparent that, despite important differences between dating and cohabitating or marital relationships, many of the precursors to dating violence are also relevant to violence against wives.

C H A P T E R 6

Wife Assault

Wife assault was first identified as an important social issue in the early 1970s. From the time the first shelters for battered women opened in Canada at this time, battered women, shelter workers, academics, and other advocates have been vocal in their demands for legal remedies to protect women from violent husbands, better treatment for abused women and their children, and public funding for shelters and other services. As awareness of the problem grew, so did government funding for research, training for health and justice workers, and services for both abused women and their violent partners. Shelters for battered women now number close to 400 across the country (Rodgers and MacDonald, 1994), and the number of treatment programs for men who batter has grown to 124 (Health Canada, 1994).

After more than two decades of research by sociologists, criminologists, psychologists, social workers, medical professionals, and others, there is now a substantial body of literature available about the correlates and consequences of wife assault. The combined results of sample surveys and qualitative case-study interviews with battered women and violent men have widened our awareness of the number of women in the population affected by violence in their marriages, the types and seriousness of their experiences, the effects of the violence on their lives and the lives of their children, and the dynamics of abusive relationships. But despite the tremendous increase in public awareness and understanding of wife battering, Canadian women continue to be threatened, assaulted, and in some cases killed by the men who profess to love them. In an average year, about 78 women are killed by their husbands and common-law partners and, in 1993, approximately 200 000 women were threatened, slapped, kicked, punched, choked, beaten, or sexually assaulted. This chapter explores the prevalence, correlates, and dynamics of battering relationships on the basis of the many surveys and research studies that have been conducted in North America and Great Britain over the past two decades.

SERIOUSNESS, TYPE, AND FREQUENCY OF ASSAULTS AGAINST WIVES

Definitions of abuse against women by their marital partners vary widely in the research literature. Some include psychological and emotional abuse, financial abuse, and rape and sexual assault, while others are restricted to physical attacks that have the possibility of resulting in injury to the victim. One method used extensively to measure violent conflicts between couples is the Conflict Tactics Scale (CTS) developed by American sociologist Murray Straus and his colleagues (see Chapter 2 for a discussion of this method). The CTS consists of 18 items designed to measure ways of handling interpersonal conflict in family relationships. Three items refer to the use of verbal reasoning techniques, such as discussion and debate; seven items attempt to estimate the use of verbal aggression and threats to harm the other person; and nine items encompass various forms of physical violence, ranging from throwing things, pushing, grabbing and shoving, and other forms of attack, to using a gun or knife (Straus, 1990a). Sexual violence is absent from the scale.

The CTS method of measuring intraspousal violence as a way of handling disputes, or slight modifications of the scale, has been applied in Canada at the national level (Lupri, 1990), in the province of Alberta (Kennedy and Dutton, 1989), in Calgary (Brinkerhoff and Lupri, 1988), and in Toronto (Smith, 1987). It has also been widely used in the United States in two national surveys (Straus and Gelles, 1990a) and in numerous small-scale surveys of random samples and convenience samples (Brush, 1990; Szinovacz, 1983; Edleson and Brygger, 1986, for example). Counting just those responses to the physical violence end of the scale, one-year rates of violence against wives reported by the Canadian CTS surveys ranged from 11 percent to 24 percent.

Decima Research conducted a national survey at the end of 1986 in which self-administered questionnaires were left behind following personal interviews (Lupri, 1989). Couples were asked to report on their own use of violence in their marriage or common-law relationship in 1986, or in their last year of the union for those previously but not currently married or cohabitating. Nationally, 18 percent of men reported using violence against their wives over a one-year period. Kennedy and Dutton (1989) used a mixed mode telephone/personal survey to interview Alberta women and estimated that 11 percent of women in that province had experienced assault by a husband or common-law partner in 1987. In a mixed format of personal interviews and self-administered questionnaires, Brinkerhoff and Lupri (1988) reported that 24 percent of Calgary men in a marriage or common-law relationship admitted to assaulting their wives in 1981. The authors attribute these extraordinarily high rates to the economic boom in that city in 1981 and the resulting social upheaval, high rates of divorce, transient population of young people, and influx of migrant workers.

Smith (1987), in a 1985 telephone survey of young Toronto women aged 18–25, used the CTS and one supplementary question to estimate that 18 percent of women in this age group had ever been assaulted by a partner and 11 percent had been victims of violence in the previous year. In 1987, in a repeat of the Toronto survey, Smith (1987) modified his sample to include women 18–50 years of age who had been married or living in a common-law relationship within the previous two years, and added three supplementary questions to the standard CTS, including one referring to acts of sexual violence by husbands. He estimated that in 1987, 36 percent of currently or recently married or cohabitating women had been victims of violence by a marital partner, 14 percent in the previous year. By comparison, Straus and Gelles estimated that 12 percent of American women had been the targets of violence by their husbands and common-law partners in 1975 and 11 percent in 1985 (Straus and Gelles, 1990c).

Statistics Canada's Violence Against Women Survey employed a methodology that was somewhat similar to these studies in the individual types of violent acts measured, but that differed in the way in which the questions about husbands' use of violence were situated within the questionnaire and how they were introduced to respondents. A random sample of Canadian women 18 years of age and over living in the 10 provinces were questioned about their partners' use of physical violence, sexual assaults, and threats to inflict physical harm, all of which are considered assaults under the Canadian Criminal Code. Unlike surveys using the CTS, which ask about methods of conflict resolution, respondents to the Violence Against Women Survey were instructed to think about times when their partners had used *violence* against them. This block of questions was situated after lengthy sections concerning experiences of sexual and physical assaults by strangers, dates, boyfriends, and other known men, which acted as sensitizing lead-in questions to the potentially more difficult section about partner violence (details about the methodology and format of the Violence Against Women Survey and the Conflict Tactics Scale are presented in Chapter 2).

The results of this survey showed that, in 1993, 29 percent of all women who had ever been married or had lived with a man in a common-law relationship had experienced at least one episode of violence by a husband or live-in partner. This figure represents over 2.6 million Canadian women. Approximately 201 000 women had suffered violence during the one-year period preceding the survey, representing 3 percent of currently married or cohabitating women.

Table 6.1 shows the prevalence of each of the 10 items that make up the definition of "wife assault" used in the Violence Against Women Survey. The most common forms of violence used by male partners were pushing, grabbing, and shoving; threatening to hit her with his fist or something else that could hurt her; slapping; throwing something at her that could hurt her; and kicking, biting, and hitting her with fists. Each of these acts affected about a million women or more. And while the percentage of women who had been beaten up, sexually assaulted, choked, or had a gun, knife, or other weapon used against them were all less than 10 percent, each of these violent acts involved between 400 000 and 800 000 women. (See Box 2.3 for the ordering of these items on the questionaire.)

The survey also indicated that the prevalence of violence was higher in former unions than in unions that were intact at the time of the interview. Fifteen percent of women living with a husband or common-law partner reported experiencing violence by those partners, while *almost half* (48 percent) of women who had been previously married or had lived in a common-law relationship in the past had been assaulted or threatened in some way by previous partners (these women may also have been in a new union). It should not be surprising that the rate of violence is higher for previous relationships. Relationships with violence are more likely to end than peaceable ones, and in some cases, the woman's decision to terminate the relationship results in a violent response from her partner.

The threefold difference in rates of violence in previous compared with current relationships may also reflect more practical considerations. Survey respondents may have greater freedom to talk to an interviewer about their experiences once they are out of an abusive relationship (although some separated women continue to be threatened and even assaulted by former partners after terminating the relationship). Women living with a violent partner may feel embarrassment, shame, and fear that prevents them from fully disclosing acts of violence to an interviewer over the telephone, despite the extra precautions taken to conduct this

TABLE 6.1

Number and Percentage of Ever-Married Women 18 Years and Over Who Reported Violence by Husbands and Common-Law Partners by Type of Assault

Type of Assault	Number in Millions	Any Partner	Current Partner	Previous Partner
			percentage	
Total women assaulted by a marital partner[1]	**2.65**	**29**	**15**	**48**
1. Pushed, grabbed, or shoved her	2.22	25	12	40
2. Threatened to hit her with his fist or anything else that could hurt her	1.69	19	7	35
3. Slapped her	1.36	15	4	30
4. Threw something at her that could hurt her	1.02	11	4	21
5. Kicked, bit or hit her with his fist	.96	11	2	22
6. Beat her up	.79	9	1	19
7. Forced her into any sexual activity when she did not want to by threatening her, holding her down, or hurting her in some way	.73	8	2	17
8. Choked her	.61	7	1	14
9. Hit her with something that could hurt her	.51	6	1	12
10. Threatened to or used a gun or knife on her	.42	5	1	10

[1] Includes common-law partners.
Figures do not add to totals because of multiple responses.

Source: Johnson and Sacco, 1995:295. Reprinted with permission.

survey (see Chapter 2 for details). Women who have taken steps to leave the man and to distance themselves from the situation may be more willing to define the assaults as violent and to relate these experiences to a survey interviewer. Together, these factors may contribute to the large difference in rates of violence in previous marriages relative to current marriages.

At first glance, the figures comparing rates of violence in previous and current marriages might suggest that a great majority of abused women eventually leave their violent partners and that, although high levels of very serious instances of assaults and battering have occurred against Canadian women, most women have been able to resolve the situation by terminating the relationship. Yet these figures are misleading because of the relative difference in the number of women currently in common-law unions or registered marriages compared with the number with previous marriages or live-in relationships. Out of the 6.69 million women currently in a marital union, 1.02 million (or 15 percent) have been assaulted by their partners. By comparison, a total of 3.74 million women have previously been in a marital union, and 1.78 million of them (or 48 percent) were victims of violence by one or more of those partners. The difference between the actual number of women who have left and those who have remained with violent men is therefore not as great as the percentages at first suggest. Later discussion in this chapter will focus on the dynamics and correlates associated with battering relationships, while Chapter 7 will discuss how these dynamics present difficulties for battered women when they make efforts to leave abusive husbands.

In a majority of cases, assaults on wives are not isolated incidents. It is evident from the high numbers of women who reported individual types of assaults relative to the total number of assaulted women that many victims experienced multiple episodes of violence. In 63 percent of all cases of wife assault, the violence occurred more than once, and 32 percent involved more than 10 episodes (see Figure 6.1). The violence reported in previous unions was more prevalent and occurred with greater frequency. Seventy-four percent of women assaulted by previous partners were subjected to multiple assaults, 41 percent on more than 10 occasions. By comparison, women currently living with abusive partners sustained violence with relatively fewer repetitions. Fifty-nine percent of women abused by a current partner reported only one incident of violence. Yet 10 percent of women living with a violent partner at the time of the interview had suffered repeated violence that occurred on more than 10 occasions, in what are commonly termed battering relationships.

FIGURE 6.1

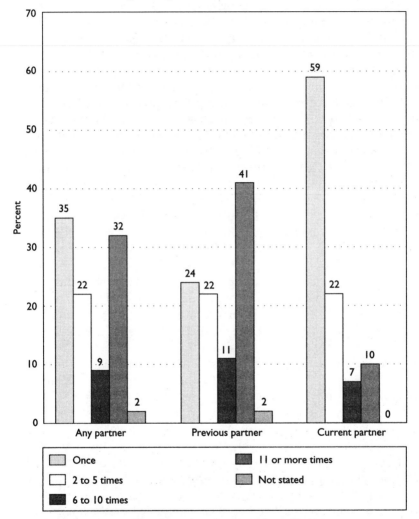

Frequency of Marital Violence

Figures may not add to 100 percent because of rounding.

Source: *Violence Against Women Survey,* Statistics Canada (1993).

Most instances of only one episode of violence occurred quite some time prior to the interview and were relatively minor incidents. Almost half (44 percent) of the women who reported one incident of violence from a current partner said it had happened at least 10 years ago. Seventy percent described the incident as a threat of assault, throwing objects, or pushing, grabbing, or shoving. In cases involving multiple episodes, increasing frequency was associated with increasingly serious acts.

In a third of all cases, women were able to halt their husbands' use of violence against them after one episode, either by leaving or threatening to leave, calling the police, or some other means. But in cases of multiple assaults, there is evidence to substantiate the oft-quoted claim that violence tends to increase over time, not only in frequency but also in intensity as the man becomes increasingly dangerous (Follingstad, 1992, for example). This is illustrated most dramatically with previous partners, who tended to inflict more serious and repeated episodes of violence. Figure 6.2 shows all types of violence as well as the most serious type ever experienced as a percentage of all women who reported violence by previous partners. The seriousness scale is a rough ordering based on the order in which these items were asked in the survey and does not take into account injury or other consequences for victims. As Figure 6.2 graphically illustrates, more than 40 percent of all women abused by a previous spouse said yes to each of having been threatened; had something thrown at them; been slapped, kicked, bitten, or hit; or had been beaten up, yet in each case fewer than 10 percent said this had been the most serious act of violence committed against them. Only 5 percent of abused women had only been threatened with assault or had objects thrown at them, the least serious items on the scale and those least likely to inflict physical injury.[1]

A significant proportion of these acts of violence had terrifying consequences for the victims. In almost half (44 percent) of all marriages with violence, a weapon was used at some point (Table 6.2). This included guns and knives in a relatively small percentage of cases (16 percent); more often these involved throwing something at the woman or hitting her with something that could hurt her. Almost half of these cases resulted in physical injury to the woman, and in almost half of the cases that involved injury, the woman received medical attention.

In 34 percent of all cases, the assaults or threats caused the woman to fear that her life was in danger. This is estimated to represent 944 000 violent unions in Canada (some women had

---

[1] There is one important qualifier to the data displayed in this way, however—that is, it is not possible to establish the sequence of events. It is assumed here that anyone who reports being hit with a fist and suffering a less serious act, such as a threat, will have been subjected to an escalation in the severity of violence. However, we cannot rule out the possibility that after hitting his spouse, a man's threats are sufficient to keep the woman intimidated and to maintain his control over her without the need to resort to further assault.

FIGURE 6.2

Type of Violence Ever Inflicted and Most Serious Type by a Previous Partner

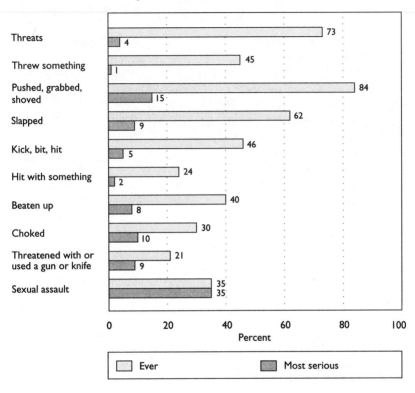

Source: Stastistics Canada, *Violence Against Women Survey,* Microdata File, Ottawa (1994a).

more than one violent relationship) (Statistics Canada, 1993a). The percentage of abused women fearing for their lives was considerably higher in unions that had ended than in current unions (45 percent of previous unions compared with 13 percent of current unions). This represents approximately 137 000 women who, living with a violent man at the time of the interview, at one time feared for their lives because of the threats, intimidation, and violence directed at them. This description of the prevalence and seriousness of violence directed against women by husbands

TABLE 6.2

Seriousness of Assaults by Husbands and Common-Law Partners

	Percentage
Total women assaulted by a marital partner	100
Threatened to use or used a weapon	44
Threw something at her that could hurt her	38
Hit her with something that could hurt her	19
Used a gun or knife	16
Suffered injury	45
Received medical attention (of those who were injured)	43
Feared her life was in danger	34

Source: Statistics Canada, "The Violence Against Women Survey," *The Daily*, November 18 (1993a).

and live-in partners illustrates the importance of including previous relationships in such studies. Studies restricted to intact marital unions, and that exclude separated and divorced women and those with previous common-law relationships, risk undercounting and misrepresenting the range and prevalence of violence in Canadian marriages.

SEXUAL VIOLENCE IN MARRIAGE

Sexual violence may not be associated with images of wife battering in the minds of many readers. Most surveys, other kinds of research, and theoretical explanations of wife battering tend to focus almost exclusively on nonsexual assaults and other types of emotional or psychological abuse. One possible explanation for the relative inattention to sexual violence in marriages is that, until very recently, the law did not recognize rape or other forms of sexual violence committed by husbands against their wives. Prior to 1983, women in Canada were not protected from sexual assaults committed by their husbands, no matter how violent or brutal the attacks. A man who raped his wife or forced her to engage in other sexual acts could not be charged with a criminal offence unless he also left evidence of injuries, and then he was open to charges of assault, not sexual assault. In fact, the law explicitly exempted wives from the law on rape in the so-called "spousal exemption." Prior to 1983, Section 143 of the Canadian Criminal Code stated that

> A male person commits rape when he has sexual intercourse with a female person *who is not his wife*,
>
> (a) without her consent, or
>
> (b) with her consent if the consent
>
>> (i)   is extorted by threats or fear of bodily harm,
>>
>> (ii) is obtained by personating her husband, or
>>
>> (iii) is obtained by false and fraudulent representations as to the nature and quality of the act.

At that time, rape was very specifically defined as "sexual intercourse" and the maximum sentence for it was life imprisonment. Other forms of sexual violence were classified under the less serious "indecent assault," another offence that did not apply to husbands.

The former law related to rape was more concerned with old-fashioned notions of the loss of the woman's reputation and marriageability once her virginity was taken than it was with the violent and assaultive nature of sexual assault. Historically, forced intercourse was considered the worst of crimes against a woman because it robbed her of her virginity and decreased her marketability as a wife (Los, 1994). Once a woman married and gave up her virginity to her husband, she also gave up the right to refuse sexual intercourse with him. Allowing charges of rape to be brought by women against their husbands was viewed as unnecessary legal intervention into the privacy of the family that would be extremely difficult to enforce, would interfere with a man's rights over his wife, and would undermine the family unit. The law considered the couple to be husband and wife even after separation, which meant that charges of rape also could not be brought against a man if he raped his wife after they were separated but not yet divorced.

Legislative changes to the Canadian Criminal Code in 1983 abolished the laws on rape and indecent assault and replaced them with three levels of sexual assault, commonly referred to as Levels I, II, and III. These offences were described in Chapter 2. They are, in descending order of seriousness: aggravated sexual assault resulting in wounding, maiming, disfiguring or endangering the life of the victim; sexual assault with a weapon, threats to a third person, or causing bodily harm; and sexual assault not involving a weapon and not resulting in bodily harm.

The Violence Against Women Survey estimates that 8 percent of ever-married or cohabiting women in Canada have been forced into sexual activity by a husband or common-law partner through the use of threats, by being held down, or by being hit or otherwise hurt in some way. The question used to estimate sexual violence in marriage contains the necessary elements to be classified as sexual assault under the Criminal Code: "Has he ever forced you into any sexual activity when you did not want to, by threatening you, holding you down, or hurting you in some way?" (Statistics Canada, 1994b:37) This 8 percent figure represents approximately 730 000 Canadian women.

Using somewhat different definitions of sexual violence, survey researchers in the United States have arrived at similar estimates of sexual violence in marriage among women in that country. Diana Russell (1990) surveyed a random sample of 930 women living in San Francisco about any incidence of sexual assault they had had at any time in their lives. Fourteen percent of the married women in the sample had experienced at least one act of sexual assault by a husband or ex-husband, some over the course of many years. Eighty-five percent of these cases included at least one completed rape. David Finkelhor and Kersti Yllo (1983; 1985) asked a representative sample of 323 Boston mothers of school-age children whether a spouse or common-law partner had ever used physical force or threats to try to have sex with them. Ten percent of these women said they had been the victims of forced sex by their husbands.

For many battered women, sexual violence forms an element of the battering relationship. Twenty-seven percent of Canadian women who were victims of physical assaults by husbands were also forced into sexual activity. Thus, among ever-married women and those who have lived in common-law relationships, the prevalence of sexual assault by spouses is 8 percent, and among battered women it is 27 percent. Other research puts this figure as high as 50 percent of battered women who have been sexually abused by a spouse (Shields and Hanneke, 1983; Russell, 1990;

Finkelhor and Yllo, 1985; Campbell, 1989; Campbell and Alford, 1989; Hanneke, Shields, and McCall, 1986).

The following quotations from women in the Canadian survey exemplify situations of sexual violence in marriage:

> He was drinking with friends and would come home and force himself on me.

> He was violent because I was not willing to have sex.

> When I did not want to have sex he would throw me out.

Sexual violence in marriage is almost always accompanied by physical assaults. Ninety-two percent of women who were sexually assaulted were also hit, slapped, punched, choked, beaten up, or threatened with guns or knives.[2] Thus, sexual violence is commonly used by battering men, and rarely are sexual attacks made by husbands who were not also physically violent. This is not the situation described by either Russell (1990) or Finkelhor and Yllo (1985); the women in their samples found sexual assault of wives to occur in the absence of battering in a substantial number of cases. But what these three studies, and others, agree on is that sexual violence is correlated with more frequent and extreme forms of violence. Victims of sexual violence by husbands experience more frequent episodes of the entire range of violent acts, from threats, pushing, and punching to using a weapon, and the violence they suffer entails more severe forms of battering than that experienced by other assaulted women (Shields and Hanneke, 1983; Russell, 1990; Finkelhor and Yllo, 1985; Frieze, 1983; Campbell, 1989). They were also more likely to suffer physical injury and more serious physical and mental health consequences than women who were battered but not sexually assaulted (Shields and Hanneke, 1983; Campbell, 1989; Campbell and Alford, 1989).

Survey questions about sexual violence in marriage may be among the most difficult for women to disclose to interviewers, and may therefore be undercounted in the studies cited here. Women who have had, or continue to be subjected to, these kinds of attacks may be ashamed and embarrassed about revealing them. Some may not be sure that they have a right to complain about acts of forced sex by husbands and so may hesitate to report them to an interviewer (Russell 1990:39). Like many people, they may hold stereotypes that rape is something that happens

---

[2] The Violence Against Women Survey does not indicate whether acts of sexual violence took place during the same episodes in which physical assaults occurred, but only that both types of assaults occurred at some point during the relationship.

between strangers and that acts of forced sex by a husband do not qualify as rape or sexual assault. Despite the publicity given to the passage of the new sexual assault law in Canada, many people seem to be unfamiliar with the details of the changes. According to a public opinion poll commissioned by the Canadian Department of Justice in 1988, 81 percent of women at that time were aware that a man can be charged with sexually assaulting his wife under the new law, although only 15 percent of women were aware of the change in legal terminology from rape to sexual assault (Roberts, 1994:15). Twenty-eight percent of women were not aware that a sexual assault can occur in the absence of sexual intercourse. Women who are unclear about how the law defines and responds to sexual violence may be reluctant to report sexual assaults by their husbands to surveys of this nature.

Sexual violence by husbands has been among the most hidden of all crimes of violence against women. Unlike battering, or sexual assaults by strangers, or even date rape, sexual violence within marriage has not been publicly scrutinized to the same extent. Stories of these types of assaults by husbands are very rarely found in the media, and tend not to be included in research studies addressing either sexual assault or wife battering. But the surveys outlined here indicate that sexual violence in marriage affects many battered women. Knowledge of this fact could help shelter workers, counsellors, and others in understanding the reactions battered women display and in providing the most appropriate supports for them (Shields and Hanneke, 1983; Campbell, 1989; Campbell and Alford, 1989).

FACTORS ASSOCIATED WITH INCREASED RISK OF WIFE ASSAULT

Before a great deal was known about battering relationships, violence by men against their wives was often assumed to be an expression of frustration against nagging or brutish women who tormented their unfortunate husbands beyond endurance. Blame was frequently laid on the female victims, who were considered to have "had it coming to them." Women who stayed with men and continued to receive beatings were perceived to be masochists who—consciously or unconsciously—enjoyed being mistreated. How else could we explain their failure to leave the situation if it were really that bad?

Blaming the victim serves a number of functions. It allows others to distance themselves from "women like that," to preserve a belief in a just world where people get what they deserve, and to deny that such things happen with any frequency (Frieze and

Browne, 1989). A belief in provocation as the cause of wife beating helps to justify the actions of the abusive partner while failing to question or challenge the right of husbands to inflict punishment on their wives. Historically, provocation has been offered as an explanation by bystanders, witnesses, police, friends, family, and agencies the victim turns to for help. When this happens, battered women may have difficulty defining the situation as anything other than their own fault. This compounds their feelings of guilt and helplessness and decreases the probability that they will be able to change the situation.

While provocation still finds favour among lay explanations for wife assault, more than two decades of research on battered women and their violent partners have provided evidence of an interplay of broad social and cultural factors in violent relationships. Sample surveys and interviews with battered women and violent men have illustrated how the prevalence of wife assault varies across populations according to various characteristics of the couple and the relationship. In particular, assaults on wives have been found to co-exist with marital conflict, the stresses and pressures associated with male unemployment and poor financial status, alcohol abuse, and early childhood exposure to violence. Other researchers have found evidence that attitudes about traditional sex roles and about the rights of husbands to assert control over wives form a component of battering relationships.

The relevance of these factors as precursors to violence against wives, and the connections among them, are described below. It will become clear throughout this discussion that assaults on wives are the culmination of a complex web of dynamics situated within ongoing relationships with emotional commitment and expectations about the rights and responsibilities of marriage.

CONFLICT IN FAMILIES

Gelles and Straus (1988) have identified several characteristics of modern families to explain why they are inherently prone to conflict. First, family members spend a great deal of time together, and their involvement with one another is emotionally intense. Family members also participate in a wide range of activities with one another, including meals and meal preparation, household chores, and recreational pursuits. As a consequence, families have many potential sources of conflict. It is inevitable that the goals of individual members will conflict on occasion and that disagreements and disputes will arise. In addition, a great deal of a family's leisure time is spent in privacy, which shields them from outside intervention. Physical violence is one possible outcome of accumulated grievances in families where violence is an acceptable method of resolving conflicts.

Within marital relationships, openness and intimacy bring the development of love and attachment, but they can also bring opportunities for emotional injury (Brinkerhoff and Lupri, 1988). People so intimately involved with each other possess personal information about each other, know their partner's weak or vulnerable spots, and know what they can say to hurt the other person. Anger and frustration have the potential to accumulate over time and to increase in intensity. The sheer range and number of activities shared by married couples, and the privacy afforded the relationship from outside influences, provide couples with ample opportunities to frustrate each other and to retaliate aggressively.

Women are particularly vulnerable to assault in marital conflicts because of the traditional power imbalance, in which they have tended to be dependent on their spouses for status and financial support. One result of this dependency is that they will often tolerate more frequent and severe levels of aggression against them that would not be tolerated if they occurred outside the family unit. Women also tend to be physically smaller and weaker than men, which makes them vulnerable to assaults and unable to retaliate in kind or to defend themselves (Sebastian, 1983). In sum, conflict and aggression are said to occur in families because frustrations and friction are common, emotional attachments and expectations among members are intense, interactions occur in private, and certain members are highly dependent on others and physically vulnerable to attack.

THE AGE OF THE MAN AND THE WOMAN

A common theme running throughout this book is the association between youth and violent victimization, whether in the form of sexual harassment, threats, or sexual or physical assaults. In all types of harassment and violence by strangers and boyfriends, younger women report far more frequent occurrences. Rates of wife assault also follow this pattern. Taking a snapshot of experiences of wife assault that occurred in the one-year period prior to the 1993 Violence Against Women Survey, 12 percent of Canadian women aged 18–24 reported at least one incident of violence by a marital partner, compared with the national average of 3 percent of all currently married (or cohabitating) women. Rates of violence declined steadily with age down to just 1 percent of women 45 years of age and over.

The age of the man and the woman are highly correlated, with men, on average, two years older than their spouses (Dumas and Péron, 1992). The higher rates of violence against young women may therefore be a reflection of the youth of their spouses. Young men are the most violence-prone group both inside and outside the family (Hirschi and Gottfredson, 1983). Rates of wife assault according to the age of male partners parallels that for female victims: 13 percent of young men in the 18–24 age group were violent toward their partners, compared with 1 percent of men 45 years of age and over (see Figure 6.3).

FIGURE 6.3

One-Year Rates of Wife Assault, by Characteristics of the Man and Type of Union

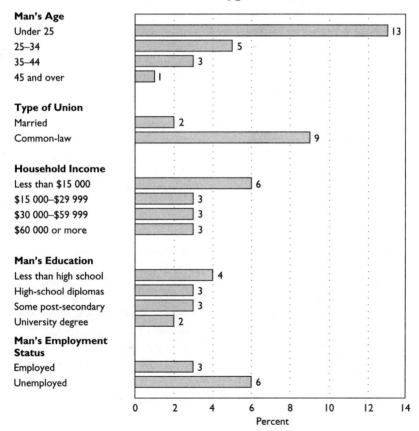

Source: *Violence Against Women Survey*, Statistics Canada (1993).

This inverse relationship between rates of wife assault and the ages of both the victim and the abuser corroborates the findings of a number of other survey researchers (Hotaling and Sugarman, 1986; Straus, Gelles, and Steinmetz, 1980; Lupri, 1989; Kennedy and Dutton, 1989; Smith, 1990b; Brinkerhoff and Lupri, 1988—although the latter indicate an increase in rates of violence at retirement age). Straus and his colleagues (1980) offer a number of explanations for the higher rates of wife assault among young couples. One possibility is that this current group of young men are more prone to violence than previous generations and that this one-year snapshot is a reflection of this particular generation of men. A second is that younger men of all generations are more predisposed to violence than older men, perhaps because of a lack of experience or maturity in resolving conflict situations, and that tendencies toward violence decrease as men age. A third possibility is that violent marriages are more likely to break up in the early stages and, consequently, that marriages that survive over the years contain lower levels of violence. As the following sections will show, the age of the man and the woman are important variables that are tied to other characteristics of the relationship; when combined with these other factors, they increase the risk of wife assaults substantially.

MARRIAGES AND COMMON-LAW UNIONS

There is a fourfold difference in rates of violence reported by women living in common-law relationships compared with women in registered marriages. In the 12-month period prior to the Violence Against Women Survey, 9 percent of cohabiting women experienced at least one incident of violence from their partners compared with 2 percent of married women. This difference is noted by other researchers whenever type of union is included as a variable (Brinkerhoff and Lupri, 1988; Kennedy and Dutton, 1989; Stets and Straus, 1989; Smith, 1987).

There are a number of important differences between common-law and married couples that might help to explain this disparity in the occurrence of wife assault. First, both men and women in common-law relationships tend to be considerably younger than their married counterparts. The Violence Against Women Survey sample, weighted to represent the Canadian female population, shows that 13 percent of men living common-law are under 25 years of age compared with 2 percent of married men; similarly, 23 percent of women living common-law are under 25 compared with 2 percent of married women. The immaturity of very young couples places them at increased risk of violence since many have not established peaceful means of working out conflict within intimate relationships. Figure 6.4 illustrates the effects of the male partner's age combined with common-law marital status. This figure shows that the overall decline in rates of violence according to the man's age is due primarily to cohabiting men. While rates do decline with age for married men (from 5 percent of men under age 25 down to 1 percent of those 45 and over), rates are higher for cohabiting men in all age groups, and they drop dramatically after age 25. The one-year rate of partner violence for cohabiting men under the age of 25 is 19 percent, six times higher than the national average of just 3 percent.

Other characteristics unique to young cohabiting men combine to increase the probability that they will commit acts of violence against their live-in partners. For example, cohabiting couples may have fewer family and community supports to call on when problems arise between them. If the young couple are living together despite disapproval from parents and other family members, potential sources of family support may be unavailable to them when they need it. Men who are isolated from their families and communities will also have less to lose in terms of a tarnished reputation if they abuse their partners because they will not feel the effects of social disapproval (DeKeseredy, 1989:59); they are also less likely to be concerned about legal action. Married men, who have a greater stake in conformity and who have more to lose in terms of reputation, are more likely to be deterred from abusing their partners by the threat of social disapproval and legal action. They are more likely to be involved in family and community networks where others would know about and express disapproval of the use of violence (Gelles, 1983). As DeKeseredy (1989) points out, if police and others regard the woman as amoral for living with a man outside of marriage, they may be less inclined to provide the couple with assistance or support. When the woman finds no support available from the police or others, there is little to deter the man from further violence.

The level of commitment of partners in marriages and common-law unions may also differ. Some cohabiting couples are seriously committed to each other and eventually marry, but many others choose to live together more for financial or convenience reasons than for reasons of commitment, and view the relationship as temporary. The majority of common-law relationships lead rapidly to either marriage or separation, with about half choosing to marry (Dumas and Péron, 1992:103). Although common-law couples now have most of the same rights and responsibilities as legally married couples, there are some financial benefits to remaining unmarried. Certain financial and tax

FIGURE 6.4

One-Year Rates of Wife Assault by Age of the Man and Type of Union

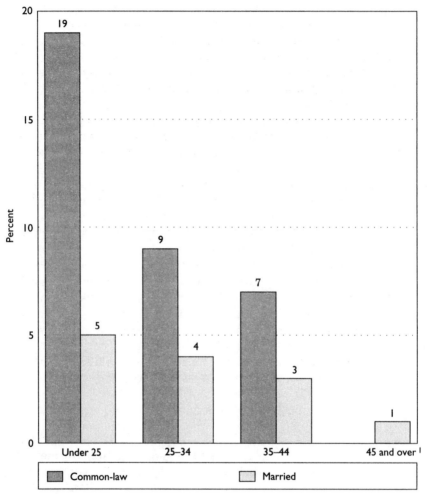

^I Figures not statistically reliable for common-law unions.

Source: Statistics, *Violence Against Women Survey,* Microdata File, Ottawa (1994a).

programs provide greater benefits to people living alone and to single parents than to married couples (Morrison and Oderkirk, 1991). Many people still choose cohabitation for these financial incentives and for the flexibility that enables them to leave their partners easily after a short period of time and with no legal ties.

Young cohabitating couples also differ from marr. in family structure and in the amount of time availabl for social activities outside the relationship. Cohabita more likely to be childless (Barr, 1993) and therefore have family responsibilities and greater flexibility regarding leisure time will be spent. When there are children in comn. law unions, they are more likely than children in registered marriages to be the product of the woman's previous relationship (Wilson, Johnson, and Daly, 1995). This higher incidence of step-children can be a source of conflict for common-law couples, and stepchildren themselves are overrepresented as victims of assault and homicide in the family (Wilson and Daly, 1992a; Daly, Singh, and Wilson, 1993).

Because of the relative youth of the partners, available leisure time, and the temporary nature of some common-law rela-tionships, alternative or additional relationships are more likely to be perceived as being accessible. This can lead to feelings of jealousy and conflict over how free time will be spent (Daly and Wilson, 1988; Ellis, 1989). In the eyes of both the couple and other people, they are not bound to the same degree as married couples to the norms that govern marriage. In fact, many people who choose cohabitation over marriage may do so in order to keep much of their independence. If couples in common-law unions invest less time and commitment in the relationship, their part-ners may be more likely than married partners to be on the lookout for alternatives (Daly and Wilson, 1988:212). When this happens—when one or both partners value their independence and have weak expectations of commitment and sexual fidelity—insecurities and tensions may run high and accusations of infidel-ity, true or false, are more likely to occur.

SOCIOECONOMIC STATUS

Unemployment, low family income, and low occupational status are commonly cited as factors that precipitate assaults by men on their wives (Kennedy and Dutton, 1989; Lupri, 1989; Smith, 1987; 1990a; 1990b; Gelles and Straus, 1988; Gelles, 1980; Finkelhor and Yllo, 1985; Lupri, Grandin, and Brinkerhoff, 1994; Hotaling and Sugarman, 1986). A poor financial situation often leads to stress, frustration, and anxiety that may culminate in violence, especially in families in which violence has become an acceptable coping response. Other researchers maintain that "status incon-sistency" is the more important factor. This occurs when a man is underemployed at an occupation much lower than his education has prepared him for, or when his wife has a higher-status occupa-tion or higher education or prestige than he does. According to resource theory, men have managed to exert power over their wives because they possess certain resources in the form of income, expertise, or status outside the family. When a man feels a loss of status in relation to his wife or peers, he may use violence at home to reinstate his authority and restore the power imbalance in his favour (Finkelhor, 1983; Gelles and Straus, 1988; Hotaling and Sugarman, 1990).

Results from the Violence Against Women Survey show low income to be a correlate of wife battering. When respondents were asked in an open-ended question how violent incidents usually begin, they commonly cited stress over finances and finding work. As Figure 6.3 shows, both family income and employment status are related to rates of violence: men living in families where the joint income is less than $15 000 and unemployed men had rates of violence twice as high as those in more affluent families and employed men. Men with low education (less than high-school graduation) also had rates of violence twice as high as men with university degrees. But, although socioeconomic factors play a role in men's tendency to use violence against their wives and partners, they are not the most important factors. The differences in rates of violence among men of various income or education levels are not large and are considerably smaller than the differences shown for other characteristics of the man and the couple, such as age and type of union.

One important intervening variable that is not often considered in analyses of the effects of socioeconomic status on wife beating is the man's age (Lupri, Grandin, and Brinkerhoff, 1994). Young men 18–24 years of age, and particularly young men living in common-law relationships, have rates of unemployment much higher than the national average and much higher than older men. In fact, 37 percent of young cohabiting men were out of work at some point during the year prior to the Violence Against Women Survey. Young couples and cohabiting couples also have lower average household incomes than older or married couples. The importance of low socioeconomic status cited in many studies of wife beating may actually be a combined effect of socioeconomic status, age, and common-law marital status, all of which are highly correlated.

Smith (1990a) offers a further explanation for the higher rates of violence found among men of lower socioeconomic status. He found, in his survey of Toronto women, that men with low income, low education, or low-status jobs were more likely than more economically advantaged men to hold traditional beliefs and attitudes about men's proper place as head of the household and were more likely to be violent toward their wives (1990a:268). Together, these findings add support to Bowker's (1983) "subculture of violence" theory that there is a substrata of men, mainly of lower socioeconomic status, who beat their wives, who hold traditional attitudes about male dominance, and provide support to one another for keeping their wives in line by using force. Bowker maintains that economic disadvantage makes it difficult for low-income men to assert a level of authority over their wives that they have learned is their due. Violence can be used to re-establish feelings of power and authority. Messerschmidt (1993:149) maintains that working-class men, who have limited power in the workplace, "develop an intense emotional dependency on the household, demanding nurturance, services, and comfort on their terms when at home." Men who lack traditional resources for demonstrating their authority, such as economic success, control, power, and status over other men and women, will "forge a particular type of masculinity that centers on ultimate control of the domestic setting through the use of violence" (1993:149).

ALCOHOL AND VIOLENCE

Excessive drinking is a common explanation for men's use of violence against their wives. But to what extent can alcohol be said to be a *cause* of wife battering? Some battered women have described how their husbands' personalities change when they have been drinking excessively and attribute the violence almost entirely to this drinking problem (Martin, 1981). On the other hand, alcohol provides battered women, who are desperate to understand why their partners hurt them the way they do, with an explanation for their husbands' behaviour. It gives them hope that, if only the man would stop drinking, the violence would also stop (Frieze and Browne, 1989; Walker, 1984; Browne, 1987; Dobash and Dobash, 1979).

Alcohol was cited as a precipitating factor by 29 percent of Canadian women when they were asked in the Violence Against Women Survey how the violence usually began (Wolff and Reingold, 1994). Many of these women perceived drinking to be the primary or sole cause of their husbands' violence against them. Others cited alcohol in combination with other factors, such as jealousy or money:

> He would spend money on alcohol, come home drunk and the fighting would start.

> When he has been drinking he becomes jealous and I have to be careful what I say.

> It usually happened when he was drinking. He was very jealous. I couldn't ever leave his sight or be two minutes late home from work.

He started drinking with his father and brother, and they both told my husband that the only way to treat a woman is to beat her up and he did.

Alcohol functions to reduce inhibitions, and alter perceptions and judgment, and in some people it can increase socially unacceptable behaviour. Excessive drinking can exacerbate ongoing difficulties in a marriage through its mood-altering effects. Rule-breaking or law-breaking behaviour is often excused when committed by someone who is under the influence of alcohol, and some people may drink with the intention of becoming violent in order to have a ready excuse for their actions (Gelles, 1974; Gelles and Straus, 1988).

According to Kantor and Straus (1990), it is not just heavy drinking but the combination of low occupational status, drinking, and approval of violence against one's wife that is associated with the greatest probability of violence. In the 1985 National Family Violence Survey in the United States, men with these characteristics had a rate of wife abuse eight times higher than others. But, those who claim to disapprove of a man slapping his wife nevertheless had higher rates of violence when they drank heavily. These men may be acting on a belief that drinking alcohol gives them a socially accepted "time out" that permits them to deny responsibility for their behaviour and to be excused for it.

Despite conflicting opinions about the precise role played by alcohol abuse in cases of wife assault, there is a correlation between heavy drinking and violence, with more severe violence perpetrated by men who are drinking at the time of the assaults. The Violence Against Women Survey found that women who are married to or living with heavy drinkers are five times as likely to be assaulted by these men than are women who live with nondrinkers (Statistics Canada, 1993a). As Figure 6.5 shows, 2 percent of women living with nondrinkers and 3 percent of those living with moderate drinkers reported that their partner had assaulted them in the year prior to the survey. The annual rate of violence for regular drinkers (those who drink at least four times per week) was triple the rate for nondrinkers (6 percent compared with 2 percent, respectively). But volume of drinking coupled with frequency increases the risk even more. The rate of violence increased to 11 percent of women whose partners are problem drinkers frequently consuming five or more drinks at a sitting.

Half of all violent men were usually drinking at the time of the assaults, and these drinkers were more likely than nondrinkers (65 percent compared with 40 percent) to use very serious acts of violence against their wives (beating up, choking, threatening with a gun or knife, or sexually assaulting). Intoxicated men were more likely to inflict injuries on their wives (56 percent compare to 33 percent), and these injuries were more likely to require medical attention (47 percent compared with 36 percent). Overall, the more a man drinks, the greater the chance that drinking will be involved in incidents of assault against his wife: 68 percent of women who say their husbands were regular heavy drinkers were typically drinking when violent. But, 28 percent of battered women who say their husbands rarely or never drink heavily nevertheless reported them to be usually drinking at the time of the assaults. These figures substantiate assertions about the ability of alcohol to reduce inhibitions and increase aggression and to allow for a "time-out" where normally unacceptable behaviour is allowed to occur (Gelles, 1980; Gelles and Straus, 1988).

As convincing as the link between alcohol and violence may be, there is not a simple cause-and-effect relationship between the

FIGURE 6.5

One-Year Rates of Wife Assault by Partners' Use of Alcohol

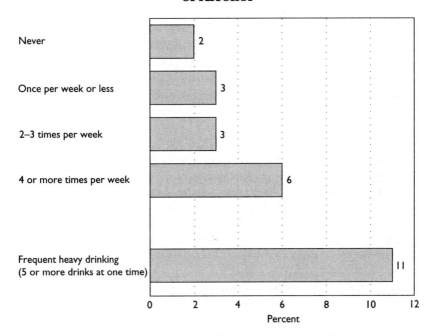

Source: *Violence Against Women Survey,* Statistics Canada (1993).

ubstantial amount of violence is perpetrated in the
, of alcohol and by abstainers and moderate drinkers.
-seven percent of assaulted women said their partner was
(or not usually) drinking at the time of the assaults. What's
,ore, even among extremely heavy drinkers, 32 percent were not
usually under the influence of alcohol when the assaults occurred.
And the majority of husbands who assaulted their wives do not
have alcohol problems. The most that can be said with confidence
is that a number of important factors come into play at the time
the blows are struck, and alcohol may be one of them.

POWER AND CONTROL

A number of authors claim that violence and threats by husbands
against their wives are best understood in terms of their coercive
utility in maintaining power and control (Daly and Wilson, 1988;
Wilson, Johnson, and Daly, 1995; Bowker, 1983; Dobash and
Dobash, 1979; 1984; 1992; Adams, 1988; Smith, 1990a; 1991;
Saunders, 1988; Bograd, 1988). In other words, violence is considered to be purposeful behaviour that serves a function for the
man—to assert control over his partner to which he feels that, as
a man and husband, he is entitled. He attempts to exert and
maintain power over her and control her through the use of physical force, intimidation, threats, and psychological abuse (Adams,
1988; Gelles and Straus, 1988).
    Feminist theorists use the concept of "patriarchy" to explain
the societal structures that foster wife battering. Patriarchy
constitutes the constellation of social relations and institutions
that award men greater status, power, and privilege over women.
It has two basic components: social structures that preserve the
dominant position of men (such as legal and financial structures),
and an ideology or set of beliefs through which this arrangement
is accepted as natural and good by the majority of the population
(Dobash and Dobash, 1979). The family is an institution that
embodies traditions, roles, and beliefs about the proper place for
men and women and thus provides both the structure and an
ideology that endorses a higher status role for men. Violence
against wives is believed to be fostered by the unequal status that
exists between men and women within marriage that historically
has been codified in law, and the acceptance of the legitimacy of
this inequality by both men and women.
    Until recently, the assertion that abusive men differed from
other men in their beliefs about appropriate roles for men and
women and about men's rights to enforce these roles was untested
with empirical data. Researchers, counsellors, and shelter workers documented in their discussions with battered women that the

violent partners of these women tended to hold very firm beliefs about men's rights to set the rules and to expect submission and obedience from their wives (Dobash and Dobash, 1979; MacLeod, 1980; 1987; Walker, 1979; Martin, 1981; Browne, 1987). But without control groups of nonviolent men for comparison, it was not possible to assess how batterers differed from other men.

Canadian sociologist Michael Smith employed a random sample of women to test this contention that men who subscribe to traditional beliefs about the natural superiority of men, and men's right to control and dominate women in intimate relationships, will have higher rates of violence against their female partners. Based on a representative sample of approximately 600 Toronto women, Smith (1990a) found that men who subscribe to traditional beliefs and who hold attitudes supportive of violence against women within the family setting are more likely to behave violently toward marital partners than men who hold more egalitarian beliefs. To assess the man's beliefs, Smith asked the women in his sample to indicate how their husbands would respond to the following four statements:

1. A man has the right to decide whether or not his wife/partner should work outside the home (36 percent agreed or strongly agreed).

2. A man has the right to decide whether or not his wife/partner should go out in the evening with her friends (32 percent agreed or strongly agreed).

3. Sometimes it is important for a man to show his wife/partner that he is head of the house (53 percent agreed or strongly agreed).

4. A man has the right to have sex with his wife/partner when he wants, even though she may not want to (18 percent agreed or strongly agreed).

Attitudes supportive of wife beating were measured via responses to six conditions under which a husband would approve of a man slapping his wife:

1. She won't do what he tells her to do (3 percent said yes).

2. She insults him when they are at home alone (4 percent said yes).

3. She insults him in public (6 percent said yes).

4. She comes home drunk (8 percent said yes).

5. She hits him first when they are having an argument (20 percent said yes).

6. He learns she has been having an affair with another man (20 percent said yes).

Smith found broader overall support for the traditional beliefs, which ranged from 18 percent to 53 percent, than for the attitudes approving of violence against wives, which ranged from 3 percent to 20 percent. Attitudes approving of violence were strongest in scenarios that have commonly been viewed as constituting provocation on the part of the wife: she hits him first, or she commits adultery. One in five women believe their husbands would feel justified using violence in these situations. The belief with the highest rating concerned the rights of men to assert themselves as head of the household.

Measuring these beliefs and attitudes against actual use of violence, Smith found that both traditional beliefs and attitudes approving of violence against wives were statistically significant predictors of whether a woman was ever beaten by her partner. And, the more traditional the beliefs and attitudes, the greater the probability that she had been beaten. Kantor and Straus (1990:214) also found that men who believe that there are certain circumstances in which they would approve of a husband slapping his wife have higher rates of violence. DeKeseredy (1989; 1990b) and DeKeseredy and Kelly (1993a) have corroborated the link between patriarchal attitudes and beliefs and abuse against female dating partners, where many of the role expectations are the same (this is discussed in Chapter 5).

Attempts to wield power and control over another person can take many forms. It can include verbal attacks, ridicule, isolation from family and friends, jealousy and unwarranted accusations about infidelity, possessiveness, damage to or destruction of property, torture or killing of pets, and threats to harm children or other family members. The effect of these acts is to attack the woman's sense of self-worth and to render her emotionally dependent and under her husband's control (Follingstad et al., 1990). This type of abuse is referred to by various writers as emotional abuse, psychological abuse, obsessiveness, and control.

The Violence Against Women Survey measured emotionally abusive and controlling acts through five separate items asking respondents to say whether or not each statement described their husbands or partners. These statements referred to the man's insisting on knowing her whereabouts, calling her names or putting her down, jealously guarding her interactions with other men, limiting her contacts with family and friends, and denying her access to the family finances. Displays of possessiveness and controlling types of behaviour on the part of husbands occurred with greater frequency than physical assaults or threats (Table

TABLE 6.3

Percentage of Previously Married Women Reporting Emotionally Abusive and Controlling Behaviour by Husbands and Common-Law Partners

Type of Emotionally Abusive Behaviour	Any Partner	Current Partner	Previous Partner
Any emotionally abusive behaviour	**35**	**17**	**59**
1. He insists on knowing who she is with and where she is at all times	22	10	36
2. He calls her names to put her down or make her feel bad	21	7	39
3. He is jealous and doesn't want her to talk to other men	19	6	38
4. He tries to limit her contact with family or friends	16	4	33
5. He prevents her from knowing about or having access to the family income, even if she asks	10	2	22

Figures do not add to totals because of multiple responses.

Source: Rodgers, 1994.

6.3). Altogether, 35 percent of all women who have ever been married or lived with a man in a common-law relationship have been subjected to at least one of these forms of abusive behaviours, compared with 29 percent who were subjected to physical assaults.

As Table 6.3 shows, the most common types of controlling behaviours measured by this survey were attempts to control her whereabouts, name-calling and put-downs, and displays of jealousy with respect to other men. Just as violence was more prevalent in previous relationships, a higher incidence of controlling behaviour was reported to have occurred in relationships that had ended than in relationships that were current at the time of the interview (59 percent compared with 17 percent, respectively). In case-study interviews with battered women, they frequently describe the erosion of self-esteem, self-confidence, and personal judgment that accompanies this type of nonphysical abuse (Follingstad et al., 1990; Martin, 1983; Walker, 1979; 1984; MacLeod, 1987). Many women in these studies portrayed the emotional abuse and humiliation as their worst battering experiences, even worse than physical assaults that resulted in serious injury, because emotional scars can last longer. The put-downs, jealousy, and obsessiveness can be especially damaging if they happen repeatedly or over long periods of time.

Controlling and emotionally abusive acts coexist with physical violence in a great many cases. Three-quarters of Canadian women who were assaulted or threatened also described their partners as controlling in one or more of these ways. A smaller proportion of relationships in which no violence was reported nonetheless contained attempts at control (18 percent). These behaviours were used with even greater frequency by men who inflicted serious violence on their wives, and as the seriousness of the assaults increased so did the type and frequency of the man's attempts to control her. Looking separately at serious, potentially life-threatening violence (beaten up, choked, threatened with a gun or knife, or violently sexually attacked) compared with less severe assaults and threats (pushing, grabbing, shoving, slapping, kicking, threats, hitting, or throwing something), it becomes clear that the husband's attempts to control his wife occur simultaneously with his use of very serious violence against her in a majority of cases. In cases of assaults by previous partners, where the most serious forms of violence occurred, extreme control was exerted in almost every case: *95 percent* of cases of serious, potentially life-threatening violence by former husbands and live-in partners were accompanied by multiple forms of jealousy, degradation, and other demonstrations of obsessiveness (Table 6.4). Extreme control was also inflicted in 79 percent of less serious instances of violence by former partners, and 59 percent of cases of serious battering in current relationships.

Rebecca and Russell Dobash (1979) conducted extensive interviews with 109 battered women in Scottish shelters in an attempt to understand how patterns of violence develop from the beginning of courtship throughout marriage. They discovered that abusive men's efforts to possess, dominate, and control their wives played a central role in their use of physical violence. The predominant theme emerging from these interviews was that violent men

Percentage of Women Who Suffered Serious and Nonserious Violence and Emotionally Abusive or Controlling Behaviour by Current and Previous Partners

Type of Emotionally Abusive Behaviour	Current Partner			Previous Partner		
	Any Violence	Serious	Less Serious	Any Violence	Serious	Less Serious
Any emotionally abusive behaviour	**49**	**59**	**39**	**89**	**95**	**79**
1. He insists on knowing who she is with and where she is at all times	27	34	22	61	70	44
2. He calls her names to put her down or make her feel bad	28	37	21	69	81	49
3. He is jealous and doesn't want her to talk to other men	19	33	12	63	72	48
4. He tries to limit her contact with family or friends	16	27	10	56	65	39
5. He prevents her from knowing about or having access to the family income, even if she asks	7	13	4	37	44	24

Figures do not add to totals because of multiple responses.

Source: Statistics Canada, *Violence Against Women Survey*, Microdata File, Ottawa (1994a).

hold very definite beliefs about the nature of the ideal relationship between husbands and wives, about the prerogatives and privileges husbands hold over their wives, and about the acceptability of physical coercion and violence to ensure compliance from their wives. Sources of conflict leading to husbands' use of violence typically involved possessiveness and sexual jealousy, followed by expectations about domestic work, and money (Dobash and Dobash, 1984).

As the following statements suggest, some respondents to the Canadian survey did not see a cause for their partners' violence other than as a symptom of anger or an uncontrollable temper (Statistics Canada, 1994a):

> No particular reason. His frame of mind. I never could gauge what would make him fly off the handle.

> You could tell when he walked in the door if you would get it or not. It could be anything.

> It builds up and he lets his anger out.

> No pattern. Anything could get him angry.

> He was frequently mad for no reason.

> He has a low frustration level.

> For nothing at all. He was always looking for an excuse.

But many, like these women, also felt that the anger stemmed from the man's feelings of insecurity and that acts of violence were used to put her down and assert his need for control (Statistics Canada, 1994a):

> It happened on a daily basis when he walked in the door. I didn't have to do anything to trigger it. He wanted to have control over everything.

> When he became frustrated with whatever and became angry, he exploded and used physical violence to make his point in an argument or to insist on whatever.

> He complained about everything. I had to serve him like a slave.

> He never wanted to be questioned about anything. He told lies and when I asked about them, he'd slap me. He was the boss. As long as he got his way, it was fine.

> It happened when he was putting me down for asking stupid questions or arguing about money or if I was going out with my girlfriends.

> When I was what he would call nagging or when he felt threatened. It all boils down to his sense of self-worth.

He got very abusive when I stood up to him.

He wanted attention but I was busy with the kids. It started because he wanted his dinner.

Jealousy, and the man's insecurities about his wife's faithfulness to him were commonly cited as precursors to the violence. Some women simply stated the cause as jealousy, while others, like the following, elaborated (Statistics Canada, 1994a):

He was just overly jealous. He would come home and ask who was there today and there was nobody but he didn't believe me. It would just give him a reason to beat me.

Arguing. Just dumb things. He was very possessive. If I went out, even with family, he'd get mad.

When I was shopping too long, or at the doctor. He accused me of having an affair with him.

He thought I was having an affair.

He was very possessive. He would lock me in the house. He would slap me when I protested. His attitude was "I am the boss. Do as I say."

When I went out alone. He never wanted me to go out alone.

If I spoke to another man, he didn't like that.

He was very possessive. Any little thing could trigger it.

In some cases, the violence was triggered by the *man's* infidelity when he reacted violently to his wife's questions about his behaviour (Statistics Canada, 1994a):

I confronted him about an affair and he became violent and threw me across the room. I lost a baby as a result of this.

I know he would sleep around, but he'd accuse me of what he was doing.

When I went out to meet him, he accused me of looking for someone else ... when he was cheating at the time.

According to the Dobashes (1979:86), these ideals about the appropriateness of male authority stem from widely held cultural beliefs about men's and women's proper spheres in marriage that present quite different rules for men and women in terms of authority, commitment, and independence. Historically, it has been expected and deemed desirable that husbands will have greater authority over major decisions that affect the household, and that they will exercise greater freedom and independence outside the confines of the family. While laws and cultural attitudes have changed over the years to remove men's legal rights of authority over women, and men have not had the legal right to physically "chastise" their wives for some time, some attitudes about the naturalness of unequal power in marriage still linger.

The abused women in the Scottish sample described a marked increase in the abusive man's independence and in his authority and control over his wife following marriage, which contrasted with an increase in his wife's isolation and her subservience to her husband's demands. His demands, and the woman's attempts to demonstrate her commitment to the man and the relationship, frequently resulted in her growing isolation from family and friends and potential sources of support. By keeping her isolated, the abuser was then able to maintain his authority over her and to reassure himself that she was his and his alone.

The Dobashes observed an increase in the abusive man's possessiveness over his wife as the relationship intensifies and he gradually attempts to control her completely. They describe how the husband's sense of ownership and control over his wife occurred almost immediately following the time the couple married or moved in together as he attempted to quickly establish his authority as head of the household. Forty-one percent of abused women in the sample were assaulted within the first six months of marriage, and 84 percent were assaulted within the first three years (1979:94). For some battered women, the abuse starts on their honeymoon and takes them completely by surprise (Bowker, 1983; Gelles and Straus, 1988). Assaults prior to marriage were less frequent, having occurred in a quarter of violent marriages. These episodes were most frequently related to the man's jealousy and were usually interpreted by the woman as isolated incidents and indications of his love for her. It was a problem that she thought would be resolved when he was sure of her commitment to him (Dobash and Dobash, 1979; Adams, 1988). Battered women generally describe their partners' behaviour toward them prior to marriage as attentive and affectionate. The men showed constant concern about the women's whereabouts and activities and expressed a desire to be together all the time (Frieze and Browne, 1989; Walker, 1984; Browne, 1987; Dobash and Dobash, 1979). By the time these men began using violence against their wives, the attentiveness and concern had become possessiveness and control, and the women had become isolated from their family and friends.

According to the Violence Against Women Survey, a relatively small proportion of assaulted women (less than 1 in 5) said the man was also violent during the time they were dating. For the majority, the violence began after they had married or moved in together, once strong emotional bonds had been established. There was a very high risk of violence against women early on in

the marital relationship, especially against women
common-law unions. The annual rate of violence in all ne
tionships (three years or less) was 8 percent and dec
relationships of longer duration. As Figure 6.6 illustrates, t
for newer common-law couples was three times the ra
marriages of the same length (12 percent compared w
percent, respectively). In fact, married couples report little variation in one-year rates of violence within the first decade of the
marriage, only dropping after 10 years. By contrast, rates of
violence reported by cohabiting couples were very high in the
first three years and dropped dramatically after that.

Both the length of time a couple has been cohabiting and
the marital status of the couple are related to their age. In the
Violence Against Women Survey, one-quarter of women in newer
unions of three years or less were under 25 years of age, and one-
half of all newer unions were common-law relationships. The
younger a person is in a common-law union, the more likely it is to
be a recent arrangement (Dumas and Péron, 1992). And, since
young people enter into common-law relationships more
frequently, they have repeated exposure to high-risk situations—
cohabiting with young men in a union of short duration.
Combining the effects of age, and type and duration of the union,
the percentage of young women living in common-law relationships for three years or less who were assaulted by a live-in
partner over a one-year period was 19 percent. In other words,
these women have a 1 in 5 chance of being the victim of violence
by their common-law partners over a one-year period.

Proponents of the "subculture of violence" and "social
support" theories point to the importance of male peers for
abusive men, peers who lend support to and reinforce the use of
violence. If the man's social networks place great value on men's
ability to dominate their wives, men who publicly display acts of
dominance will gain status and respect in the eyes of their peers
(Messerschmidt, 1993). Many researchers have shown that men
who receive social support from their male peers in their use of
violence are more likely to abuse their wives and girlfriends than
men who receive no such support (Bowker, 1983; Smith, 1991;
DeKeseredy, 1988; 1990b; DeKeseredy and Kelly, 1993b; Kanin,
1985; Alder, 1985). Social support can take the form of attachments to male peers through networks of friends who abuse their
own partners, guidance and advice from these friends that abuse
of wives and girlfriends is all right, and approval for violence from
male peers. Attitudes, beliefs, and behaviours of male dominance
are reinforced by like-minded peers who provide important
support for men who abuse their intimate partners, including a
"vocabulary of adjustment" that enables them to view themselves

FIGURE 6.6

One-Year Rates of Wife Assault by Length of Time Married or Living Together and Type of Union

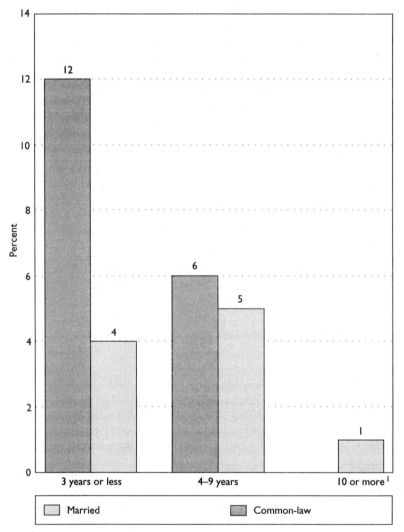

[1] There were too few common-law couples coresiding for 10 years or more to make statistically reliable estimates for that group.

Source: Statistics Canada, *Violence Against Women Survey,* Microdata File, Ottawa (1994a).

as normal and respectable people despite their violent behaviour (Kanin, 1985).

Without specifically testing for the existence of traditional attitudes and beliefs, other researchers have found a positive relationship between the frequency of abusive men's contacts with their male friends and the frequency and severity of beatings inflicted on their wives (Bowker, 1983; Dobash and Dobash, 1979). Young men, and particularly young men in common-law relationships, have more discretionary leisure time and are therefore more often involved in social activities with male peers and more frequently influenced by them. If these peers also support and encourage abuse and dominance over female partners, this would help to explain the higher rates of violence by young cohabiting men (Ellis, 1989).

Husbands who subscribe to beliefs about a man's rights to obedience, respect, loyalty, and dependency from his wife tend to be extra vigilant about situations that threaten these claims. Evolutionary psychologists Martin Daly and Margo Wilson use the term "sexual proprietariness" to describe men's feelings of entitlement over their female partners, and they argue that violence may be used in response to threats to these entitlements (Daly and Wilson, 1988; Wilson, Johnson, and Daly, 1995). Whether violence is used will depend on the woman's attractiveness to other men (determined by such factors as her age), her autonomy, and the costs of using violence. Daly and Wilson argue that male sexual proprietariness and violence are more likely to be present in common-law unions where the man feels less secure of his partner's commitment to him, where women tend to be younger on average and therefore more attractive to other men as potential mates, where the couple are more autonomous and have more leisure time, and where the social repercussions to the man for using violence are less important to him.

SEPARATION

Battered women may face increased danger when they threaten or take steps to leave their violent husbands. Threats from the woman to end the relationship may be perceived by the man as representing a serious challenge to his control over her and may result in increased violence against her or even death (Daly and Wilson, 1988; Wilson, Johnson, and Daly, 1995). It is at the time of separating from a violent husband that some women are at serious risk of being killed: between 1974 and 1992, rates of wife killings for married women who were separated from their husbands were six times as high as rates for women still cohabitating at the time of the homicide (Wilson and Daly, 1994). Police officers investigating these cases confirmed a history of domestic violence in 80 percent of cases involving separated couples compared with 35 percent of couples who were living together at the time of the killing.

According to the Violence Against Women Survey, 19 percent of Canadian women who had separated from violent partners said the assaults and intimidation continued following the separation, and in a third of the cases of continued abuse, the violence actually *increased* in severity following the separation. A smaller proportion (8 percent) said the violence actually began at a time of separation. These figures exclude those women who were assaulted when they made threats to leave their violent spouse and were intimidated into staying with him. Frieze (1983) found that leaving or threatening to leave was the factor most often associated with sexual assaults by husbands, and Finkelhor and Yllo (1985) found rape of wives to be more prevalent during periods of separation.

The pattern of increased violence following separation fits with explanations of power and control as a causal factor in wife beating. If the violent partner's motive is to be rid of her, he need only wait out her departure (Wilson, Johnson, and Daly, 1995). But the violence continues and often escalates when the woman attempts to escape his control. Most people are familiar with media accounts of women who are killed after being pursued by an estranged husband. In these cases, violence may be used to express anger toward the woman and to punish her for her decision to leave him, or as a desperate attempt to maintain control over the situation. If the couple have become isolated from outside support as a result of the battering and he feels he will have nothing without her, there may be a feeling that he has nothing to lose by killing her. (See Chapter 7 for more about this.)

PREGNANCY

Pregnancy is a time of great joy for the majority of couples. But it may also be a time of stress and anxiety as the couple contemplate and look forward to their new roles as parents and to the changing structure of their lives. For a controlling and possessive man, his partner's pregnancy may represent to him a threat to his exclusive control over her and to her exclusive attention and affection toward him. The Violence Against Women Survey found that 21 percent of battered women were assaulted during pregnancy, representing approximately 560 000 women, and in 40 percent of these cases, the abuse began at that time. Men who assaulted their wives during pregnancy were among the most violent: their victims were four times as likely as other abused women to say they experienced very serious violence (beaten up, choked, threatened with a gun or knife, or sexually assaulted). Just over 100 000 women who were assaulted during pregnancy suffered a miscarriage or other internal injuries as a result.

A study of Ontario women attending hospitals, clinics, and private doctors' offices for prenatal care determined that 7 percent had been physically abused during the pregnancy, and a majority of these women reported an increase in the severity of the abuse during the pregnancy (Stewart and Cecutti, 1993). Two of the most important risk factors for abuse during pregnancy identified in this study were the youth of the woman and the fact that she was likely to be unmarried or living in a common-law union.

Like other socioeconomic factors and common-law marital status, pregnancy is closely tied to age. The fact that women experience a higher incidence of violence during their childbearing years also puts them at higher risk of violence during the time when they are pregnant. But there are aspects other than age that increase a woman's vulnerability at this time. She is more physically vulnerable as her capacity to defend herself is diminished, and she becomes more economically dependent on the father of the child as she makes plans to stop working temporarily or for the long term. Pregnancy and early child rearing also increase the woman's isolation in the household and away from outside contacts, factors that increase her dependence on the abuser and her vulnerability (MacLeod, 1980).

EXPOSURE TO VIOLENCE IN CHILDHOOD

What role does witnessing violence against one's mother in childhood play in learning to use violence later in life? Many researchers have noted a positive relationship between men's exposure to their father's violence and the tendency to later use violence against their own wives (Straus, Gelles, and Steinmetz, 1980; Kalmuss, 1984; Hotaling and Sugarman, 1986; Fagan, Stewart, and Hansen, 1983; see also Widom, 1989). The explanation for this observed "cycle of violence" stems from social learning theory, which suggests that children will learn aggressive approaches to resolving conflict if they have been exposed to violence at home and see greater benefit to using these strategies than nonviolent means. Children will grow up learning to use violence if they have role models for such behaviour within the family, few alternative role models, and a family environment that accepts such behaviour as appropriate.

Psychologist Peter Jaffe and his colleagues at the London Family Court Clinic, in their work with battered women and their children, report a wide range of emotional, developmental, and behavioural effects of exposure to wife battering in these children (Jaffe, Wolfe, and Wilson, 1990; Jaffe, Wilson, and Wolfe, 1986; see also Davis and Carlson, 1987). These include significant emotional trauma in the form of fear, anxiety, confusion, and anger as the children cope with the unpredictability and insecurity that accompanies their father's violent outbursts. Intimidation, terror, and violence form their earliest impressions of marriage and family life that sometimes exist throughout their lives. They learn that violence is the basis of power and control in families, that women have fewer rights and less value than men, and that fathers have a right to use violence against their wives.

Jaffe and his colleagues assert that the difficulties experienced by boys, in particular, are similar in seriousness to the difficulties exhibited by boys who have been abused themselves (Jaffe, Wilson, and Wolfe, 1986; Jaffe et al., 1986b). Girls tend to become passive and withdrawn as they witness the assaults and see that their mothers are powerless to stop them. In such situations, the children are left to feel helpless, and both girls and boys feel partly responsible for the abuse. Young boys strongly identify with their father and may have conflicting and very confusing feelings about what their father has done (Jaffe, Wolfe, and Wilson, 1990). They tend to act out and become aggressive, disobedient, and destructive. The severity of the violence against the mother tends to be associated with the degree of adjustment problems in male children (Jaffe et al., 1986a).

Child welfare legislation in the Atlantic provinces and Saskatchewan have responded to these allegations about the negative effects of exposure to violence by including "children living in situations of severe domestic violence" under the criteria of children in need of state protection. Children who are exposed to domestic violence, like those who are battered, sexually abused, or neglected, are considered children at risk and may be removed from their home and taken under the care of child welfare authorities.

The problem-solving strategies that are presented to children in violent homes typically exclude positive negotiating skills. These children are provided with poor training for negotiating conflicts within the family of origin, or with their own mates and children later on. In homes where wife battering occurs, children tend to learn either passive or aggressive strategies to solve problems and are less likely to know assertive strategies or how to arrive at a mutual compromise (Jaffe, Wilson, and Wolfe, 1986). They are significantly more likely than other children to condone violence as a means of resolving conflict in relationships (Jaffe, Wilson, and Wolfe, 1988). Children exposed to wife battering are also likely to misinterpret the intentions, thoughts, and feelings of other people.

The greater probability of adjustment problems in children of battered women stems from a variety of factors related to the violence, in addition to their exposure to violent role models. These children live with higher degrees of stress and dysfunction within the family that accompanies the assaults on their mothers, an absence of close emotional attachment to their parents, and a fear that they or their mothers will be physically injured (Jaffe, Wolfe, and Wilson, 1990:55). Because much abuse happens in low-income families and those with alcoholic men, the added stresses associated with poverty and alcoholism contribute to the dysfunction in the family caused by the abuse. In addition, there may be sudden or repeated separations from friends, school, and familiar surroundings, and these can be emotionally upsetting for children and can exacerbate the family's economic situation.

Children in battering families also suffer as victims of ineffective parenting from their battered mothers when they are most in need of support and stability. A woman who is threatened, intimidated, assaulted, and physically injured by an abusive husband may be impaired in her ability to provide adequate nurturance, support, or supervision for her children (Jaffe, Wolfe, and Wilson, 1990:22). Children of battered women suffer abnormal or disrupted bonding to their mothers, and may be caught in the violence themselves. As a result of the extreme unpredictability of events in their lives, the children's normal routine is disrupted, as well as their daily activities, the structure in their lives, and the nurturance and guidance they receive from their primary care-givers. The ensuing poor interaction between the parents and child, and the child's unmet emotional and physical needs, place the child at increased risk of behavioural and emotional disorders. These children may begin acting out in response to their chaotic surroundings at a time when their mother's ability to cope with them is at its lowest. These factors may precipitate problems at school and with peers that, in turn, aggravate problems at home.

The number of children who have been exposed to wife assault in their homes can be estimated from a question on the Violence Against Women Survey that asked respondents whether their children ever witnessed any of the incidents of violence. In 39 percent of marital relationships with violence, victims said their children had been witnesses. There is no information available about the total number of marital relationships that had children on which to calculate the percentage of violent marriages with children in which the children witnessed the violence against their mothers. This figure would be higher than the 39 percent if in some marriages there were no children at risk. Nevertheless, we can calculate that if 2.65 million women have been assaulted by a spouse, and in 39 percent of these cases children witnessed the violence, at a minimum, one million children (many of whom are now adults) were exposed to the trauma of watching their mothers being abused. The average number of children per couple is now approximately two, but this has been higher in previous years, which means that *at least* two million children have been exposed to the effects of violence in their homes. No details were provided about the nature of the exposure, whether the children actually saw the assaults taking place, whether they were in another part of the house where they could hear what was going on, or whether they saw the aftereffects, such as bruises or other injuries. These figures may undercount the number of children exposed to their mothers' abuse because of the tendency for some women to minimize or deny the presence of children when the violence is taking place by claiming that they were sleeping, in another part of the house, or playing outside. From interviews with children of battered women, researchers and clinicians have found that almost all can describe detailed accounts of violence that their parents didn't know they had witnessed (Jaffe, Wolfe, and Wilson, 1990:21).

Responses to this survey also add support to links established in other research between exposure to wife assault as a child and use of violence as an adult. Respondents were asked whether, to the best of their knowledge, their own father was ever violent toward their mother, and whether their husband's father (both current and previous spouses) was ever violent toward his mother. The possible responses were "yes/think so," "no/don't think so," and "no father present." On the basis of these questions, 1 in 6 (17 percent) Canadian women reported that assaults on their mothers had occurred. This was also true for the husbands of 9 percent of currently married or cohabitating women, and 17 percent of husbands from previous marriages.

Despite the possibility that a margin of error exists in this question if some respondents were mistaken about or unaware of the existence of violence by either their own fathers or their husbands' fathers, the evidence points to a relationship between reports of childhood experiences and adult experiences of abuse. Men who witnessed their mothers being abused were up to three times as likely to be violent toward their own wives compared with men who grew up in nonviolent homes. As Figure 6.7 shows, rates of violence toward wives were 12 percent in current marriages where the man had not been exposed to violence as a child, but 36 percent in marriages where the man had witnessed abuse. Witnessing violence also had an effect on spouses in former relationships, but rates were much higher for both men exposed

and those not exposed to violence in childhood
percent, respectively, were violent toward thei
According to sex role theory, boys and gir
that is appropriate to their gender through cultu
a process of socialization. North American cultur

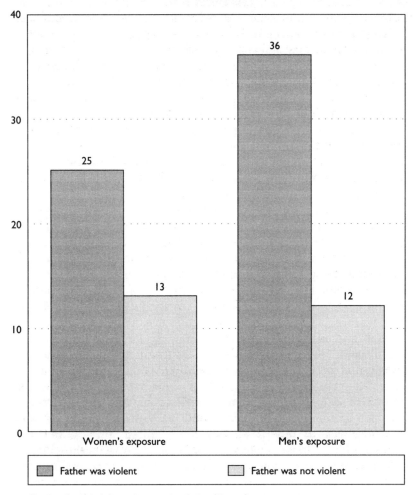

F I G U R E   6 . 7

**Rates of Wife Assault by Exposure to Violence
in Childhood**

Graph refers to violence in current relationships only.

Source: *Violence Against Women Survey,* Statistics Canada (1993).

oughness in males and submissiveness in females, and who witness wife battering are exposed to the extreme s of these stereotypes. They see the prominent man in their ves asserting his will over his wife in a most brutal fashion; many also see their mothers powerless to stop the abuse and outsiders unwilling to interfere. They may see indifference to their mothers' plight on the part of other family members, neighbours, and witnesses. Girls who witness violence inflicted on their mothers may be learning lessons about a woman's obligations to her husband, regardless of the harm he may do her. Girls may also learn a sense of helplessness if violence recurs in their adult life. Hotaling and Sugarman (1986), in a review of the literature on wife battering, found exposure to parental violence to be the only consistent risk marker in women's victimization. The Canadian Violence Against Women Survey shows that women who were exposed to wife battering while growing up had rates of violence directed at them by their own husbands that were almost twice as high as women who grew up in nonviolent environments (see Figure 6.7). The pattern was also strong in previous battering relationships, where 67 percent of women who witnessed violence while growing up suffered violence from husbands compared with 43 percent of women who were not exposed to violence in childhood.

From what this survey tells us about children of battered women, it appears that many of these children are witnessing very severe forms of violence against their mothers. When children were exposed to assaults on their mothers, in 61 percent of cases the women suffered physical injuries, and in 52 percent of cases the violence was so serious that the women feared for their lives. Many male children in turn carry these lessons into adulthood and severely abuse their own wives. Battered wives of men who were exposed to violence in childhood tend to suffer more serious and repeated assaults than wives of men without this early exposure. These women are more frequently beaten, choked, threatened with a gun or knife, or sexually assaulted, and are more likely to suffer physical injury as a result of the attacks. They also suffer more frequent episodes of violence. These lessons can also be generalized to premarital intimate relationships. In a random survey of undergraduates in the United States, Gwartney-Gibbs and her colleagues found a correlation between the severity of abuse inflicted by young men on their dating partners and the severity of wife-battering episodes these men witnessed as children (Gwartney-Gibbs, Stockard, and Bohmer 1987:279).

Although the evidence is compelling, there are exceptions to the cycle of violence theory that do not make for a simple cause-and-effect relationship between early exposure to assaults on mothers and later use of the same tactics. While it is true that the rate of wife beating is much higher for men who have witnessed violence by their own fathers, it is also true that the majority of abusive men were not exposed to violence in childhood. And, over half the men who did have this exposure have not been violent toward their own wives. Thus, while there is empirical support for the theory that violence is transmitted from one generation to another through modelling and reinforcement, other factors can intervene to break the cycle. Situations or experiences other than a nonviolent home can also intervene in the man's life to influence him to use violence to intimidate or coerce his wife in the absence of violent role models. Certainly, not all men who witness violence against their mothers will grow up to be abusers. It has been demonstrated that children from abusive homes are at risk of a host of behavioural and emotional problems, including an increased tendency to act aggressively, both in childhood and later on in marriage, but to label them as potential wife-beaters may set them up for failure in their adult relationships.

SUMMARY

This chapter identifies a wide range of factors that have been shown to be associated with acts of violence against wives. We cannot know for certain whether any of these factors are direct *causes* of violence against wives, only that they are somehow associated with the violence or they occur jointly. Together, they increase the likelihood that violence will occur.

The interconnections among these factors suggest a few salient themes. The economic dependency and social isolation that accompany the traditional role of women in marriage may increase their vulnerability to violence and decrease their ability to change an abusive situation once it begins. Vulnerability to violence may rise during pregnancy and early child rearing, when women's dependence on their husbands for financial support is greatest. If other factors, such as cohabitation, weaken ties between the couple and community supports, isolation can increase and social repercussions against the man for using violence may be less effective.

Theories of power and control tie together many of the risk markers, including common-law marital status, the youth of the man and the woman, separation, and pregnancy. Young couples may more frequently encounter episodes of marital conflict that they are unable to resolve peaceably because of immaturity or because they have not yet established other ways of settling differences within the relationship (Ellis, 1989). Traditional beliefs about the rights and prerogatives of husbands over their wives may be more easily threatened in common-law unions, where feelings of commitment may be tenuous and where one or both partners continue to pursue their independence and autonomy outside the relationship. Young cohabiting men may respond to insecurities about the sexual fidelity of their young wives with fears and accusations of adultery that then culminate in violence. In addition, threats to feelings of entitlement in intimate relationships can present themselves in other ways that find greater prominence in cohabitating unions, such as male unemployment and low income. Violence may be used in these situations as a tool to regain lost status and establish feelings of authority and control.

A learned readiness to use violence and an acceptance of violence as an appropriate and effective response to stress are also important precursors to acts of aggression committed against wives. Witnessing wife battering in childhood can have harmful effects on a child's emotional development and opportunities for learning positive negotiating skills. Children who witness battering learn that violence has a place in intimate relationships. Very often the extent of abuse witnessed by the children of battered women is severe, and these lessons are carried on into the child's adult relationships. Alcohol and stresses associated with economic disadvantage may be mediating factors that enhance feelings of insecurity and lower inhibitions toward violence.

In the next chapter, we see how violence against wives can escalate into murder—of either the wife or the husband—and how women who try to leave a violent relationship can actually endanger their lives more, leaving them with few options but to put up with the abuse.

C H A P T E R **7**

Spousal Killings: When the Violence Turns Lethal

Wife battering that increases in frequency and severity over a long period of time risks becoming lethal. Spousal killings are usually preceded by a long history of violence directed at the woman, but it is not always the woman who is killed. Sometimes the battered woman kills her brutal husband in self-defence or in defence of her children or someone else.

Homicide data collected by the police and supplied to Statistics Canada show only slight year-to-year fluctuations in the number of spousal killings over the past two decades (Figure 7.1). The number of women killed by their husbands or common-law partners has remained fairly stable, with an average of 78 women killed each year between 1974 and 1993. The number of men killed by wives and common-law partners during the same period averaged 24. Each year, wife killings outnumber husband killings by a ratio of about 3:1. In the case of husband killings, the majority seem to represent an act of desperation on the part of a severely battered woman who kills because she fears being killed herself. Men who kill their wives often do so as a final act of brutality after years of abusing their partners.

When considering homicides in general, the circumstances and characteristics of incidents involving male and female victims differ in important ways. Overall, men have much higher rates of homicide victimization than women. In 1993, for example, 67 percent of all homicide victims were male and 33 percent were female (Canadian Centre for Justice Statistics, 1993b). Males also accounted for 87 percent of all those accused of committing homicide that year. But spousal killings represent a substantial proportion of all homicides against women in a given year, and only a very small proportion of all killings involving male victims. By comparison, men are more likely to be killed by a stranger or an acquaintance. Between 1991 and 1993, over half of solved homicides against women were committed by a spouse, an ex-spouse

FIGURE 7.1

Number of Women and Men Killed by Spouses, 1974–1993

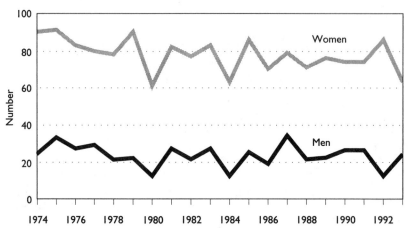

Source: Canadian Centre for Justice Statistics, Homicide Survey (1995). Unpublished data.

or another intimate partner. This includes 39 percent by spouses and ex-spouses and 13 percent by boyfriends and lovers. For men, the percentages killed by spouses and ex-spouses and lovers were much lower, at 6 percent and 2 percent, respectively (Table 7.1 and Figure 7.2). Eighty percent of men were killed by friends, acquaintances, or strangers compared with only 32 percent of women. Murders by intimate partners have remained the dominant type of murder of women for over 30 years (Silverman and Kennedy, 1993).

Over the years, women have accounted for about 12 percent of offenders in homicide incidents and about 40 percent of victims (Silverman and Kennedy, 1993). Women's involvement in lethal violence as both offenders and victims is much more likely to be tied to their intimate relationships than to people they know outside the family or to strangers. The reverse is true for men. Men are more than twice as likely to be killed by a stranger than by an intimate partner; women, on the other hand, are over five times as likely to be killed by a spouse or other intimate partner than by a stranger.

When women do the killing, they are also three times as likely to kill spouses than strangers, while men are slightly more likely to kill strangers than spouses. When homicides are commit-

FIGURE 7.2

Relationship to Offender by Gender of Victim in Solved Homicides, 1991–1993

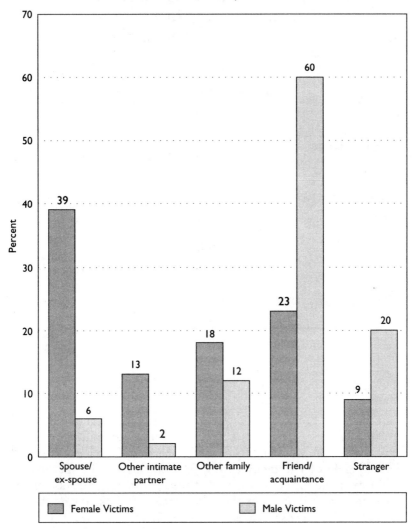

Source: Canadian Centre for Justice Statistics, Homicide Survey (1995).

ted among people related to each other through kinship or marriage, women were identified as the perpetrators in 23 percent and men in 77 percent of cases. In comparison with other types of homicides, women make up only 7 percent of all people accused of homicides among acquaintances and strangers, while

T A B L E   7 . 1

Percentage Distribution of Solved Homicides, by Gender of Victim and Relationship of Offender to Victim, Canada, 1991–1993

Relationship of Offender to Victim	Gender of Victim					
	Female		Male		Total	
	No.	%	No.	%	No.	%
Spouse	172	28	71	5	243	12
Ex-spouse	68	11	10	1	78	4
Other intimate partner	80	13	28	2	108	6
Other family	110	18	157	12	267	14
Friend/acquaintance	141	23	793	60	934	48
Stranger	54	9	259	20	313	16
Total	**625**	**100**	**1318**	**100**	**1943**	**100**

Percentages do not add to 100 due to rounding.

Source: Canadian Centre for Justice Statistics, Homicide Survey, Unpublished data (1993b).

men make up the vast majority (93 percent). When men kill their spouses, they are also more likely to commit suicide afterward, something that women rarely do (31 percent for men compared with 4 percent for women). Familicides, the killing of a spouse and children in one incident, are almost uniquely a male phenomenon, with males as offenders in about 90 percent of these incidents.

According to research conducted by Wilson and Daly (1992b), other Western industrialized nations such as Australia, England and Wales, Scotland, and Denmark exhibit sex ratios of spousal killings that closely approximate Canada's. The United States, by contrast, is the one country they studied in which the ratio of male to female victims in spousal homicides is almost even. That is, women kill husbands in the United States approximately as often as men kill wives, and in some American cities, women actually outnumber men in spousal killings. One interpretation of this lack of gender disparity in spousal homicides might be that the greater availability of firearms in the United States serves to equalize the advantages men have over women in terms of size and strength in marital conflicts. Exploring this possibility, Wilson and Daly found no difference in the sex ratio of shooting deaths compared with other types of killings. In fact, women are even more lethal relative to men in cases not involving guns than in shooting deaths. The authors also found that the involvement of women in spousal homicides is not a reflection of a more general trend toward greater involvement of women in homicides in general. What they did find is that the higher incidence of female perpetrators was specific to African-American couples and not to other ethnic groups, and that this may be caused by a higher incidence of other risk factors for spousal violence in African-American couples (such as common-law relationships and stepchildren from previous unions).

This chapter explores the trends and patterns in homicides involving spousal partners and some of the legal remedies offered by the Canadian Parliament and the Supreme Court of Canada. We begin with an examination of sociodemographic and other precursors that affect the risk of either a woman or a man being killed by a spouse.

FACTORS ASSOCIATED WITH INCREASED RISK OF SPOUSAL HOMICIDE

To what extent are incidents of wife killings similar to incidents of serious battering that do not result in death? What are the factors that elevate the risk of homicide for women in battering relationships? Are there common risk factors in cases of lethal and nonlethal violence?

Police statistics and case studies suggest that spousal killings and nonlethal assaults on wives share certain similarities in circumstances, motives, and dynamics. Although some wife killings are the result of sudden, unforeseeable attacks by depressed or mentally unstable husbands and are unrelated to a history of violence in the family, most do not seem to fit this description. Spousal homicides are often preceded by warning signs of trouble in the family. In 54 percent of cases that occurred in Canada between 1991 and 1993, police stated that they knew about previous incidents of violence in the family (Canadian Centre for Justice Statistics, 1993b). Police were actually more likely to report a history of violence in cases in which husbands were killed (68 percent) than in cases in which wives were killed (52 percent).

These figures likely underestimate the actual incidence of battering in the histories of spousal homicide victims considering that a
very high percentage of violent incidents don't come to the attention of the police. (See Chapter 8 for more on this.)

Information available from the police adds other clues about
the dynamics of spousal killings and the role of provocation and
self-defence. Police made the attribution that the victim was "the
first to use or threaten to use physical force or violence in the incident" in 45 percent of husband killings in which police had the
knowledge to answer this question compared with only 7 percent
of wife killings (Canadian Centre for Justice Statistics, 1993b).
This fits with descriptive case studies that report that when wives
killed husbands, most were reacting to a history of abuse inflicted
by their husbands in which the battering that preceded the lethal
incident was the "last straw" (Browne, 1987). Half of the wife killings were also preceded by a history of violence in the family, but
rarely was the husband acting to protect himself from violence
initiated by his wife. More often, wife killings are a culmination of
a long period of battering inflicted by a violent husband.

It was noted in Chapter 6 that marital relationships characterized by a young couple living in a common-law union, with low
income and periods of unemployment, heavy use of alcohol on the
part of the man, and a climate of control and possessiveness
toward the woman, are correlated with the man's use of violence
against the woman. Many of these factors have also been cited as
important contributors to spousal killings. Other precursors to
lethal violence cited in the literature include weapons in the
home, use of weapons in prior violent incidents, threats to kill,
serious injury to the victim in prior incidents, sexual abuse in the
battering relationship, violence committed during pregnancy,
violence against the children, threats or fantasies of homicide or
suicide, isolation of both the abuser and the battered woman from
support systems, rage, depression, and the woman's attempt to
leave an abusive relationship (Sonkin, Martin, and Walker, 1985;
Hart, 1988; Campbell, 1992a; 1992b; Kellerman and Mercy, 1992;
Kellerman et al., 1993).

In a study of police and coroners' records of 551 women killed
by intimate partners between 1974 and 1990 in Ontario, Crawford and Gartner (1992) highlighted the offender's rage over the
actual or impending separation as the motive for the homicide in
45 percent of cases where a motive could be established. In
another 15 percent of cases, the motive appeared to be the offender's suspicions about his partner's unfaithfulness. In fact, threats
on the woman's part to end the relationship and the husband's
suspicions of infidelity are the factors that seem to motivate many

violent men to commit the ultimate violent act against their wives.

Jacquelyn Campbell (1992a; 1995) has developed a statistical risk-assessment tool called the Danger Assessment Instrument to aid clinicians in assessing battered women's risk of potentially lethal violence. Recognizing that prediction of dangerousness is a very inexact science, Campbell asserts that clinicians neverthe-less have an ethical responsibility to warn battered women of the potential for escalating violence and homicide if certain warning signs are present. She maintains that because battering is the most frequent precursor to spousal homicide, prediction should be designed around characteristics related to abuse. The Danger Assessment Instrument is based on retrospective research studies of spousal homicides and correlates of homicide that Campbell has developed and tested on samples of battered women. She recommends using it as a basis for discussion with battered women by shelter workers, health-care professionals, social work-ers, and counsellors. The instrument includes items about increases in the frequency and severity of abuse, guns in the house, forced sex, use of drugs and alcohol, threats to kill her, attempts to control her actions, extreme jealousy, violence during pregnancy, threats or attempts at suicide by either the man or the woman, violence against the children, and violence outside the home.

Wilson, Johnson, and Daly (1995) studied the commonalities and differences among cases of lethal and nonlethal violence against wives described in the Canadian Homicide Survey (Cana-dian Centre for Justice Statistics, 1993a) and the national survey on violence against women. A number of factors common to battering relationships were found in wife killings. These include common-law marital status, the youth of the man (in legal but not common-law unions), estrangement, and manifestations of extreme controlling and proprietary behaviour by the man toward his wife. Over the past two decades in Canada, the homicide rate was about eight times greater for women in common-law unions than for women in registered marriages, a factor that was also present in nonlethal cases of wife battering. As discussed in the previous chapter, common-law marital status is correlated with a number of factors that increase the probability of marital conflict and violence, such as poverty, unemployment, the presence of stepchildren, and the youth of the man and the woman. Young men committed higher rates of wife killings than did older men (in legal unions) in a pattern similar to but less pronounced than in nonlethal assaults. As well, risk of deadly violence was substan-tially higher for separated couples than for married couples who were living together: between 1974 and 1992, rates of wife killings were six times higher for separated wives than for those still living with the accused at the time of the killing (Wilson and Daly, 1994). Many men increase the level of battering against their wives when the women take steps to leave.

The claim that a large proportion of wife killings are motivated in some sense by the husbands' concerns about losing their proprietary rights over their wives may seem puzzling. As Wilson and her colleagues point out, when a woman is pursued and killed by a man she has left, the motive cannot be merely to be rid of her, nor can it simply be to hang on to her. If that were the case, killing her would be counterproductive. Wife killings by estranged husbands have been interpreted as the desperate attempts by husbands to reassert control over their wives, whom they have been able to control effectively up to that point through threats and violence (Wilson, Johnson, and Daly, 1995). The thought of doing without their wives is intolerable to them. As their wives are leaving with the children, these men might see everything important to them being taken away. At the point of desertion, some feel very strongly that "If I can't have you, no one can" (Campbell, 1992a; Wilson and Daly, 1992a).

In a comprehensive case study, Angela Browne (1986; 1987) interviewed 42 women who were facing charges for murder or attempted murder in Denver, Colorado, in the death or serious injury of their intimate partners, and compared them to a group of women who had been involved in abusive relationships that had stopped short of homicide. Browne examined the killings in the context of the abusive relationships, and the impact the abuse had on the women's assessment of the danger and of alternatives available to them. From these interviews, police and hospital records, and the testimony of witnesses, acquaintances, employers, and service providers, Browne identified several factors that increased the probability that a woman would kill her battering husband:

- Each of the women in the sample of female homicide offenders had a history of being physically abused by the man she killed.

- Men in the homicide group were more likely to have drug or alcohol problems.

- Women who had committed homicide sustained more frequent violent acts and more serious injuries.

- Sexual violence was more frequent and more brutal for women in the homicide group.

- Male homicide victims were more likely to have threatened to kill themselves and other people.

- The women themselves were also more likely to have made threats to kill the abuser or themselves.

Browne found that there were many "cries for help" prior to the lethal incident, and that almost all of the women in her study had attempted to flee the situation and had sought outside intervention against the violence.

WHY DO BATTERED WOMEN STAY?

It may seem incomprehensible to many readers that a woman would stay with a violent man and tolerate increasingly serious threats and abuse until her life and safety are in jeopardy. Her apparent inaction in the face of increasing danger to herself and her children is often misinterpreted as an indication that the violence cannot be as bad as she maintains, or that she has a masochistic desire to be beaten. Why women don't simply leave violent partners is perhaps the most perplexing question in this field of study.

There are many factors that contribute to a woman's dependency on her spouse that may not be apparent to outsiders. Dependency can take the form of economic reliance on the man if the woman has little formal training or has been out of the workforce for several years. She may worry about bringing herself and her children to a life of poverty if she is faced with supporting her children on her own. This is a realistic concern, as 60 percent of all single mothers in Canada live in poverty (Statistics Canada, 1995). The woman's only option may be to flee to a shelter, uproot her children, and apply for welfare. After years of abusive and degrading treatment from her spouse, the woman may also suffer low self-esteem and emotional dependency on him. Her self-confidence and sense of self-worth may be undermined to the point where she thinks herself incapable of managing outside the marriage on her own. If she has been isolated from possible sources of outside support, it may be difficult for her to obtain help; in addition, her opinions about herself will be more strongly influenced by his negative comments and his assaults against her than by anything else (Browne, 1987).

For many battered women, the decision to stay, to leave, or to return to an abusive husband is not a simple one. Some women leave at the first sign of trouble and never return. Others successfully manage to stop the violence and keep the marriage together. Others may take steps to leave but find that there are too few resources or expertise among the various agencies they turn to for help to provide them with realistic alternatives.

In interviews with women who had effectively ended the abuse without leaving their partners, Bowker (1983) found that certain strategies worked better than others. Threatening to leave or get a divorce and obtaining the support of friends, family, and social service agencies were more effective than either a passive or an aggressive defence at the time the assaults were taking place. But many women want to stay because of a deep sense of commitment to the relationship. The battering typically starts after strong emotional bonds have been developed between the couple, and may start or continue after children have arrived. Many women stay despite the violence for the companionship of marriage, the social status that marriage brings, to avoid the stigma of divorce, or to avoid poverty. For many women, the over-all benefits of the marriage outweigh the occasional episodes of violence (Gelles and Straus, 1988).

Among women who reported wife assault to the Violence Against Women Survey, 43 percent had left their partners either for a short while or permanently because of abuse. In their study of women in Scottish shelters, Rebecca and Russell Dobash (1979) found that women rarely leave a violent relationship just once and never return. The vast majority of women in their shelter sample (88 percent) left at least once, and the majority of these left more than once. Half of those who left spent less than one week away from home before returning. For some, this decision is influenced by the threat of further violence. Some women, when they make attempts to leave their partners, are tracked down and beaten in retaliation (Browne, 1987). Over 130 000 women in Canada have at some point feared for their lives because of a man who is currently abusing them, and 30 percent of these women have never left the men, even for a short while. It may seem inexplicable to many readers that a battered woman would not flee to save her own life, unless we consider the possibility that she stays *because* her life has been threatened. Threats of serious injury or even death by a violent partner are taken seriously by battered women, who have come to know the batterer's capacity for violence. Some of the women in Browne's sample returned to extremely violent men because they could not cope with the stress and anxiety of living in hiding and in constant fear of being hunted down. They felt that, if they were living with the man, at least they knew where he was and could monitor his behaviour.

The Dobashes (1979:144) summarized their impressions of the complexities inherent in the decision to terminate a battering relationship:

The pattern of staying, leaving, and returning reflect the complex pushes and pulls of the numerous personal, social and material factors that motivate the battered woman. The pattern of leaving and returning and the reasons for doing so change over time as the woman's perceptions of her position change and as the couple's relationship deteriorates.

According to the Violence Against Women Survey, women's decisions to leave a violent partner are motivated by factors related to the severity of the violence, reporting to the police, and having children who witnessed the violence (Rodgers, 1994). As Table 7.2 indicates, women were more likely to leave as the situation escalated, especially to the point where they fear for their lives or were injured, or when they got to the point where they called the police for protection. In some cases, the police may be a catalyst for change if they assist the woman to leave, offer to take her to a safe place, or advise her of shelters or other services that are available to her. Many women make the decision to leave when the violence begins to affect their children. But even very serious violence does not ensure that a battered woman will leave the situation. Thirty-seven percent of women who were injured in an assault by their husbands did not leave; neither did 40 percent of those threatened with a gun or knife, nor 43 percent of those who feared for their lives.

Children are also a primary consideration in the decision to return to an abusive spouse. Seventy percent of women who left their partners eventually returned home at least once (Statistics Canada, 1994a). The most common reasons given for their decision to return were "for the sake of the children" (31 percent), wanting to give the relationship another try (24 percent), the husband "promised to change" (17 percent), and a lack of money or place to go (9 percent).

The social role of wife and mother may create difficulties for women when they are faced with increasing violence from a spouse. For many women, their role entails a sense of responsibility for the well-being of the family and the success of the marriage (Browne, 1987; Stanko, 1985). The identity of many women tends to be defined in relation to their husbands, homes, and families, so that the failure of the relationship becomes the women's personal failure, even when there is severe violence inflicted against them. The abuser may blame the woman for his attacks on her, and she may accept this interpretation, particularly if she is isolated from other people and does not receive outside help. Rather than retaliating or fleeing, many women resort to negotiation and conciliation in response to assaults by a spouse, in part because this is a safer approach than any other, and in part because it is

T A B L E 7 . 2

Factors Influencing Women's Decisions to Leave Violent Partners

Factors	Percent Who Left Violent Partners
Total	**43**
Most serious type of violence ever experienced	
1. Threatened to hit her	—
2. Threw something at her	—
3. Pushed, grabbed, or shoved	20
4. Slapped	20
5. Kicked, bit, or hit her with his fist	42
6. Hit her with something	—
7. Beat her up	70
8. Choked her	60
9. Used a gun or knife on her	60
10. Sexual assault	62
Feared for her life	57
Injured	63
Reported to the police	74
Children witnessed the violence	60
— not statistically reliable	

Source: Statistics Canada, *Violence Against Women Survey,* Microdata File, Ottawa (1994a).

consistent with their social training to maintain family relationships and to try to smooth over difficult patches in the marriage.

The previous chapter included a discussion of the cyclical patterns of spousal violence from one generation to the next, where women who had been exposed to wife assault in childhood suffered higher rates of abuse by their own spouses in adulthood.

This has led some researchers to predict that these childhood lessons will lead to increased feelings of helplessness in the face of danger and a greater willingness to tolerate abuse. Contrary to these assertions, survey data show that women who witnessed violence were slightly more likely than others to leave an abusive husband, at least for a short time (49 percent of those exposed to violence in childhood compared with 40 percent of others). They were also no more likely than other women to return to an abusive husband following a separation.

The testimonies of women who had killed their husbands in Browne's (1987) sample illustrate how dangerous separation can be for severely battered women. These women were often brutally beaten for even mentioning a separation; thus, leaving the abuser is often no guarantee of freedom from further violence. These women felt themselves to be hopelessly trapped in a desperate situation. Both staying and attempting to leave meant the possibility of serious injury. Women in these situations reacted to the level of threat and violence directed at them by choosing the responses that seemed most likely to minimize the immediate danger and increase their chances of survival. They tended to withdraw from outside contacts after an attack rather than taking action to escape, and became overwhelmed by feelings of helplessness and fear. As the violence directed against them increased in frequency and severity, their perceptions of their options narrowed and they focused only on avoiding and surviving another attack. Although they were frequently living in terror of the man, they were constrained by his threats of harm or death if they attempted to leave.

Browne (1987) explains the psychological effect that increasing violence can have on a victim's perceptions of her alternatives. She maintains that women in increasingly dangerous situations are constantly reassessing the limits of their tolerance, and that eventually a certain level of abuse becomes normal in the relationship as the women adjust to it. In the end, they are enduring levels of violence that they never could have imagined in the beginning. Often, just prior to the homicide, there was a sudden change in the pattern or the severity of the violence that indicated to them they might not survive the next time. When they realized they could neither escape the situation nor survive within it, they responded with lethal violence.

THE BATTERED WOMAN DEFENCE

Until recently, the courts showed little leniency toward battered women who killed their abusive partners. In fact, it was very difficult for these women to obtain an acquittal unless the killing occurred during the course of a direct attack against her.

The relevant sections of the Criminal Code relating to the defence of self-defence are Sections 34 through 37. The law with respect to self-defence has three major stipulations:

(1) persons are entitled to use force to protect themselves against attack if the degree of force used is no more than is necessary to defend themselves,

(2) the danger must be imminent, and,

(3) there must be a reasonable apprehension of death or grievous bodily harm.

A person must believe, on reasonable grounds, that there is no other way she can save herself from death or grievous bodily harm. The belief that the degree of force used was necessary to prevent this harm must be shown to be reasonable from an objective point of view. Where the actions of the accused person fail to measure up to these criteria, a conviction is likely to result.

The criteria that have caused the greatest difficulty for battered women accused of killing their abusive spouses are the legal requirements of "reasonableness" and "imminent danger." Lethal violence used in self-defence was not considered justified if used in retaliation for a past assault or in anticipation of an upcoming assault that is not imminent or immediate (Comack, 1993). The concept of reasonableness is based in common law, on the notion of what the "reasonable man" might do under similar circumstances. If the judge or jury found that the beliefs and actions of the accused were ones that a "reasonable man" would have followed, a plea of self-defence could succeed. This test was designed to provide a universally applicable standard by which the actions of all accused persons could be assessed as justifiable under the circumstances.

Women who killed their spouses at a time when they were not having to defend themselves from an attack had great difficulty convincing the court that they did not have the opportunity to escape the battering situation at some point. A battered woman was rarely able to satisfy the legal requirement of imminence, since her experiences and perceptions of danger were rarely those experienced by reasonable men. As judges and juries were unlikely ever to have been in the same position of ongoing abuse as a battered woman, their perceptions of imminent danger were likely to vary significantly from hers.

Judges had the authority to determine that only the immediate circumstances surrounding the incident were relevant to the case, at which point the woman's history of abuse became irrelevant in considering the reasonableness of her actions. Once the single incident culminating in a homicide was removed from the context of prolonged abuse, it became even more difficult for a judge or jury to understand that a battered woman's actions may have been a reasonable response to what she perceived to be imminent danger. A look, a gesture, or a verbal threat of death to a woman experienced in anticipating her husband's violent outbursts could be perceived by her as constituting an imminent threat to her life, but the courts had difficulty understanding how this could be perceived to be "imminent" without an overt attack against her.

A 1983 ruling in the case of *R. v. Whynot* by the Nova Scotia Court of Appeal reinforced the legal meaning of these principles in cases of women who kill battering husbands. The case involved a woman who shot and killed her husband while he lay unconscious in his truck after drinking heavily. The man had physically abused the accused woman on a number of occasions, and on that night he had threatened to kill her son. In convicting the woman, the court ruled that self-defence did not apply: "In my opinion, no person has the right in anticipation of an assault that may or may not happen, to apply force to prevent the imaginary assault." This ruling cut off the availability of self-defence for women in ongoing battering relationships.

The doctrine of self-defence was fundamentally altered by the Supreme Court decision of *R. v. Lavallee* in 1990. This case focused primarily on issues relating to the admissibility of expert testimony as court evidence, but it was a pivotal case because it recognized the significance of battering within the context of spousal homicides (Noonan, 1993). The case concerned Angelique Lyn Lavallee, a Manitoba woman who had shot her common-law husband in the back of the head while he was walking away from her. According to the accused woman's statement to police, their relationship was punctuated with violent attacks against her. During a party at their home on the night of the killing, her partner Kevin Rust had threatened to kill her when all the guests had left. That night, he had hit her several times, which made her fearful of another beating. While in the bedroom, he handed her a loaded gun, which she fired through a window screen. He then loaded a second shot, which she pointed at herself. At this point, he said to her, "Wait till everybody leaves, you'll get it then," followed by "Either you kill me or I'll get you." As he walked out of the bedroom, she shot him in the back of the head.

The facts of the case show that at the moment the shot was fired, an attack on Ms. Lavallee was not underway, and under case law current at the time, the self-defence plea would not have been successful. The expert testimony of a psychiatrist with extensive experience in the treatment of battered women was allowed in order to support a defence of self-defence. The defence attempted to prove extenuating circumstances that the accused was suffering from "the battered woman syndrome," which had been accepted in various American states for over a decade. The psychiatrist explained Ms. Lavallee's ongoing terror of Mr. Rust, her inability to escape the relationship despite the violence, and the continuing pattern of abuse that put her life in danger. He testified that, in his opinion, the woman's actions constituted the final desperate act of a woman who sincerely believed that she would be killed that night.

The jury in the lower Manitoba court acquitted Ms. Lavallee, and the Crown appealed on several grounds: since Ms. Lavallee herself did not testify and several of the points made by the doctor were not in her sworn statement, the testimony of the psychiatrist was considered hearsay evidence and inadmissible; the jury was not properly instructed as to the weight to be attached to the expert testimony; and there was no precedent for the introduction of expert testimony on the consequences and effects of wife battering. This appeal succeeded, and Ms. Lavallee appealed to the Supreme Court of Canada, which decided unanimously to acquit her of the charge of murder.

With respect to the admission of expert testimony, the Supreme Court ruled that

> Expert testimony is admissible to assist the fact-finder in drawing inferences in areas where the expert has relevant knowledge of experience beyond that of the lay person. It is difficult for the lay person to comprehend the battered wife syndrome. It is commonly thought that battered women are not really beaten as badly as they claim, otherwise they would have left the relationship. Alternatively, some believe that women enjoy being beaten, that they have a masochistic strain in them. Each of these stereotypes may adversely affect consideration of a battered woman's claim to have acted in self-defence in killing her partner. Expert evidence can assist the jury in dispelling these myths.
>
> Expert testimony relating to the ability of an accused to perceive danger from her partner may go to the issue of whether she "reasonably apprehended" death or grievous bodily harm on a particular occasion. Expert testimony pertaining to why an accused remained in the battering relationship may be relevant in assessing the nature and extent of the alleged abuse. By providing an explanation as to why an accused did not flee when she perceived her life to be in danger, expert testimony may also assist the jury in assessing the reasonableness of her belief that killing her batterer was the only way to save her own life. (*R. v. Lavallee*, 1990:889)

The court ruled that, in this case, expert testimony was properly admitted in order to assist the jury in determining whether the defendant had a reasonable apprehension of death or grievous bodily harm and believed on reasonable grounds that she had no alternative but to shoot in order to protect herself. On the point of inadmissibility of hearsay evidence, the court argued that each specific fact underlying the expert's opinion need not be proven in evidence, as long as there is some admissible evidence to establish the foundations for the opinion. There was independent evidence from medical records that Ms. Lavallee was battered repeatedly and brutally by Mr. Rust over the course of their relationship, and that she made several trips to hospital for injuries including severe bruises, a fractured nose, multiple contusions, and a black eye, although she had made up excuses to explain her injuries on these occasions. One of the physicians stated that he disbelieved her explanation on one such occasion that she had sustained her injuries by falling from a horse. A friend of the couple also testified that he had seen Mr. Rust beat up Ms. Lavallee on several occasions.

In writing for the court, Madame Justice Bertha Wilson stated that

> Expert evidence on the psychological effect of battering on wives and common law partners must, it seems to me, be both relevant and necessary in the context of the present case. How can the mental state of the appellant be appreciated without it? The average member of the public (or of the jury) can be forgiven for asking: Why would a woman put up with this kind of treatment? Why should she continue to live with such a man? How could she love a partner who beat her to the point of requiring hospitalization? We would expect the woman to pack her bags and go. Where is her self-respect? Why does she not cut loose and make a new life for herself? Such is the reaction of the average person confronted with the so-called "battered wife syndrome." We need help to understand it and help is available from trained professionals. (R. v. Lavallee, 1990:871)

Madame Justice Wilson challenged the requirement of imminent attack when she argued that requiring "a battered woman to wait until the physical attack is underway before her apprehensions can be validated by law would ... be tantamount to sentencing her to 'murder by installment'" (R. v. Lavallee, 1990:883). The rationale for the imminence rule was designed to ensure that there was no significant time lag between the original assault and the response, where the second assault was motivated by revenge rather than self-defence. This makes sense in the case of a barroom brawl between two men of comparable size and strength. However, Madame Justice Wilson wrote that expert testimony of the effects on women of ongoing violence is necessary to assess the woman's state of mind at the time of the killing and her ability to repel an assault made against her by her husband. The court reasoned that without expert testimony about the context of battering relationships, it might be difficult for a jury to understand why the woman would continue to live with an abusive partner despite the danger to her own life. That is where expert testimony can provide useful insights. This ruling allowed expert testimony to assist judges and juries in determining the reasonableness of the victim's fear and her mental state at the time she pulled the trigger.

The basis for the Supreme Court decision allowing evidence of the battered woman syndrome to demonstrate the reasonableness of the defendant's actions stems from Lenore Walker's theory of the cycle of violence. According to Walker (1979; 1989), the cycle of violence in battering relationships has three distinct phases that can vary in time and intensity. The first is the tension-building phase, during which time minor assaults, psychological abuse, and verbal put-downs occur. The woman tries to calm the man either by becoming nurturing and compliant and responding to his every demand, or by staying out of his way. Women who have been battered over a period of time know that these minor incidents usually intensify, and they do what they think will prevent the man's anger from escalating. This is followed by an acute battering incident. Nothing the woman does during this stage can avert his rage and an attack on her, and she may be severely injured in the attack.

The final stage is a phase of calm, loving contrition in which the batterer apologizes for his actions and begs her forgiveness. His kindness toward her during this phase acts to restore her positive feelings toward him. The woman desperately wants to believe that the abuse will never happen again, and in the early stages of the battering relationship she does believe. It is very hard for her to leave the relationship at this point because this is when the positive aspects of the marriage come through. Later on, as the cycle continues, she ceases to believe that the violence will stop. By then he is no longer as contrite, and the violence and his threats of death and injury have increased. In very severe cases of battering, fear of being killed replaces the belief that he will stop beating her as the motivation for staying with him.

Walker (1989) maintains that women acquire a state of "learned helplessness" in battering situations. Learned helplessness is a theory of social learning that if organisms are subjected to negative reinforcement or punishment regardless of attempts to avert it, they may come to accept that their behaviour has no effect on controlling what happens to them even after solutions are presented to them. Battered women who are subjected to assaults and other abuse, no matter how careful they are to avoid antagonizing the abuser, have been found to suffer from feelings of helplessness and loss of control over their situation. As nothing they do lessens the risk of a violent response, they cease trying to assert control over the situation and become compliant, passive, and submissive. Even when an opportunity for escape presents itself, the victim may remain passive, unconvinced that her actions can have any effect. Many battered women go to great lengths to try to control any external factors that might upset the man during the first and third phases. But as a woman's control over the battering diminishes, she learns that she is powerless to stop the cycle from continuing, acquires the tendencies of learned helplessness, and adapts coping rather than escape responses. Walker asserts that living constantly with fear can make the woman unaware of the seriousness of her situation.

Some experts on wife battering object to Walker's typification of battered women as psychologically deficient. Dobash and Dobash (1992) and Comack (1993), for example, maintain that because only some women will conform to this helpless stereotype, only some women will be helped by the testimony of experts and the battered woman defence.

Nevertheless, the Lavallee case sets an important precedent in Canadian criminal law. It allows the introduction of expert testimony containing hearsay evidence as long as it has evidentiary support, and it acknowledges the battered woman syndrome. But this ruling does not signify that all battered women who kill abusive partners will be guaranteed an acquittal. If a judge or jury finds that, under the circumstances of the battering relationship, the woman had a reasonable fear of grievous bodily harm or death and used the amount of force necessary to defend herself, she is entitled to an acquittal (Noonan, 1993). However, if the defence fails to meet these standards, a conviction of first- or second-degree murder could result, followed by a minimum prison term of 10 and 25 years, respectively, before eligibility for parole.

At the time of writing, Justice Minister Allan Rock had agreed to appoint an independent panel to review the cases of about 15 women serving prison sentences for killing their abusive husbands (Bindman, 1995). The Canadian Association of Elizabeth Fry Societies had lobbied the federal government for more than two years to review the cases of women who were convicted and imprisoned before the 1990 Lavallee case. These women were convicted of manslaughter or murder without consideration of their history of abuse by the men they killed. The panel will make recommendations to the federal government, which will then decide whether to release the women, shorten their sentences, or order new trials.

ANTI-STALKING LEGISLATION

In the early 1990s, there were several highly publicized cases of women being stalked and harassed by men they were once involved with and seriously injured or killed. The killing of Patricia Allen, an Ottawa woman, is one well-known example. Ms. Allen was hunted down by her estranged husband and shot through the chest with a crossbow while she left a dentist's office early one morning in 1992. Terri-Lynn Babb, a Manitoba woman, was also stalked and harassed for more than a year before she was killed by a man who was a patient at a hospital where she worked. These deaths and other incidents like them prompted the federal government to draft anti-stalking laws for inclusion in the Criminal Code.

New anti-stalking, or criminal harassment, legislation was passed by the Canadian Parliament in August 1993. It was intended to protect people (usually women) who live in fear of someone (often a male ex-spouse or other intimate partner) who is following, harassing, and intimidating them. Women in these situations are often in a position of trying to escape an intimate partner or otherwise ending a relationship, and often violence is attempted or threatened by the ex-partner. However, the law is not specific about the object of the harassment or stalking. The stalked person could be a celebrity, an employer, a rival, a stranger, or anyone else, so long as the pursuit of that person causes him or her to fear for his or her safety (Cooper, 1994). Police statistics show that, in 1994, three-quarters of victims in incidents of criminal harassment were female, and in these cases spouses and ex-spouses accounted for 35 percent of offenders, casual acquaintances for 28 percent, and close friends (including intimate partners) for 18 percent (Hendrick, 1995). Ten percent of cases involved strangers to the victim.

According to then Minister of Justice Pierre Blais, speaking in the House of Commons, the new law is meant to cover situations such as "repeatedly following someone; spending extended periods of time watching someone's home or place of work; making repeated telephone calls to someone or her friends, making contact with someone's neighbours or co-workers; and contacting and possibly threatening someone's new companion, spouse or children" (House of Commons, *Debates*, May 6, 1993:19015). Much of the behaviour that constitutes stalking is obsessive, persistent, and repetitive (McCormack, 1993). The essence of the law is that actions like these, some of which may seem innocuous, under the circumstances can cause the victim to fear for her safety, even in the absence of direct threats. The implied threat of injury in these actions was considered by the lawmakers to hold the potential for substantial psychological harm. The law is not intended to punish criminal conduct that hasn't yet occurred, but to punish harm that has already been perpetrated by virtue of the psychological harm of the threat of violence and injury, and fear of what the person might be capable of doing (Lytwyn, 1994; Cooper, 1994).

The law on criminal harassment, under Section 264 of the Criminal Code, states

(1) No person shall, without lawful authority and knowing that another person is harassed or recklessly as to whether the other person is harassed, engage in conduct referred to in subsection (2) that causes that other person reasonably, in all the circumstances, to fear for their safety or the safety of anyone known to them.

(2) The conduct mentioned in subsection (1) consists of

(a) repeatedly following from place to place the other person or anyone known to them;

(b) repeatedly communicating with, either directly or indirectly, the other person or anyone known to them;

(c) besetting or watching the dwelling-house, or place where the other person, or anyone known to them, resides, works, carries on business or happens to be; or

(d) engaging in threatening conduct directed at the other person or any member of their family.

While subsections 2 (a), (b), and (c) relate to repeated acts, 2(d) provides for one-time acts that cause the victim to fear for his or her safety.

Criminal harassment is a hybrid offence punishable by a maximum term of imprisonment of five years and/or a fine of $2000.

Not only must the Crown show that the victim was harassed, it also must establish that the conduct caused the victim to "reasonably" fear for her safety or the safety of anyone known to her. The reasonableness of the fear may be assessed in light of all the circumstances of the event and in the context of the relationship between the victim and the accused, which may include a history of abuse (Lytwyn, 1994). Relevant circumstances might include the accused's conduct, the previous relationship between the two, any previous restraining orders and bail conditions, the number and frequency of contacts, and conduct aimed at the defendant's children, employer, or new partner (McCormack, 1993).

To improve the strength of the anti-stalking law, Section 515 relating to bail conditions was amended simultaneously. A person charged with criminal harassment can now be prohibited from possessing a firearm or ammunition as a condition of bail. The law also states that the judge must consider as a condition of bail that the accused not communicate with any witness or other person or be prohibited from going to any specified place (which could include the family home or the victim's place of work).

The anti-stalking provisions of the Criminal Code represent a response by the federal government to the high risk of battered women to violence and intimidation by estranged partners who refuse to be rejected. The provisions acknowledge the risk posed by abusive partners who threaten violence, particularly those who may follow through on plans to intimidate or to cause injury. The law does not require that a physical assault took place, and so provides a lower threshold for police intervention.

SUMMARY

The numbers of women and men who are killed by their spouses each year in Canada has remained steady over the past two decades. However, an examination of the risk factors suggests that many could have been prevented with intervention. The majority of killings of both wives and husbands seem to evolve out of ongoing violent relationships, many of which were previously known to outsiders. Many of the same correlates of nonlethal assaults on wives, particularly very serious battering relationships, are present in spousal homicides. Broader awareness of these correlates could help professionals working with battered women to intervene at critical stages to prevent the violence from turning lethal.

There has been a gradual appreciation of the complexity of factors that influence a battered woman's decisions to end or continue the relationship in the face of ongoing threats to her safety. The battered woman defence and the criminal harassment legislation are two legal remedies that have recently become available to Canadian women that recognize the vicious cycle of wife battering and the very real danger to abused women of separating from violent or extremely controlling partners. The next and final chapter will address the consequences of violence for women and their efforts to seek help through the justice system and other means.

C H A P T E R   8

In the Aftermath of Violence

The preceding chapters have focused on the range of correlates and causative factors, both theoretical and empirical, that are associated with incidents of violence against women. The research reviewed in this text reveals a breadth of factors that extend to social, cultural, historical, personal, and situational precursors. This final chapter will examine the consequences of violence for female victims, the steps women take to obtain help from others, and the role played by the criminal justice system in responding to women's calls for help.

THE CONSEQUENCES OF VIOLENCE

The consequences of violent victimization are often difficult to quantify. The of experiences categorized in this text and by the criminal law as "violence" is very broad, ranging from threats and unwanted touching to vicious rapes, battering, and murder. The extent of harm inflicted is also very broad. Many on the less serious end of the scale result in no visible scars. In cases of sexual assault, injuries may be internal and concealed from outsiders. But the emotional or psychological impact, which can be difficult to assess and often remains invisible, can have a much more profound effect on the victim's long-term health and well-being.

Canadian women responding to the Violence Against Women Survey said they had been physically injured in 45 percent of all cases of wife assault and 22 percent of violent sexual attacks. In 1 in 5 cases of wife assault and 1 in 20 incidents of violent sexual attack, victims sought and received medical care. This may not accurately reflect the actual number of injuries that required medical care, however, as the tendency for many women is to try to conceal their injuries and the nature of the attack causing the injuries.

The most frequent types of injuries to assaulted women were bruises, followed by cuts, scratches, and burns, and fractured and broken bones. Fifteen percent of women who said their husbands had been violent toward them during pregnancy suffered miscarriages or other internal injuries as a consequence of the assaults. Fifteen percent of women who suffered a violent sexual attack also received internal injuries as a result.

Emotional effects can be the result of a single violent incident, or an accumulation of threats, or what are generally considered to be less serious events, over time. We saw in Chapter 3 how experiences of violence and noncriminal sexual harassment can affect women's feelings of vulnerability and fear. This type of worry about personal safety can linger for a long time, and may carry over into other situations that are unrelated to the specific event.

When women were asked about the emotional impact of violent experiences on their lives, they gave a range of effects, including anger, loss of trust and confidence, and increased fear. Their responses varied depending on their relationship to the perpetrator. As Table 8.1 indicates, about 30 percent of assaulted women said they were angry about what had happened to them, and about 10 percent said they felt ashamed or guilty. Women assaulted by strangers were most likely to say the experience made them more cautious and less trusting, and more fearful. Victims of wife assault were more likely than others to state that the experience had lowered their self-esteem and made them depressed and anxious. Victims of dating violence were more likely than others to say that the experience had created problems for them in the way they relate to men.

One way women have coped with ongoing abuse in their lives has been by using alcohol, medication, or illicit drugs. Overall, one-quarter of victims of wife assault turned to alcohol, medication, or other drugs to help them cope with the situation (Rodgers, 1994). Substance abuse was a more significant problem for women who also suffered emotional abuse in addition to violence (used by 31 percent of these women), and by women who suffered violence serious enough to cause physical injuries (41 percent of this group). While drug and alcohol abuse offers a short-term remedy by alleviating the immediate pain and turmoil for women in abusive situations, in the long run it represents an additional threat to their safety as the substances cloud the women's judgment and may cause them to miscalculate the level of danger they are facing (Dobash and Dobash, 1979).

TABLE 8.1

Emotional Effects of Violence by Spouses, Dates and Boyfriends, and Strangers

Emotional Effects	Spouses	Dates and Boyfriends	Strangers
		percent	
Angry	30	31	32
More cautious/less trusting	18	32	36
Fearful	21	27	31
Lowered self-esteem	18	12	7
Ashamed/guilty	10	11	9
Problems relating to men	10	16	6
Depressed/anxious	14	6	4
Upset/confused/frustrated	4	4	5
Shocked/disbelief/disgusted	3	4	5
Increased self-reliance	10	2	3
Other[1]	13	6	3
No emotional effects	13	9	12

Figures do not add to totals because of multiple responses.

[1] Includes sleeping problems, hurt, disappointment.

Source: Statistics Canada, "The Violence Against Women Survey," *The Daily*, November 18, Shelf Table 13 (1993).

Seeking Help

The nature of sexual violence and wife assault creates problems for victims following the event. These experiences are deeply personal, and for many victims they bring with them feelings of embarrassment and humiliation that prevents the women from obtaining help to cope with the consequences. As Table 8.1 shows, only 13 percent of women abused by spouses reported no emotional effects, and 10 percent had the positive effect of increased self-reliance having discovered personal strength while coping with the situation. When asked directly what they found to be especially helpful in dealing with the abuse, the largest response category was "relying on herself," given by 1 in 4 women (Statistics Canada, 1994a). But by keeping the experience private, a great many women don't receive the support they need to change the situation.

Table 8.2 illustrates the help-seeking behaviour of assaulted women. It shows that three-quarters of women sought support of some kind from someone, usually a friend or family member. Victims of wife assault were equally likely to confide in friends as in family members, while for sexual assault victims, friends were preferred over family. This is perhaps due to a desire to keep sexual activity private from parents and siblings, even when it is forced. As we saw in the preceding discussions of stranger and dating violence, most victims of sexual assault are young women under 25 years of age. Forced sexual activity at a young age may result in a great deal of guilt and confusion, particularly if perpetrated by an acquaintance or intimate partner.

A consistent proportion of about one-quarter of battering relationships were reported to the police, to a social service, or to a doctor or other medical professional. A much smaller but consistent proportion of sexual assaults (6 percent) were reported to these helping agencies. Ministers and other clergy members were least likely to be sought out as possible sources of support to either battered or sexually assaulted women.

These findings confirm the work of Bowker (1983) and Gelles and Straus (1988) in the United States, who found that informal sources of help are commonly chosen by battered women over legal avenues. However, these help-seeking actions are often closely connected; women who involved the police were more than twice as likely to contact a social service agency than women who did not involve the police (49 percent compared with 19 percent, respectively) (Statistics Canada, 1994a). This reflects the policies of police in many jurisdictions to work closely with shelters and other services for abused women and to make referrals to these services.

TABLE 8.2

Help-Seeking Behaviour of Assaulted Women by Type of Assault

Source of Support	Wife Assault	Sexual Assault
	percent	
Total who told someone	**77**	**74**
Friends/neighbours	45	51
Family	44	38
Police	26	6
Social service	24	6
Doctor	23	6
Clergy	7	2
Told no one	**22**	**25**

Figures do not add to totals because of multiple responses.

Source: Statistics Canada, "The Violence Against Women Survey," *The Daily*, November 18, Shelf Table 18 (1993).

Perhaps the most intriguing aspect of Table 8.2 is the very considerable proportion of violent events that victims kept entirely to themselves. In approximately one-quarter of all cases of wife assault and sexual assault, victims told no one before disclosing the event to a Statistics Canada interviewer. Two important messages are conveyed by these figures. One is the very hidden nature of some forms of violence in women's lives, even some very serious, potentially life-threatening events. Judging by the description of some of these events, the seriousness of the assault does not appear to be the sole reason for not seeking help. While the majority of unreported wife-assault cases were less harmful, 18 percent involved injury to the victim, a figure that represents approximately 111 000 battered women (Rodgers, 1994). Ten percent of women who had been beaten up, choked, sexually assaulted, or had a gun or knife used against them, and

18 percent of those who feared their lives were in danger from an abusive spouse, had never told anyone prior to their participation in the survey.

The second point to be drawn from these figures is that there are important benefits to sample surveys that go to women themselves for a description of their experiences instead of relying on police statistics or clinical populations, which hear about only a fraction of all violent events.

There has been much discussion about the effects on children of witnessing wife battering, especially the potential for the pattern to repeat itself as these children form intimate relationships of their own later in life. Survey data show that women who were exposed to wife battering in childhood were twice as likely as women who did not witness violence to suffer the same abuse themselves. But we also find that women who had witnessed violence did not respond differently once violence occurred. They were no more likely than other women to return to a violent husband once they left. And, contrary to assumptions that these women have certain beliefs about the legitimacy or appropriateness of violence in intimate relationships, they were slightly more likely than other women to seek support from friends and relatives and from helping agencies, particularly social services designed to assist female victims of violence.

THE DECISION TO INVOLVE THE CRIMINAL JUSTICE SYSTEM

The decision to invoke the weight of the criminal justice system against an abusive husband is not taken lightly by most battered women. For a very few, it is an option that is exercised at the first sign of trouble. As shown in Table 8.3, only 6 percent of women assaulted only once called on the police to intervene. One-fifth of women assaulted between 2 and 5 times called the police, as did one-quarter with 6 to 10 episodes. Those battered on a recurring basis of more than 10 times called on the police in half of all cases. From these data we cannot determine the sequence of events, however. Some women who reported recurring instances of violence may have called the police very early on, which, if the police response was ineffective, may have enraged the man and caused him to increase his level of violence against the woman.

Other factors related to the severity of the violence and whether children were involved also influence women's decisions to call on the police for help against abusive husbands. Table 8.3 shows that women were almost three times as likely to call the

TABLE 8.3

Factors Influencing Women's Decisions to Report Battering to the Police

Factors	Percent Who Involved Police
Total percentage who reported	**26**
Frequency of violence episodes	
Happened once	6
2 to 3 times	21
4 to 5 times	18
6 to 8 times	24
9 to 10 times	26
More than 10 times	49
Most serious type of violence	
Threatened to hit her	—
Threw something at her	—
Pushed, grabbed, or shoved	7
Slapped	—
Kicked, bit, or hit her with his fist	—
Hit her with something	—
Beat her up	25
Choked her	40
Used a gun or knife on her	58
Sexual assault	43
Children witnessed	
Yes	43
No	16
Injured	
Yes	43
No	12
Feared for her life	
Yes	55
No	11

— not statistically reliable

Source: Statistics Canada, *The Violence Against Women Survey,* Microdata File, Ottawa (1994a).

police if they had children who witnessed the violence, about four times as likely if they were injured, and five times as likely if they feared their lives were in danger. They were more likely to call the police if they had had a weapon used against them (58 percent) than if subjected to less serious forms of violence.

Some might argue that this is an appropriate use of the criminal justice system and that relatively minor assaults can and should be dealt with by the people involved without police intervention, which may result in charges eventually being dropped or withdrawn. However, if we turn these percentages around to see who is *not* reporting to the police, we find that women are unlikely to call the police until they have been beaten up, and that well over half of all women who have been beaten up or choked in the course of marital violence did *not* report the abuse to the police. Almost half of all abused women who feared for their lives also did not seek help from the police; neither did more than half of those who were injured and one-third of those who got medical treatment (Statistics Canada, 1994a).

The majority of very serious sexual assaults also were not reported to the police. For example, 80 percent of violent sexual attacks by strangers were not reported; nor were 80 percent of incidents resulting in physical injury to the victims, 43 percent of those requiring medical treatment, and 65 percent of those carried out with a weapon (Statistics Canada, 1994a). The significantly higher proportion of assaults with medical treatment coming to the attention of the police may reflect the interagency cooperation that exists between hospitals and police in many Canadian communities, where medical staff have been trained to collect forensic evidence and victims are offered support in taking the case to the police. A critical question for criminal justice practitioners remains, however: why do so many women who are seriously hurt in violent crimes not see the criminal justice system as offering a viable solution to their problem?

Table 8.4 presents the responses of wife-battering victims who had been injured or feared for their lives when asked why they had not notified the police. A surprising proportion in both groups felt that the situation was too minor to warrant the attention of the police, despite the severity of the assaults. They were less likely to say that they didn't want their husbands arrested than they were to say that they feared retaliation from him, particularly those who feared for their lives. Significant proportions felt shame and embarrassment about what had happened to them and wanted to keep the incident private, despite their fear and injury. Comparable proportions stated that they did not want to get involved with the police, thought the police could not help them, and felt they did not want or need help.

TABLE 8.4

Reasons for Not Reporting Wife Battering to the Police, by Women Who Were Injured or Feared for Their Lives

Reasons	Injured	Feared for her life
	percent	
Too minor	20	15
Feared retaliation by the offender	14	21
Wanted to keep the incident private	17	14
Did not want to get involved with the police	11	12
Thought the police could not help	10	13
Shame or embarrassment	9	9
Didn't want or need help	9	6
Did not want the offender arrested	4	4

Figures do not add to totals because of multiple responses.

Source: Statistics Canada, *The Violence Against Women Survey,* Microdata File, Ottawa (1994a).

THE RESPONSE OF THE CRIMINAL JUSTICE SYSTEM

For centuries, wife battering was seen as a private family problem. It was seen not to pose a serious threat to public order and therefore was not a matter for criminal justice intervention. The inaction of the criminal justice system in response to wife battering continued long after a husband's legal rights of chastisement over his wife had been abolished. This followed from the widespread belief that what goes on in the privacy of the home is not a matter for state intervention (Dobash and Dobash, 1979; Schneider, 1994). Police officers considered that their primary role in domestic violence cases was to calm the people involved and restore order, and that once that was accomplished, their job was done (Jaffe, Hastings, Reitzel, and Austin, 1993). There was also a widely accepted presumption on the part of police, other helping professionals, and the public that battered women who wanted to could simply leave a violent relationship, and if they stayed, the situation couldn't be as serious as they claimed.

Recent developments, such as legal reform, mandatory charging policies, and other government initiatives, have moved wife battering and sexual assault from the private to the public realm. The criminalization of these particular forms of violence resulted from a gradual process of defining and perceiving them as dangerous to the social order and not just to individual victims, as well as from a better understanding of the dynamics and consequences of these experiences (Pleck, 1989).

A continent-wide move toward laying criminal charges against men accused of assaulting their spouses began during the early 1980s. This movement was spurred on in the United States by the U.S. Attorney General's Task Force on Family Violence, which recommended that family violence be treated as a crime; by several lawsuits brought against police departments for failing to protect battered women who called for help; and in part by the Minneapolis Domestic Violence Experiment published in 1984 (Sherman and Berk, 1984). This was the first randomized controlled experiment of the effectiveness of arrest in domestic violence cases. Cases of domestic violence reported to the police were randomly assigned to one of three possible outcomes: arrest, advice to the couple or mediation, or removing the suspect from the home for a brief period. The researchers found that dispensing advice or removing the suspect doubled the woman's risk of further violence over a six-month follow-up, compared with arresting the suspect. On the basis of this evidence, mandatory arrest was quickly adopted by police departments across the United States.

In Canada, mandatory charging policies were implemented by police departments across the country in the early 1980s. At the same time, sexual assault laws were changed to permit men to be charged with sexual assaulting their wives, and the Canada Evidence Act was revised to allow women to testify against their husbands (Jaffe, Hastings, Reitzel, and Austin, 1993). The decision to adopt mandatory charging policies was influenced in large part by the lobby efforts of shelter workers and other advocates for battered women. These policies were intended to improve the way the justice system dealt with cases of domestic violence, and to increase the number of charges laid and the number of successful prosecutions. By emphasizing the criminal nature of wife assault, mandatory charging was also intended to encourage women to report these offences to the police by demonstrating that they would be taken seriously. It would establish a standard for police response and give women immediate and guaranteed access to criminal justice protection.

Mandatory charging policies give police the authority to lay charges against a suspect where there is reasonable and probable grounds to believe that an assault has occurred regardless of whether there are witnesses to the crime. The philosophy of mandatory charging is grounded in the belief that female victims often lack sufficient power in the marital relationship to repel the offender or convince him to change his behaviour, and that the power of the police will help to right this imbalance. Prior to mandatory charging policies, women could be required to bring charges against their husbands independently, which could antagonize abusers into further violence. Women were often too intimidated to state their preference for arrest while the abusive spouse was present, and so charges often were not laid unless injuries were serious or the police or someone else witnessed the assault. The presence of the police and the laying of criminal charges provide immediate protection from violence, and give women who are ready to end the relationship an opportunity to leave with police protection (Dutton et al., 1992).

The deterrent function of mandatory charging is both general and specific. The threat of arrest and public exposure is meant to send a message to all citizens that wife abuse is morally and legally wrong, and the arrest of individual violent men is expected to deter them from further assaults on their wives. As Dutton et al. (1992) point out, arrest makes the man's violence public, which may increase informal social pressures from friends and family to cease his abusive behaviour. In addition, the power dynamic within the relationship may shift as a consequence of arrest. The increased visibility of the violence can generate social support for the victim and challenges from the man's community to his perceived right to abuse his wife. Public condemnation of the abuse may make the woman less likely to blame herself and more likely to take assertive action to end the relationship or to notify the police or other people in the future. Victims who know police will take their complaints seriously may gain strength and some control over their lives (Dutton et al., 1992).

When the police did intervene in wife battering or sexual assault cases reported to the Violence Against Women Survey, very few resulted in criminal charges being laid against a perpetrator and even fewer resulted in court appearances. Only 26 percent of violent marriages were ever reported to the police, and 28 percent of these resulted in criminal charges (Statistics Canada, 1993a). However, once charges were laid, the majority, 79 percent, proceeded to court. The figures are considerably lower for sexual assaults. Only 6 percent were reported to the police; 34 percent of these resulted in charges, and 46 percent of these proceeded to court. Of the total number of wife assault and sexual assault cases, only 6 percent and 1 percent, respectively, resulted in a court appearance by an accused person.

Unfortunately, it is not possible from this survey to track changes in rates of reporting over time. It seems likely, given recent changes in societal attitudes and criminal justice policies concerning wife battering, that women may have become more willing to seek help from the police in recent years and that police and Crown prosecutors may be more willing to proceed with charges and prosecution (Statistics Canada, 1993a). But this survey asked about experiences of violence that had occurred at any point in the respondent's adult lifetime and, therefore, can neither support nor refute this claim. The incidents captured by this survey spanned the time during which the policy was implemented and cannot be used to assess its effectiveness.

In the perception of the female victims, the response of the police was effective in decreasing or stopping their partners' violence in 45 percent of reported cases (Rodgers, 1994). There was no change in the men's behaviour following police intervention in 40 percent of cases, and the violence actually increased in 10 percent of cases. When charges were laid, victims were more likely to say that the level of violence had decreased, although the difference between these cases and those for which charges were not laid was small (51 percent said the violence had decreased compared with 43 percent for which the police responded but did not lay charges). The percentage who said the violence decreased rose to 58 percent when the police referred the woman to services in the community (Statistics Canada, 1994a).

STUDIES ON THE EFFECTS OF ARREST

Other research in Canada has shown that arrest of violent spouses can be beneficial in curbing assaults on wives. Peter Jaffe and his colleagues at the London Family Court Clinic in London, Ontario, have monitored the charging policy and the level of repeat violence of men against their female partners prior to and following the implementation of the policy in that city. They note that only 3 percent of incidents of wife assault that were reported to the police in 1979 resulted in a criminal charge, even though 20 percent of the victims needed medical attention. By 1990, police were laying charges in 89 percent of these cases (Jaffe, Hastings, Reitzel, and Austin, 1993). The authors found substantial reductions in violence, according to both police files and interviews with victims, in cases where charges were laid (Jaffe, Wolfe, Telford, and Austin, 1986). They also found increased satisfaction among victims with the help received from police. Victims whose partners had been charged by police described a higher degree of support from the police officers and were made to feel less to blame than victims interviewed prior to the mandatory charging policy.

While these results are encouraging, the authors caution that they may not be generalizable to other communities because of the very active way in which the city of London has organized to respond to domestic violence. Through the London Coordinating Committee to End Woman Abuse, service agencies in the community, including police, probation, courts, Crown attorneys, family and children's services, the London Family Court Clinic, women's shelters, nonresidential referral and counselling services for women, and counselling programs for men, have joined forces to develop a coordinated and integrated approach to helping abused women, their partners, and their children. In addition, the London Police Force has developed crisis units and specialized training programs in order to improve the way in which its officers respond to battered women (London Family Court Clinic, 1991). Communities lacking this level of coordination may witness different reactions to mandatory charging policies than those measured by the London researchers.

Some studies show that the effects of arrest can be enhanced with counselling for the male batterers. In Vancouver, psychologist Donald Dutton (1986) compared rates of reoffending among men who had been charged and received treatment with those who had been charged but did not receive treatment. Over a two-and-a-half-year follow-up, just 4 percent of those who received treatment were rearrested for assault, compared with 40 percent of men in the untreated group. However, the effects of arrest may be short-lived, lasting only as long as the man has some contact with justice authorities. Dutton notes that the sharpest increases in the rate of reoffending occurred after probation supervision had expired, when the men were no longer under the control of the criminal justice system.

Replications of the Minneapolis Domestic Violence Experiment in six American cities have produced conflicting results (Schmidt and Sherman, 1993). Arrest worked to deter some offenders but increased the rates of violence by others. In some cases where arrest reduced violence in the short term, it actually increased it over the long term. One fairly consistent finding, however, was that arrest seemed to have a greater deterrent effect for employed men and for white men, but had the opposite effect for unemployed and African-American men. This led the authors of the Minneapolis experiment to speculate that the effects of punishment depend on how much the offender has to lose from the social consequences of arrest (Sherman, Schmidt, and Rogan, 1992). Since middle-class men have higher status in the community, they have more to lose by being publicly identified as abusive. Alternatively, arrest may serve to grant power to the woman and take away what little status and control lower-class men have, which primarily consists of control in the domestic sphere (Stark, 1993). This increases their anger and rage toward their wives, which escalates into assaults against them. Middle-class men have other avenues open to them through which to regain status following arrest, such as employment, income, and education. The results of the replication experiments have led the originators of the Minneapolis experiment to renounce mandatory arrest policies, particularly in cities with large ghetto populations and high unemployment rates, because such policies are likely to backfire in these settings (Sherman, Schmidt, and Rogan, 1992).

On the basis of this research and their personal experience with wife-battering cases, some police officers, academics, and groups who provide services to battered women have grown sceptical about the ability of the justice system to deter abusive men and to provide relief to victims. Initially, there was great optimism about the potential deterrent effect of the mandatory charging policy. It held the promise of great symbolic change in sending a clear message that violence is unacceptable and will not be tolerated. The hope was that it would help reduce the incidence of wife assault by punishing individual offenders and by promoting a broader social message that eventually would become internalized and widely accepted. But over the past decade of working with this policy, many battered women, police officers, and service providers have become frustrated with the way in which discretion is removed from both police and victims. Crown prosecutors in some jurisdictions are compelled to take a case to court regardless of the victim's wishes, and can even subpoena an unwilling victim to testify in court. Mandatory charging may also have the unintended effect of reducing the willingness of women to report to police (Mederer and Gelles, 1989). Many women call the police for reasons other than having their husbands arrested, such as wanting the violence to stop and exerting some control over the situation. If victims fear losing control over the outcome, they may not call. In a sense, the justice system can end up working against those it is supposed to protect, giving them less, not more, control over the course of events (MacLeod, 1995b).

A "zero tolerance" policy on wife assault in Winnipeg removed all discretion from police and committed them to lay charges whenever a complaint was made. An unanticipated consequence was that the abusive spouse could counter-charge his wife when police appeared on the scene. Police were then forced to charge the woman as well (MacLeod, 1995a:22). The solution has been to have the police present details of the charge to the Crown attorney, who then makes a decision on whether to proceed.

One underlying justification for the implementation of the mandatory charging policy was that domestic violence is a crime like any other and should be countered with criminal charges. But wife battering is *not* a crime like any other. Unlike crimes that occur outside the milieu of the family, victims are living with their assailants; they often have strong emotional, financial, and physical bonds; many share children; and very often they want the relationship to continue. All of these factors create complications for both victims and police officers called to the scene of the crime. The difficulties are exacerbated in situations where community-level supports for the victim and her children are lacking. Mandatory charging policies and the best intentions on the part of the police officer may have little effect on alleviating the violence over the long term if the woman lives in an area with no shelters or counselling services for either herself or her husband, and if she has no family support, no financial resources, and no forseeable way of supporting herself and her children. In these circumstances, the woman's isolation and dependence on her husband continues after charges are laid, making it difficult for her to escape the violent marriage. Without other community supports working cooperatively with the efforts of the criminal justice system to address the problem, many feel that these efforts are only temporary.

INNOVATIVE APPROACHES TO COUNTERING WIFE BATTERING

In addition to mandatory charging policies, a number of innovative projects have emerged to address the problem of wife battering in a comprehensive fashion. The following are just a few examples.

THE WINNIPEG FAMILY VIOLENCE COURT

The Winnipeg Family Violence Court began operation in 1990 specifically to handle cases of spouse abuse, child abuse, and abuse of elderly people. This new initiative evolved out of public pressure and a perception that the sentences imposed in wife assault cases in particular were lenient, inappropriate, and unjust compared to the sentences imposed in other types of crimes (MacLeod, 1995a:21).

Spouse abuse is defined by the court as cases of violence perpetrated by legal and common-law spouses, former spouses, and other current or former intimate partners. Ninety percent of spouse abuse cases involve female victims and male offenders. The goals of the court are threefold: (1) to expedite court processing, (2) to increase victim cooperation and reduce case attrition, and (3) to provide appropriate sentencing that would protect victims, such as mandated treatment for abusers and monitoring through probation supervision (Ursel, 1994). The court was created to ensure that cases of family violence were prosecuted as rigorously as other cases of violence, while at the same time recognizing the uniqueness of violent incidents in which victims are highly bonded to and dependent on offenders.

A preliminary assessment of the first two years of the functioning of the court indicates that the court has had some success in meeting these goals (Ursel, 1994). Court processing time averaged about three months per case despite continuing increases in the volume of cases. This was achieved primarily by allocating more court time and court staff to these cases. More modest success was achieved with respect to reducing case attrition. The percentage of spousal assault cases that were withdrawn or dismissed declined significantly in the first year of the court's operation, but increased again in the second year. There is evidence here that a very rigorous police charging policy may have a negative effect on the success rate for prosecutors of these cases. According to Ursel:

> The difference may be the result of a substantial change in police charging practice in relation to spousal assault. Crown attorneys in the Family Violence Court report that as a result of an increasingly rigorous charging policy on the part of the police, they must deal with increasing numbers of cases in which the evidence is weak or ambiguous or in which the victim/witness may be reluctant to testify. (Ursel, 1994:11–12)

With respect to the goals of more appropriate sentencing, the number of cases resulting in probation supervision tripled in the first two years of operation and those resulting in jail sentences doubled, while the use of fines and conditional discharges declined substantially. Court-mandated treatment for offenders was ordered for 53 percent of all persons sentenced, and half of these involved completion of a batterers treatment group. Alcohol treatment was designated in 39 percent of all cases. The increased use of probation and these additional conditions effectively increased the level of monitoring and supervision of offenders from what had been the case in general court.

The success of this court in reaching its goals may be attributed to a number of innovative factors. The specialized nature of this court led to the selection of specially trained judges and prosecutors who are knowledgeable about issues related to violence in families and intimate relationships and are less likely to hold attitudes that are biased against victims. In addition, the court has, as a component of the prosecutorial process, The Women's Advocacy Program, which provides support for women throughout their involvement with the justice system. The availability of knowledgeable and highly trained professionals may serve to increase the confidence of victims in the system and reduce the frequency with which they withdraw from testifying against the abuser. The end result has been to elevate the status of family violence cases from low-priority cases to complex cases that require highly skilled personnel (MacLeod, 1995a).

A current challenge facing the Manitoba correctional system as a direct result of the success of the charging and prosecution policies is the deluge of cases with court-mandated treatment orders. Between 1983 and 1993, the number of cases in which charges were laid increased from 629 to about 4000. The impact on the correctional system was a tenfold increase in treatment orders for batterers from 80 to 800 (MacLeod, 1995a). With no new sources of funding available, resources have had to be reallocated from counselling for other types of crimes to counselling for abusive men.

SASKATCHEWAN VICTIMS OF DOMESTIC VIOLENCE ACT

The Saskatchewan Victims of Domestic Violence Act is scheduled to come into effect in late 1995. This act strengthens civil legislation that is designed to provide police with tools, in addition to the criminal law, to help victims of family violence in times of crisis. Three types of remedies are provided by this legislation (Turner, 1995):

1. Emergency intervention orders are available 24 hours a day from a number of specially recruited and trained justices of the peace. These orders can give victims exclusive possession of the family home, restrain abusers from communicating with or contacting victims or members of her family, and order a police officer to supervise the removal of personal belongings from the family home.

2. Victim Assistance Orders can provide additional remedies, such as monetary compensation for losses suffered as a result of the violence (such as legal or moving expenses, dental expenses, or temporary possession of the car or other personal property), or increase the range of constraints on the offender regarding contact or communication with the victim or her family.

3. Warrants of Entry enable a designated person to enter a building to examine the situation and, if necessary, to remove the victim, when there is a concern that the person is unable to act on her own. This provision would be used primarily with elderly persons or those with disabilities.

The victim, the police, or anyone else can apply for any of the above orders. Violation of any part of this act is a criminal offence. Police are authorized to arrest without a warrant anyone who breaches an order.

The development and implementation of this legislation took place in a partnership approach involving the provincial government, crisis intervention agencies, community members, police, and other support services for victims. It arose out of frustration on the part of the police and others with the constraints and limitations of the criminal law in intervening in the early stages of wife battering. Twenty-two justices of the peace have been recruited throughout the province to hear and grant emergency intervention orders. They have been selected on the basis of their experience and knowledge about family violence issues and were specially trained. Every police officer in the province will also receive training about the procedures under the new legislation, how this legislation will be used in conjunction with the criminal law, as well as general issues in the dynamics of family violence.

COMMUNITY CONFERENCING

In response to what they view as the failure of the traditional criminal justice system to adequately curb male violence, John Braithwaite and Kathleen Daly (1994) propose an alternative community-based approach. The *community conferencing strategy* is an approach borrowed from the indigenous Maori people of New Zealand. It has been used for centuries by the Maori to deal with sexual abuse and family violence and recently has been adapted to the white New Zealand culture to respond to juvenile crime. Community conferencing is also under way in Australia and is being tested in three communities in Newfoundland (MacLeod, 1995c).

Braithwaite and Daly summarize the failure of the criminal justice system to respond to male violence under three main points:

1. Because most acts of sexual assault and wife beating are not reported to the police, and many that are reported do not result in conviction, most men who commit these crimes are not held accountable.

2. Because conviction is a rare event, men who are prosecuted for sexual violence or wife beating likely have entrenched patterns of violence that are resistant to rehabilitation.

3. Women who report crimes of violence against them are re-victimized by a confrontational criminal justice process that demeans and degrades them.

Rather than protecting women from male violence, intervention by police can actually increase the risk of violence for some women, especially poor minority women with unemployed partners, as demonstrated by the Minneapolis experiment.

A central assumption of community conferencing is that shaming and apology are more effective strategies than punishment in reaffirming community values, so long as they occur within an environment of concern for the victim and the offender and are followed by reintegration back into the community. Whereas the criminal justice experience is stigmatizing for both victims and offenders and reinforces denial by the offender, community conferencing is designed to open dialogue among all parties affected and to encourage the admission of responsibility and regret.

The context for community conferencing is "communities of concern" made up of the victim's and the offender's caring friends and family members who, it is argued, are better equipped to challenge the acceptability of violence and to intervene in family violence than are justice officials. In the Newfoundland project, it is social service or justice officials who recommend to the Family Group Conferencing coordinator that certain families suffering from abuse take part in the program. Other people outside the immediate friendship-and-family network with specialized knowledge of the dynamics of family violence may also attend the conference to assist participants in their deliberations (MacLeod, 1995c). The theory is that discussion of the harm and distress caused to the victim, her family, and the offender's family will instil shame in the offender and motivate him to change. Communities and extended families are better able to watch over the offender, obtain assurance from victims that the violence has not continued, enforce agreements about abstaining from alcohol, and act as a visible reminder to the abuser that the abused person has a safe haven should the violence recur.

This approach stands in opposition to traditional legal systems that enforce standard strategies for responding to law violations. By contrast, the community conference empowers communities to devise solutions that are culturally appropriate to the people involved and to the circumstances of the event. The effectiveness of this strategy lies in the threat of criminal punishment that can be imposed should the process fail. It signals to the violent man that he is better off responding before the case is brought before the courts, where an uncertain fate awaits him.

Figure 8.1 illustrates Braithwaite and Daly's enforcement pyramid through which the process of community conferencing progresses. Once a community conferencing approach has been established and the shamefulness of violence is internalized among community members, this internalization is assumed to prohibit acts of violence. If his conscience fails him, the social disapproval that the abuser imagines will be forthcoming from his community should inhibit further violence on his part. If the fear of social disapproval is not present, someone must confront him about the violence. If family members are too intimidated to confront him, the police must be called and a warrant for arrest issued. The presence of the police and a suspended warrant give the woman a measure of protection and hang over the man as a threat during the community conference. Such measures are not enacted until several attempts at conferencing have been made and have shown to be ineffective in deterring the man from further violence.

The conferencing strategy is not proposed at all costs. If at any time either the victim or the offender feels that her or his civil rights are being violated or that she or he is unhappy with the process, both are free to allow the arrest warrant to be activated and to face the criminal court.

The community conferencing strategy is seen to be preferable to the criminal justice system, which tends to treat each reported incident of battering in isolation from the rest in that it monitors patterns of offending with the backup of the state. The community approach also provides a means of exposing male violence that is not dependent on the courage of victims to endure the criminal justice process and does not end up revictimizing women. Although it does not hinge on the man admitting guilt, this is often the outcome when he begins to appreciate the impact of his actions on the victim, her family, and his family. The sanctions agreed to by both parties are often less than a court might impose but definitely more than would have been imposed had the complaint not been reported or had been withdrawn.

Domestic Violence Enforcement Pyramid

J. Braithwaite and K. Daly, "Masculinities, violence and communitarian control," in T. Newburn and E. Stanko (eds.), *Just Boys Doing Business?* (London: Routledge, 1994), p. 197. Reprinted with permission.

This approach can benefit many more women than the traditional approaches by encouraging more women to come forward, confronting the offender and thus holding him accountable, receiving some redress for the wrong done, and perhaps helping the woman to find the courage to testify in court should the conferencing process break down. Another advantage is enabling communities to bring violence to light at earlier stages and to intervene earlier in the lives of violent offenders. The community conference can provide a forum in which abused women who want to avoid breaking up their families and bringing the stigma of criminal charges against their husbands can find support among community members who will challenge his behaviour. Unlike the traditional justice system, community conferencing opens up possibilities for apology, reaffirmation of community values, and dialogue among all affected parties (Braithwaite and Day, 1994).

SUMMARY

Most assaulted women suffer a variety of emotional and physical effects, but their reaction to these is not typically to call on medical, legal, or religious services. They are most likely to call on the support of family and friends, which, in some of these cases, may be the most beneficial approach for the women involved. A point of concern for justice practitioners, however, is that most battered women do not report their husbands to the police, even when the consequences for the women are very serious. In fact, a great many battered women stay with extremely violent men without seeking help from the police and without the potential benefit of outside support for themselves, their partners, or their children. As elaborated in the last few chapters, the dynamics involved in battering relationships, and in women's decisions to leave their partners and to make the situation public by involving the police, are complex, and the decision to break from the situation can be very difficult.

C H A P T E R 9

Summing Up

The intention of this book was to synthesize current theoretical, methodological, and empirical debates in the field of violence against women, with a focus on the experiences of Canadian women. Some of the empirical findings add support to theories and ideas put forth by other researchers, and some suggest new ways of looking at and responding to the problem.

Theories of social learning, sex role socialization, and power and control within traditional male–female relationships seem to have the greatest utility as theoretical explanations for men's use of violence against female strangers, dating partners, and spouses. Social learning theory looks at how violence can be learned within a child's family and social environment as an appropriate means of solving everyday problems if the consequences are perceived to be positive and if opportunities for learning alternatives are weak or absent. An empirical link between childhood exposure to wife battering in male children and the tendency to inflict violence on one's own wife in adulthood is one of the most common research findings cited in the family violence literature. Messages about the appropriateness of using violence are especially potent for male children, who grow up with cultural images of masculine power and toughness.

However, there are sufficient exceptions to the rule to caution against accepting this as a simple cause-and-effect relationship. Many abusive men are *not* exposed to violence in childhood, and a great number of men whose mothers were battered are not violent toward their own wives. Nevertheless, there is compelling evidence that children growing up in violent homes are at risk of emotional, developmental, and behavioural problems, including increased aggression in both childhood and adulthood, which warrant early identification, treatment, and support for these families.

Sex role theory expands on the principles of social learning but views gender as a critical component of the socialization process. According to sex role theory, cultural messages about appropriate male and female behaviour script the passage of children into adulthood. Men who relate strongly to masculine ideals of toughness and dominance over women, but who feel insecure in their ability to achieve these ideals personally, may respond by asserting their will over their wives and girlfriends and may use violence to achieve it.

Evolutionary theory attributes the higher risk of wife battering among young couples living in low-income, common-law unions to the feelings of possessiveness that can accrue when either partner feels insecure about the future of the relationship, and additional leisure time opens up possibilities for the young woman to attract a new mate, particularly one who has greater status or financial resources. In fact, many young common-law couples may perceive the union to be temporary and may be actively looking for alternative mates, which increases the risk that fears and accusations of infidelity will occur. Suspicions or threats of infidelity, and threats to end the relationship, are common precursors to both serious battering and wife killings. Some researchers assert that men's perceived right of entitlement over their female mates is an evolutionary manifestation that in extreme cases is carried out to the point of killing the woman.

Feminist theories of power and control further expand on sex role and social learning theories by incorporating historical analyses of social structures that have tolerated and, in some cases, explicitly approved of sexual violence and wife battering. Men are assigned roles of higher status over women, and legal and social structures in Western society have served to reinforce and legitimate this superior status. Thus the sex roles that men and women learn have great legitimacy in the broader culture and cannot be altered significantly without also altering the structures that support the differential status awarded to men and women.

Other researchers have offered innovative variations on traditional routine activities theory that incorporate parts of sex role theory and take account of social roles of men and women in dating situations. Traditional application of routine activities theory looks primarily at demographic characteristics that increase an individual's proximity to risky places and people. Young women are considered to be at greatest risk of dating violence because their leisure activities provide greater opportunities for social interaction with males of the same age and for dating situations. But a variation on this theory also takes into account the ways in which men and women typically relate to each other in dating situations that reflect traditional assumptions about their social roles and certain male privileges. Men tend to assume greater control and decision-making power over the circumstances surrounding the date, the mode of transportation, and the sequence of events. Men's assumed role to initiate and control the situation may lead to misinterpretations of the women's willingness to engage in sexual activity. The more traditional the participants' views about sex roles, the more likely such misinterpretation will occur and the more likely force will be felt to be justifiable.

Alcohol abuse is also commonly cited as a precursor to wife battering and other forms of violence in general. While there is some empirical support for this, the link cannot be said to be directly causal. Although many battered women have reported a cessation in the violence following alcohol treatment for their partners, research suggests that heavy drinking is often coupled with other factors, such as low economic status and attitudes approving of violence toward wives, which may be more important as explanatory variables. When other risk factors are also present in the relationship, such as the youth of the couple, common-law marital status, low income, bouts of male unemployment, exposure to violence in childhood, or peers supportive of wife abuse, alcohol may exacerbate an already tense situation and elevate the risk of violence.

At the conclusion of this book, it is obvious that the answer to the commonly asked question "Why does she stay?" is not as straightforward as might first appear. Women and men in battering relationships are often joined by marital bonds that are not unlike those that keep nonviolent couples together and committed to the marriage throughout difficult times. In most battering relationships, the violence escalates over a period of time amidst positive periods that keep the woman hoping for change. For many women, the benefits of the marriage overshadow the abuse until it becomes unbearable, both physically and emotionally. By that point, a woman may have become trapped in an increasingly deadly situation with no perceived means of escape.

Canadian courts and legislators have recognized the cycle that can trap battered women and the danger of separation in cases of escalating violence. The plea of self-defence is now open to battered women who kill their mates if it can be proved that, under the circumstance of the ongoing relationship, the woman had a reasonable fear of serious injury and believed that lethal force was necessary to defend herself. The law on criminal harassment offers protection to women who feel threatened by the harassing actions of a spouse or an ex-spouse. While it is too soon for the results of a federal government evaluation of this law, its intent was to recognize the risks that sometimes accompany women's attempts to extricate themselves from violent, threatening, or extremely controlling relationships.

What, then, are the possible solutions to the ongoing problem of male violence against women? Debates continue about the most appropriate role for the criminal justice system in cases of wife battering. There is conflicting evidence about the effectiveness and the viability of mandatory charging policies for police and

Crown prosecutors that remove discretion and control from all players, the victim, the police, and the Crown. But regardless of whether the actions taken by the criminal justice system are discretionary or not, it seems likely that the police will remain a primary component of the societal response to wife battering and one of the few options available to a great many women who lack family support or financial resources to alter their situation. Consequently, we must endeavour to monitor and evaluate police responses to these events in order to increase the benefits and reduce the costs to the women involved.

It is also critical that we continue to develop alternatives to seeking punishment through the criminal justice system. Significant numbers of sexually assaulted and battered women choose not to involve the police. These are highly personal experiences, and few women make the decision to report to the police without serious thought. In some cases, the disadvantages of reporting the incident outweigh the benefits to the woman involved, particularly if she perceives the incident to be minor. But many very serious cases of sexual violence and battering go unreported for reasons related to fear of the violent partner, shame, and embarrassment on the part of the victim, and distrust of the justice system.

We must recognize the limitations of the criminal justice system. It is cumbersome and unpredictable and can take control away from those whom it was designed to help. It cannot, nor should it, be expected to provide the entire solution to social problems. Wife battering and sexual violence, like many other criminal justice issues such as youth crime and prostitution, are not only legal issues—they are also issues for educators, health professionals, religious leaders, and community organizations. What is needed to effect a significant reduction in various forms of violence against women is a change in public consciousness, where violence will not be tolerated, coupled with prevention efforts, which challenge traditional roles for men and women in intimate relationships. Formal social controls have real limits in deterring acts that are so rarely dealt with through these avenues. What is needed is an increase in the informal social controls against violence where communities and individuals feel a personal responsibility to act. Models for this type of strategy are mass public education campaigns similar to those for impaired driving and anti-smoking, in which attitudes effectively have been changed in part due to regulatory controls but in large measure because of significant changes in public tolerance and awareness. Efforts have begun in this direction in communities, schools, parent groups, and other settings across the country. The next challenge is to raise wife assault and sexual violence to the level of serious public and societal problems for which all citizens feel a responsibility.

REFERENCES

Adams, David. 1988. "Treatment Models of Men Who Batter: A Profeminist Analysis." In Kersti Yllo and Michele Bograd (eds.), *Feminist Perspectives on Wife Abuse*. Newbury Park, CA: Sage, 176–99.

Adler, Zsuzsanna. 1987. *Rape on Trial*. London, UK: Routledge & Kegan Paul.

Agnew, R.S. 1985. "Neutralizing the Impact of Crime." *Criminal Justice and Behavior* 12:221–39.

Alder, C. 1985. "An Exploration of Self-Reported Sexually Aggressive Behaviour." *Crime and Delinquency* 31:306–31.

Attorney General's Task Force on Family Violence. 1984. *Final Report*. Washington, DC: U.S. Department of Justice.

Bachman, Ronet. 1994. *Violence Against Women: A National Crime Victimization Survey Report*. Washington, DC: Bureau of Justice Statistics.

Bachman, Ronet, and Bruce Taylor. 1994. "The Measurement of Family Violence and Rape by the Redesigned National Crime Victimization Survey." *Justice Quarterly* 11(3):499–512.

Bachman, Ronet, and Linda Saltzman. 1995. *Violence Against Women: Estimates from the Redesigned Survey*. Washington, DC: Bureau of Justice Statistics.

Bandura, Albert. 1977. *Social Learning Theory*. Englewood Cliffs, NJ: Prentice-Hall.

Barr, Lynn. 1993. *Basic Facts on Families in Canada: Past and Present*. Ottawa: Statistics Canada.

Belknap, Joanne. 1987. "Routine Activity Theory and the Risk of Rape: Analyzing Ten Years of National Crime Survey Data." *Criminal Justice Policy Review* 2(4):337–56.

Benson, Dennis, Catherine Charlton, and Fern Goodhart. 1992. "Acquaintance Rape on Campus: A Literature Review." *College Health* 40:157–65.

Bersani, Carl, and Huey-Tsyh Chen. 1988. "Sociological Perspectives in Family Violence." In Vincent Van Hasselt, Randall Morrison, and Alan Bellack (eds.), *Handbook of Family Violence*. New York: Plenum Press, 57–86.

Biderman, A.D., and J.P. Lynch. 1990. *Understanding Crime Incidence Statistics*. New York: Springer-Verlag.

Bindman, Stephen. 1995. "Women Who Killed Abusers Win Review." *Ottawa Citizen*, July 14, A3.

Bograd, Michele. 1988. "Feminist Perspectives on Wife Abuse: An Introduction." In Kersti Yllo and Michelle Bograd (eds.), *Feminist Perspectives on Wife Abuse*. Newbury Park, CA: Sage, 11–26.

Bowker, Lee. 1983. *Beating Wife Beating*. Toronto: Lexington Books.

Boyle, Christine. 1994. "The Judicial Construction of Sexual Assault Offences." In Julian Roberts and Renate Mohr (eds.), *Confronting Sexual*

Assault: A Decade of Legal and Social Change. Toronto: University of Toronto Press, 136–56.

Braithwaite, John, and Kathleen Daly. 1994. "Masculinities, Violence and Communitarian Control." In Tim Newburn and Elizabeth Stanko (eds.), *Just Boys Doing Business? Men, Masculinities and Crime.* London, UK: Routledge, 189–213.

Brinkerhoff, Merlin, and Eugen Lupri. 1988. "Interspousal Violence." *Canadian Journal of Sociology* 13(4):407–34.

Browne, Angela. 1987. *When Battered Women Kill.* New York: Free Press.

———. 1986. "Assault and Homicide at Home: When Battered Women Kill." In Michael J. Saks and Leonard Saxe (eds.),*Advances in Applied Social Psychology.* Hillsdale, NJ: Lawrence Erlbaum, Associates, 57–79.

Browning, James, and Donald Dutton. 1986. "Assessment of Wife Assault with the Conflict Tactics Scale: Using Couple Data to Quantify the Differential Reporting Effect." *Journal of Marriage and the Family* 48:375–79.

Brownmiller, Susan. 1975.*Against Our Will: Men, Women and Rape.* New York: Simon & Schuster.

Brush, Lisa. 1990. "Violent Acts and Injurious Outcomes in Married Couples: Methodological Issues in the National Survey of Families and Households." *Gender and Society.* 4:56–67.

Burt, Martha R. 1991. "Rape Myths and Acquaintance Rape." In Andrea Parrot and Laurie Bechhofer (ed.),*Acquaintance Rape: The Hidden Crime.* New York: John Wiley & Sons, 26–40.

———. 1980. "Cultural Myths and Supports for Rape."*Journal of Personality and Social Psychology* 38(2):217–30.

Campbell, Jacquelyn. 1995. "Prediction of Homicide of and by Battered Women." In *Assessing Dangerousness: Violence by Sexual Offenders, Batterers, and Child Abusers.* Thousand Oaks, CA: Sage, 96–113.

———. 1992a. "The Danger Assessment Instrument: Risk Factors of Homicide of and by Battered Women." In Carolyn Rebecca Block and Richard Block (eds.), *Questions and Answers in Lethal and Non-Lethal Violence: Proceedings of the First Annual Workshop of the Homicide Research Working Group.* Washington, DC: National Institute of Justice, 27–38.

———. 1992b. "If I Can't Have You, No One Can: Power and Control in Homicide of Female Partners." In J. Radford and D. Russell (eds.),*Femicide: The Politics of Women Killing.* New York: Twayne Publishers, 99–113.

———. 1989. "Women's Responses to Sexual Abuse in Intimate Relationships." *Health Care for Women International* 10:335–46.

Campbell, Jacquelyn, and Peggy Alford. 1989. "The Dark Consequences of Marital Rape." *American Journal of Nursing* 89:946–49.

Canadian Centre for Justice Statistics. 1993a. Revised Uniform Crime Reporting Survey. Unpublished data.

———. 1993b. Homicide Survey. Unpublished data.

———. 1990. "Conjugal Violence Against Women." *Juristat Service Bulletin* 10(7).

Cate, R., J. Henton, J. Koval, F. Christopher, and S. Lloyd. 1982. "Premarital Abuse: A Social Psychological Perspective." *Journal of Family Issues* 3(1):79–90.

Catlin, Gary, and Susan Murray. 1979. *Report on Canadian Victimization Survey Methodological Pretests*. Ottawa: Statistics Canada.

Check, James, and Ted Guloien. 1989. "Reported Proclivity for Coercive Sex Following Repeated Exposure to Sexually Violent Pornography, Nonviolent Dehumanizing Pornography, and Erotica." In D. Zillmann and J. Bryant (eds.), *Pornography: Research Advances and Policy Considerations*. Hillsdale, NJ: Erlbaum, 159–84.

Check, James, and Neil Malamuth. 1985. "An Empirical Assessment of Some Feminist Hypotheses about Rape." *International Journal of Women's Studies* 8(4):414–23.

———. 1983. "Sex-Role Stereotyping and Reactions to Depictions of Stranger versus Acquaintance Rape." *Journal of Personality and Social Psychology* 45:344–56.

Chodorow, Nancy. 1974. "Family Structure and Feminine Personality." In M. Rosaldo and L. Lamphere (eds.), *Woman, Culture and Society*. Stanford, CT: Stanford University Press, 43–66.

Clark, Lorenne, and Debra Lewis. 1977. *Rape: The Price of Coercive Sexuality*. Toronto: The Women's Press.

Clark, Scott, and Dorothy Hepworth. 1994. "Effects of Reform Legislation on the Processing of Sexual Assault Cases." In J. Roberts and R. Mohr (eds.), *Confronting Sexual Assault: A Decade of Legal and Social Change*. Toronto: University of Toronto Press, 113–35.

Cohen, Lawrence, and Marcus Felson. 1979. "Social Change and Crime Rate Trends: A Routine Activity Approach." *American Sociological Review* 44:588–608.

Coleman, Diane, and Murray Straus. 1990. "Marital Power, Conflict and Violence in a Nationally Representative Sample of American Couples." In Murray Straus and Richard Gelles (eds.), *Physical Violence in American Families: Risk Factors and Adaptions to Violence in 8,145 Families*. New Brunswick, NJ: Transaction, 287–304.

Comack, Elizabeth. 1993. "Feminist Engagement with the Law: The Legal Recognition of the Battered Woman Syndrome." *The CRIAW Papers*. Ottawa: Canadian Research Institute for the Advancement of Women.

Cooper, Mary. 1994. *Criminal Harassment and Potential for Treatment: Literature Review and Annotated Bibliography*. Vancouver: B.C. Institute on Family Violence.

Crawford, Maria, and Rosemary Gartner. 1992. *Woman Killing: Intimate Femicide in Ontario, 1974–1990*. Toronto: Women We Honor Action Committee.

Daly, Martin, Lisa Singh, and Margo Wilson. 1993. "Children Fathered by Previous Partners: A Risk Factor for Violence Against Women." *Canadian Journal of Public Health* 84:209–10.

Daly, Martin, and Margo Wilson. 1988. *Homicide.* New York: Aldine de Gruyter.

Davis, Liane, and Bonnie Carlson. 1987. "Observation of Spouse Abuse: What Happens to the Children?" *Journal of Interpersonal Violence* 2(3):278–91.

DeKeseredy, Walter. 1990a. "Male Peer Support and Woman Abuse: The Current State of Knowledge." *Sociological Focus* 23(2):129–39.

———. 1990b. "Woman Abuse in Dating Relationships: The Contribution of Male Peer Support." *Sociological Inquiry* 60(3):236–43.

———. 1989. "Woman Abuse in Dating Relationships: An Exploratory Study." *Atlantis* 14(2):55–62.

———. 1988. "Woman Abuse in Dating Relationships: The Relevance of Social Support Theory." *Journal of Family Violence* 3(1):1–13.

DeKeseredy, Walter, and Ronald Hinch. 1991. *Woman Abuse: Sociological Perspectives.* Toronto: Thompson Educational Publishing.

DeKeseredy, Walter, and Katharine Kelly. 1995. "Sexual Abuse in Canadian University and College Dating Relationships: The Contribution of Male Peer Support." *Journal of Family Violence* 10(1):41–53.

———. 1993a. "Woman Abuse in University and College Dating Relationships: The Contribution of the Ideology of Familial Patriarchy." *Journal of Human Justice* 4(2):25–52.

———. 1993c. "The Incidence and Prevalence of Woman Abuse in Canadian University and College Dating Relationships." *Canadian Journal of Sociology* 18(2):137–59.

DeKeseredy, Walter, and Brian MacLean. 1990. "Researching Women Abuse in Canada: A Realist Critique of the Conflict Tactics Scale." *Canadian Review of Social Policy* 25:19–27.

Dobash, Rebecca Emerson, and Russell Dobash. 1992. *Women, Violence and Social Change.* London, UK: Routledge.

———. 1979. *Violence Against Wives.* New York: The Free Press.

Dobash, Russell, and Rebecca Emerson Dobash. 1988. "Research as Social Action: The Struggle for Battered Women." In K. Yllo and M. Bograd (eds.), *Feminist Perspectives on Wife Abuse.* Newbury Park, CA: Sage, 51–74.

———. 1984. "The Nature and Antecedents of Violent Events." *British Journal of Criminology* 24:269–88.

Dobash, Russell, Rebecca Emerson Dobash, Margo Wilson, and Martin Daly. 1992. "The Myth of Sexual Symmetry in Marital Violence." *Social Problems* 39(1):71–91.

Dumas, J., and Y. Péron. 1992. *Marriage and Conjugal Life in Canada.* Ottawa: Statistics Canada, Catalogue No. 91-534.

Dutton, Donald. 1986. "The Outcome of Court-Mandated Treatment for Wife Assault: A Quasi-Experimental Evaluation." *Violence and Victims* 1(3):163–75.

Dutton, Donald, Stephen Hart, Leslie Kennedy, and Kirk Williams. 1992. "Arrest and the Reduction of Repeat Wife Assault." In Eve Buzawa and Carl Buzawa (eds.), *Domestic Violence: The Changing Criminal Justice Response.* Westport: Auburn House, 111–27.

Edleson, Jeffrey, and Mary Pat Brygger. 1986. "Gender Differences in Reporting of Battering Incidences." *Family Relations* 35:377–82.

Ellis, Desmond. 1989. "Male Abuse of a Married or Cohabiting Female Partner: The Application of Sociological Theory to Research Findings." *Violence and Victims* 4(4):235–55.

Fagan, Jeffrey, Douglas Stewart, and Karen Hansen. 1983. "Violent Men or Violent Husbands? Background Factors and Situational Correlates." In David Finkelhor, Richard Gelles, Gerald Hotaling, and Murray Straus (eds.), *The Dark Side of Families: Current Family Violence Research.* Newbury Park, CA: Sage, 49–67.

Ferraro, Kathleen, and John Johnson. 1983. "How Women Experience Battering: The Process of Victimization." *Social Problems* 30(3):325–39.

Ferraro, Kenneth, and Randy LaGrange. 1987. "The Measurement of Fear of Crime." *Sociological Inquiry* 57(1):70–101.

Finkelhor, David. 1983. "Common Features of Family Abuse." In David Finkelhor, Richard Gelles, Gerald Hotaling, and Murray Straus (eds.), *The Dark Side of Families: Current Family Violence Research.* Newbury Park, CA: Sage, 17–28.

Finkelhor, David, and Kersti Yllo. 1985. *License to Rape: Sexual Abuse of Wives.* New York: The Free Press.

———. 1983. "Rape in Marriage: A Sociological View." In David Finkelhor, Richard Gelles, Gerald Hotaling, and Murray Straus (eds.), *The Dark Side of Families: Current Family Violence Research.* Newbury Park, CA: Sage, 119–30.

Follingstad, Diane, Elizabeth Hause, Larry Rutledge, and Darlene Polek. 1992. "Effects of Battered Women's Early Responses on Later Abuse Patterns." *Violence and Victims* 7(2):109–28.

Follingstad, Diane, Larry Rutledge, Barbara Berg, Elizabeth Hause, and Darlene Polek. 1990. "The Role of Emotional Abuse in Physically Abusive Relationships." *Journal of Family Violence* 5(2):107–20.

Frieze, Irene. 1983. "Investigating the Causes and Consequences of Marital Rape." *Signs: Journal of Women in Culture and Society* 8(3):532–53.

Frieze, Irene Hanson, and Angela Browne. 1989. "Violence in Marriage." In Lloyd Ohlin and Michael Tonry (eds.), *Family Violence.* Chicago: University of Chicago Press, 163–218.

Gartner, Rosemary, and Anthony Doob. 1994. "Trends in Criminal Victimization: 1988–1993." *Juristat Service Bulletin* 14(13).

Gelles, Richard. 1983. "An Exchange/Social Control Theory." In David Finkelhor, Richard Gelles, Gerald Hotaling, and Murray Straus (eds.),

The Dark Side of Families: Current Family Violence Research. Newbury Park, CA: Sage, 151–65.

————. 1980. "Violence in the Family: A Review of Research in the Seventies." *Journal of Marriage and the Family* 42:873–85.

————. 1979. *Family Violence.* Beverly Hills, CA: Sage.

————. 1974. *The Violent Home: A Study of Physical Aggression Between Husbands and Wives.* Newbury Park, CA: Sage.

Gelles, Richard, and Murray Straus. 1988. *Intimate Violence: The Causes and Consequences of Abuse in the American Family.* New York: Simon & Schuster.

Gelsthorpe, Loraine, and Allison Morris (eds.). 1990. *Feminist Perspectives in Criminology.* Milton Keynes, UK: Open University Press.

Giles-Sims, J. 1983. *Wife-Battering: A Systems Theory Approach.* New York: Guilford.

Gilligan, Carol. 1982. *In a Different Voice.* Cambridge, MA: Howard University Press.

Gordon, Margaret, and Stephanie Riger. 1989. *The Female Fear.* London, UK: Collier Macmillan Publishers.

Groth, A.N., A.W. Burgess, and L.L. Holmstrom. 1977. "Rape: Power, Anger and Sexuality." *American Journal of Psychiatry* 134(11):1239–43.

Groth, Nicholas, and J. Birnbaum. 1979. *Men Who Rape.* New York: Plenum Press.

Gwartney-Gibbs, Patricia, Jean Stockard, and Susan Bohmer. 1987. "Learning Courtship Aggression: The Influence of Parents, Peers and Personal Experiences." *Family Relations* 36:276–82.

Hanmer, Jalna, and Sheila Saunders. 1984. *Well-Founded Fear: A Community Study of Violence to Women.* London, UK: Hutchison & Co.

Hanneke, Christine, Nancy Shields, and George McCall. 1986. "Assessing the Prevalence of Marital Rape." *Journal of Interpersonal Violence* 1(3):350–62.

Harney, Patricia, and Charlene Muehlenhard. 1991. "Factors that Increase the Likelihood of Victimization" In Andrea Parrot and Laurie Bechhofer (eds.), *Acquaintance Rape: The Hidden Crime.* New York: John Wiley & Sons, 159–75.

Hart, B. 1988. "Beyond the 'Duty to Warn': A Therapist's 'Duty to Protect' Battered Women and Children." In Kersti Yllo and Michelle Bograd (eds.), *Feminist Perspectives on Wife Abuse.* Newbury Park, CA: Sage, 234–48.

Health Canada. 1994. *Canada's Treatment Programs for Men Who Abuse Their Partners.* Ottawa: National Clearinghouse on Family Violence.

Hendrick, Dianne. 1995. "Canadian Crime Statistics, 1994." *Juristat Service Bulletin* 15(12).

Henton, J., R. Cate, J. Koval, S. Lloyd, and F. Christopher. 1983. "Romance and Violence in Dating Relationships." *Journal of Family Issues* 4:467–82.

Hilton, Zoe. 1993. "Police Intervention and Public Opinion." In Zoe Hilton (ed.), *Legal Responses to Wife Assault*. Newbury Park, CA: Sage, 37–61.

Hindelang, M.J., M.R. Gottfredson, and J. Garofalo. 1978. *Victims of Personal Crime: An Empirical Foundation for a Theory of Personal Victimization*. Cambridge, MA: Ballinger.

Hirschi, T., and M. Gottfredson. 1983. "Age and the Explanation of Crime." *American Journal of Sociology* 89:552–84.

Hotaling, Gerald, and David Sugarman. 1990. "A Risk Marker Analysis of Assaulted Wives." *Journal of Family Violence* 5(1):1–13.

———. 1986. "An Analysis of Risk Markers in Husband to Wife Violence: The Current State of Knowledge." *Violence and Victims* 1(2):101–24.

Hough, Michael, and Patricia Mayhew. 1983. *The British Crime Survey*. Home Office Research Study No. 76. London: Her Majesty's Stationery Office.

House of Commons Debates. May 6, 1993. *Hansard* 132(247):19015–24.

Huesmann, L. Rowell, and Neil Malamuth. 1986. "Media Violence and Antisocial Behaviour: An Overview." *Journal of Social Issues* 42(3):1–6.

Jaffe, Peter, Elaine Hastings, Deborah Reitzel, and Gary Austin. 1993. "The Impact of Police Laying Charges." In Zoe Hilton (ed.), *Legal Responses to Wife Assault: Current Trends and Evaluation*. Newbury Park, CA: Sage, 62–95.

Jaffe, Peter, Susan Kaye Wilson, and David Wolfe. 1986. "Promoting Changes in Attitudes and Understanding of Conflict Resolution Among Child Witnesses of Family Violence." *Canadian Journal of Behavioural Science* 18(4):357–66.

Jaffe, Peter, Susan Kaye Wilson, and David Wolfe. 1988. "Specific Assessment and Intervention Strategies for Children Exposed to Wife Battering: Preliminary Empirical Investigations." *Canadian Journal of Community Mental Health* 7:157–63.

Jaffe, Peter, David Wolfe, Anne Telford, and Gary Austin. 1986. "The Impact of Police Charges in Incidents of Wife Abuse." *Journal of Family Violence* 1(1):37–49.

Jaffe, Peter, David Wolfe, and Susan Kaye Wilson. 1990. *Children of Battered Women*. Newbury Park, CA: Sage.

Jaffe, Peter, David Wolfe, Susan Wilson, and Lydia Zak. 1986a. "Family Violence and Child Adjustment: A Comparative Analysis of Girls' and Boys' Behavioral Symptoms." *American Journal of Psychiatry* 143(1):74–77.

———. 1986b. "Similarities in Behavioral and Social Maladjustment among Child Victims and Witnesses to Family Violence." *American Journal of Orthopsychiatry* 56(1):142–46.

Johnson, Holly. 1996. "Sexual Assault." In Leslie W. Kennedy and Vincent F. Sacco (eds.), *Crime Counts*. Scarborough, ON: Nelson, 133–49.

———. 1995. "Violence Against Women: A Special Topic Survey." In R. Silverman, J. Teevan, and V. Sacco (eds.), *Crime in Canadian Society* (5th ed.). Toronto: Harcourt Brace & Co., 210–21.

———. 1988. "Wife Abuse." *Canadian Social Trends* (Spring), 17–20.

Johnson, Holly, and Vincent F. Sacco. 1995. "Researching Violence Against Women: Statistics Canada's National Survey." *Canadian Journal of Criminology* 37(3):281–304.

Junger, Marianne. 1987. "Women's Experiences of Sexual Harassment: Some Implications for Their Fear of Crime." *British Journal of Criminology* 27(4):358–83.

Kalmuss, Debra. 1984. "The Intergenerational Transmission of Marital Aggression." *Journal of Marriage and the Family* 46:11–19.

Kalmuss, Debra, and Murray Straus. 1990. "Wife's Marital Dependency and Wife Abuse." In Murray Straus and Richard Gelles (eds.), *Physical Violence in American Families: Risk Factors and Adaptions to Violence in 8,145 Families*. New Brunswick, NJ: Transaction, 369–82.

Kanin, Eugene. 1985. "Date Rapists: Differential Sexual Socialization and Relative Deprivation." *Archives of Sexual Behavior* 14(3):219–31.

———. 1984. "Date Rape: Unofficial Criminal and Victims." *Victimology: An International Journal* 9(1):95–108.

Kantor, Glenda Kaufman, and Murray Straus. 1990. "The 'Drunken Bum' Theory of Wife Beating." In Murray Straus and Richard Gelles (eds.), *Physical Violence in American Families: Risk Factors and Adaptions to Violence in 8,145 Families*. New Brunswick, NJ: Transaction, 203–24.

Kellerman, Arthur, and James Mercy. 1992. "Men, Women and Murder: Gender-Specific Differences in Rates of Fatal Violence and Victimization." *Journal of Trauma* 33(1):1–5.

Kellerman, Arthur, Frederick Rivara, Norman Rushforth, Joyce Banton, Donald Reay, Jerry Francisco, Ana Loggi, Janice Prodzinski, Bela Hackman, and Grant Somes. 1993. "Gun Ownership as a Risk Factor for Homicide in the Home." *New England Journal of Medicine* 329:1084–91.

Kelly, Liz. 1988. *Surviving Sexual Violence*. Minneapolis: University of Minnesota Press.

———. 1987. "The Continuum of Sexual Violence." In Jalna Hanmer and Mary Maynard (eds.), *Women, Violence and Social Control*. Atlantic Highlands, NJ: Humanities Press, 46–60.

Kennedy, Leslie, and Donald Dutton. 1989. "The Incidence of Wife Assault in Alberta." *Canadian Journal of Behavioural Science* 21:40–54.

Kennedy, Leslie, and David Forde. 1990. "Routine Activities and Crime: An Analysis of Victimization in Canada." *Criminology* 28(1):137–51.

Koss, Mary. 1992. "The Underdetection of Rape: Methodological Choices Influence Incidence Estimates." *Journal of Social Issues* 48(1):61–75.

———. 1989. "Hidden Rape: Sexual Aggression and Victimization in a National Sample of Students in Higher Education." In Maureen Pirog-

Good and Jan Stets, *Violence in Dating Relationships: Emerging Social Issues.* New York: Praeger, 145–68.

Koss, Mary, and Christine Gidycz. 1985. "Sexual Experiences Survey: Reliability and Validity." *Journal of Consulting and Clinical Psychology* 53:422–23.

Koss, Mary, Christine Gidycz, and Nadine Wisniewski. 1987. "The Scope of Rape: Incidence and Prevalence of Sexual Aggression and Victimization in a National Sample of Higher Education Students." *Journal of Consulting and Clinical Psychology* 55(2):162–70.

Koss, Mary, and Cheryl Oros. 1982. "Sexual Experiences Survey: A Research Instrument Investigating Sexual Aggression and Victimization." *Journal of Consulting and Clinical Psychology* 50(3):455–57.

LaGrange, Randy, Kenneth Ferraro, and Michael Supancic. 1992. "Perceived Risk and Fear of Crime: Role of Social and Physical Incivilities." *Journal of Research on Crime and Delinquency* 29(3):311–34.

Laner, Mary, and J. Thompson. 1982. "Abuse and Aggression in Courting Couples." *Deviant Behavior* 3:229–44.

Lavoie, F., M. Jacob, J. Hardy, and G. Martin. 1989. "Police Attitudes in Assigning Responsibility for Wife Abuse." *Journal of Family Violence* 4:369–88.

Linz, Daniel. 1989. "Exposure to Sexually Explicit Materials and Attitudes Toward Rape: A Comparison of Study Results." *Journal of Sex Research* 26(1):50–84.

London Family Court Clinic. 1991. *Wife Assault as a Crime: The Perspectives of Victims and Police Officers on a Charging Policy in London, Ontario from 1980–1990.* Ottawa: Department of Justice.

Los, Maria. 1994. "The Struggle to Redefine Rape in the Early 1980s." In Julian Roberts and Renate Mohr (eds.), *Confronting Sexual Assault: A Decade of Legal and Social Change.* Toronto: University of Toronto Press, 20–56.

Lupri, Eugen. 1989. "Male Violence in the Home." *Canadian Social Trends* 14:19–21.

Lupri, Eugen, Elaine Grandin, and Merlin Brinkerhoff. 1994. "Socioeconomic Status and Male Violence in the Canadian Home: A Reexamination." *Canadian Journal of Sociology* 19(1):47–73.

Lytwyn, T. H. 1994. "Preliminary Thoughts on the Meaning of Section 264: Criminal Harassment in Canada." Unpublished paper.

MacLeod, Linda. 1995a. "Expanding the Dialogue: Report of a Workshop to Explore the Criminal Justice System Response to Violence Against Women." In Mariana Valverde, Linda MacLeod, and Kirsten Johnson (eds.), *Wife Assault and the Canadian Justice System.* Toronto: Centre for Criminology, University of Toronto, 10–32.

———. 1995b. "Policy Decisions and Prosecutorial Dilemmas: The Unanticipated Consequences of Good Intentions." In Valverde, MacLeod, and Johnson (eds.), *Wife Assault*, 47–61.

———. 1995c. "Family Group Conferencing: A Community-Based Model for Stopping Family Violence." In Valverde, MacLeod, and Johnson (eds.), *Wife Assault*, 198–204.

———. 1987. *Battered but Not Beaten: Preventing Wife Battering in Canada*. Ottawa: Canadian Advisory Council on the Status of Women.

———. 1980. *Wife Battering in Canada: The Vicious Circle*. Ottawa: Canadian Advisory Council on the Status of Women.

Mahoney, Martha. 1994. "Victimization or Oppression? Women's Lives, Violence and Agency." In Martha Albertson Fineman and Roxanne Mykitiuk (eds.), *The Public Nature of Private Violence*. New York: Routledge, 59–92.

Makepeace, James. 1989. "Dating, Living Together and Courtship Violence." In Maureen Pirog-Good and Jan Stets (eds.), *Violence in Dating Relationships: Emerging Social Issues*. New York: Praeger, 94–107.

———. 1986. "Gender Differences in Courtship Violence Victimization." *Family Relations* 35:383–88.

———. 1981. "Courtship Violence among College Students." *Family Relations* 30:97–102.

Malamuth, Neil. 1989. "Predictors of Naturalistic Sexual Aggression." In Maureen Pirog-Good and Jan Stets (eds.), *Violence in Dating Relationships: Emerging Social Issues*. New York: Praeger, 218–40.

———. 1981a. "Rape Proclivity among Males." *Journal of Social Issues* 37(4): 138–57

———. 1981b. "The Effects of Mass Media Exposure on Acceptance of Violence against Women: A Field Experiment." *Journal of Research in Personality* 15:436–46.

Malamuth, Neil, and John Briere. 1986. "Sexual Violence in the Media: Indirect Effects on Aggression Against Women." *Journal of Social Issues* 42(3):75–92.

Margolin, Gayla, Linda Gorin Sibner, and Lisa Gleberman. 1988. "Wife Battering." In Vincent Van Hasselt, Randall Morrison, and Alan Bellack (eds.), *Handbook of Family Violence*. New York: Plenum Press, 89–117.

Martin, Del. 1981. *Battered Wives*. San Francisco: Volcano Press.

McCormack, Hilary. 1993. "Prosecuting the Stalker: The New Criminal Harassment Provision." Paper presented at the Ontario Crown Attorneys Conference, Clevelands House, May.

McLeod, M. 1984. "Women against Men: An Examination of Domestic Violence Based on an Analysis of Official Data and National Victimization Data." *Justice Quarterly* 170–93.

McNeill, Sandra. 1987. "Flashing: Its Effect on Women." In Jalna Hanmer and Mary Maynard (eds.), *Women, Violence and Social Control*. Atlantic Highlands, NJ: Humanities Press International, 93–109.

Medea, A., and K. Thompson. 1974. *Against Rape*. New York: Farrar, Straus and Giroux.

Mederer, Helen, and Richard Gelles. 1989. "Compassion or Control: Intervention in Cases of Wife Abuse" *Journal of Interpersonal Violence* 4(1):25–43.

Meithe, Terance. 1995. "Fear and Withdrawal from Urban Life."*Annals of the American Academy of Political and Social Science* 539:14–27.

Meithe, Terance, Mark Stafford, and Scott Long. 1987. "Social Differentiation in Criminal Victimization: A Test of Routine Activities/Lifestyles Theories." *American Sociological Review* 52:184–94.

Mercer, Shirley Litch. 1988. "Not a Pretty Picture: An Exploratory Study of Violence against Women in High School Dating Relationships."*Resources for Feminist Research* 17(2):15–23.

Messerschmidt, James W. 1993. *Masculinities and Crime*. Lanham, MD: Rowman & Littlefield.

Miedzian, Myriam. 1995. "Learning to Be Violent." In Einat Peled, Peter Jaffe, and Jeffrey Edleson (eds.), *Ending the Cycle of Violence*. Thousand Oaks, CA: Sage, 10–24.

Morgan, David. 1987. "Masculinity and Violence." In Jalna Hanmer and Mary Maynard (eds.), *Women, Violence and Social Control*. Atlantic Highlands, NJ: Humanities Press International, 180–92.

Morrison, Richard, and Jillian Oderkirk. 1991. "Married and Unmarried Couples: The Tax Question." *Canadian Social Trends* (Summer):15–20.

Muehlenhard, Charlene. 1989. "Misinterpreted Dating Behaviors and the Risk of Date Rape." In Maureen Pirog-Good and Jan Stets (eds.),*Violence in Dating Relationships: Emerging Social Issues*. New York: Praeger, 241–56.

Muehlenhard, Charlene, and Melaney Linton. 1987. "Date Rape and Sexual Aggression in Dating Situations: Incidence and Risk Factors."*Journal of Counseling Psychology* 34(2):186–96.

Noonan, Sheila. 1993. "Strategies of Survival: Moving Beyond the Battered Woman Syndrome." In Ellen Adelberg and Claudia Currie (eds.), *In Conflict with the Law: Women and the Canadian Justice System*. Vancouver: Press Gang, 247–70.

O'Grady, B. 1991. "Crime, Violence and Victimization: A Newfoundland Case." In R. Silverman, J. Teevan, and V. Sacco (eds.), *Crime in Canadian Society*, 79–91.

Ogrodnik, Lucie. 1994. "Canadian Crime Statistics, 1993."*Juristat Service Bulletin* 14(14).

Pagelow, M. 1981. *Battering: Victims and Their Experience*. Beverly Hills, CA: Sage.

Pleck, Elizabeth. 1989. "Criminal Approaches to Family Violence, 1640–1980." In Lloyd Ohlin and Michael Tonry (eds.), *Family Violence*. Chicago: University of Chicago Press, 19–57.

R. v. Chase, [1987], 37 C.C.C. (3d) 97 (S.C.C.).

R. v. Daviault [1994], 3 S.C.R. 63–132.

R. v. Lavallee (1990), 1 S.C.R. 852–900.

R. v. Pappajohn [1980], 2 S.C.R. 120.

R. v. Whynot (1983), 37 C.R. (3d) 198 (N.S.C.A.).

Roberts, Julian V. 1994. *Criminal Justice Processing of Sexual Assault Cases.* Ottawa: Statistics Canada.

Roberts, Julian V., and Robert Gebotys. 1992. "Reforming Rape Laws." *Law and Human Behavior* 16(5):555–73.

Roberts, Julian, and Michelle Grossman. 1994. "Changing Definitions of Sexual Assault: An Analysis of Police Statistics." In Julian Roberts and Renate Mohr (eds.), *Confronting Sexual Assault: A Decade of Legal and Social Change.* Toronto: University of Toronto Press, 57–83.

Rodgers, Karen. 1994. "Wife Assault: The Findings of a National Survey." *Juristat Service Bulletin* 14(9).

Rodgers, Karen, and Garry MacDonald. 1994. "Canada's Shelters for Abused Women." *Canadian Social Trends* (Autumn):10–14.

Rodgers, Karen, and Georgia Roberts. 1995. "Women's Non-Spousal Multiple Victimization: A Test of the Routine Activities Theory." *Canadian Journal of Criminology* 37(3):363–91.

Roscoe, Bruce, and Nancy Benaske. 1985. "Courtship Violence Experienced by Abused Wives: Similarities in Patterns of Abuse." *Family Relations* 34:419–24.

Russell, Diana. 1990. *Rape in Marriage.* Bloomington: Indiana University Press.

———. 1984. *Sexual Exploitation: Rape, Child Sexual Abuse and Workplace Harrassment.* Beverly Hills, CA: Sage.

Sacco, Vincent F. 1990. "Gender, Fear and Victimization: A Preliminary Application of Power-Control Theory." *Sociological Spectrum* 10:485–506.

Sacco, Vincent F., and Holly Johnson. 1990. *Patterns of Criminal Victimization in Canada.* Ottawa: Minister of Supply and Services.

Sacco, Vincent F., Holly Johnson, and Robert Arnold. 1993. "Urban–Rural Residence and Criminal Victimization." *Canadian Journal of Sociology* 18(4):433–53.

Sacco, Vincent F., and Leslie W. Kennedy. 1994. *The Criminal Event.* Scarborough, ON: Nelson.

Sanday, Peggy Reeves. 1990. *Fraternity Gang Rape.* New York: New York University Press.

Saunders, Daniel. 1988. "Wife Abuse, Husband Abuse or Mutual Combat: A Feminist Perspective on the Empirical Findings." In K. Yllo and M. Bograd (eds.), *Feminist Perspectives on Wife Abuse.* Newbury Park, CA: Sage, 90–113.

Saunders, D., and P. Size. 1986. "Attitudes about Woman Abuse among Police Officers, Victims, and Victim Advocates." *Journal of Interpersonal Violence* 1:25–42.

Schechter, Susan. 1982. *Women and Male Violence.* Boston: South End Press.

Scheppele, Kim Lane. 1983. "Through Women's Eyes: Defining Danger in the Wake of Sexual Assault." *Journal of Social Issues* 39(2):63–81.

Schmidt, Janell, and Lawrence Sherman. 1993. "Does Arrest Deter Domestic Violence?" *American Behavioral Scientist* 36(5):601–9.

Schneider, Elizabeth. 1994. "The Violence of Privacy." In Martha Albertson Fineman and Roxanne Mykitiuk (eds.), *The Public Nature of Private Violence*, 36–58.

Schwartz, Martin D., and Walter DeKeseredy. 1988. "Liberal Feminism on Violence against Women." *Social Justice* 15(3–4):213–21.

Sebastian, Richard, 1983. "Social Psychological Determinants." In David Finkelhor, Richard Gelles, Gerald Hotaling, and Murray Straus (eds.), *The Dark Side of Families: Current Family Violence Research.* Newbury Park, CA: Sage, 182–92.

Sheffield, Carole. 1989. "The Invisible Intruder: Women's Experiences of Obscene Phone Calls." *Gender and Society* 3(4):483–88.

Sherman, Lawrence, and Richard Berk. 1984. "The Specific Deterrent Effects of Arrest for Domestic Assault" *American Sociological Review* 49:261–72.

Sherman, Lawrence, Janell Schmidt, and D. Rogan. 1992. *Policing Domestic Violence: Experiments and Dilemmas.* New York: The Free Press.

Shields, Nancy, and Christine Hanneke. 1983. "Battered Wives' Reactions to Marital Rape." In David Finkelhor, Richard Gelles, Gerald Hotaling, and Murray Straus (eds.), *The Dark Side of Families: Current Family Violence Research.* Newbury Park, CA: Sage, 132–48.

Shields, William, and Lea Shields. 1983. "Forcible Rape: An Evolutionary Perspective." *Ethology and Sociobiology* 4:115–36.

Skogan, Wesley. 1990. *Disorder and Decline: Crime and the Spiral of Decay in American Neighborhoods.* New York: The Free Press.

———. 1986. "Methodological Issues in the Study of Victimization." In Ezzat Fattah (ed.), *From Crime Policy to Victim Policy: Reorienting the Justice System.* London, UK: Macmillan, 80–116.

———. 1984. "Reporting Crimes to the Police: The Status of World Research." *Journal of Research in Crime and Delinquency* 21(2): 113–37.

Skogan, Wesley, and Michael Maxfield. 1981. *Coping with Crime.* Beverly Hills, CA: Sage.

Silverman, Robert, and Leslie W. Kennedy. 1993. *Deadly Deeds: Murder in Canada.* Scarborough, ON: Nelson.

Smith, Michael D. 1994. "Enhancing the Quality of Survey Data on Violence Against Women: A Feminist Approach." *Gender and Society* 8(1):109–27.

———. 1993a. "Obscene and Threatening Telephone Calls to Women: Data from a Canadian National Survey." Paper presented at the Canadian Sociology and Anthropology Association Meeting, Ottawa, June.

———. 1993b. "Women's Fear of Male Violence." *Canada Watch* 1:68–70.

———. 1991. "Male Peer Support of Wife Abuse." *Journal of Interpersonal Violence* 6(4):512–19.

———. 1990a. "Patriarchal Ideology and Wife Beating: A Test of a Feminist Hypothesis." *Violence and Victims* 5(4):257–73.

———. 1990b. "Sociodemographic Risk Factors in Wife Abuse: Results from a Survey of Toronto Women." *Canadian Journal of Sociology* 15(1):39–58.

———. 1988. "Women's Fear of Violent Crime: An Exploratory Test of a Feminist Hypothesis." *Journal of Family Violence* 3(1):29–38.

———. 1987. "The Incidence and Prevalence of Women Abuse in Toronto." *Violence and Victims* 2:33–47.

Solicitor General Canada. 1985. *Female Victims of Crime*. Canadian Urban Victimization Survey, Bulletin 4.

Sommers, Evelyn, and James Check. 1987. "An Empirical Investigation of the Role of Pornography in the Verbal and Physical Abuse of Women." *Violence and Victims* 2(3):189–209.

Sonkin, D., D. Martin, and L. Walker. 1985. *The Male Batterer: A Treatment Approach*. New York: Springer.

Stanko, Elizabeth. 1995. "Women, Crime and Fear." *Annals of the American Academy of Political and Social Science* 539:46–58.

———. 1990a. *Everyday Violence: How Men and Women Experience Sexual and Physical Danger*. London, UK: Pandora.

———. 1990b. "When Precaution Is Normal: A Feminist Critique of Crime Prevention." In Loraine Gelsthorpe and Allison Morris (eds.), *Feminist Perspectives in Criminology*. Milton Keynes, UK: Open University Press, 173–83.

———. 1988. "Fear of Crime and the Myth of the Safe Home: A Feminist Critique of Criminology." In K. Yllo and M. Bograd (eds.), *Feminist Perspectives on Wife Abuse*. Newbury Park, CA: Sage, 75–88.

———. 1987. "Typical Violence, Normal Precaution: Men, Women and Interpersonal Violence in England, Wales, Scotland and the USA." In Jalna Hanmer and Mary Maynard (eds.), *Women, Violence and Social Control*. Atlantic Highlands, NJ: Humanities Press International, 122–34.

———. 1985. *Intimate Intrusions: Women's Experiences of Male Violence*. London, UK: Unwin Hyman.

Stark, Evan. 1993. "Mandatory Arrest of Batterers: A Reply to Its Critics." *American Behavioral Scientist* 36(5):651–80.

Statistics Canada. 1995. *Women in Canada*, 3rd ed., Catalogue No. 89-503.

———. 1994a. *Violence Against Women Survey*. Microdata file. Ottawa.

———. 1994b. *Violence Against Women Survey. Questionnaire Package*. Ottawa.

———. 1993a. "The Violence Against Women Survey," *The Daily*, November 18.

———. 1993b. *General Social Survey*. Microdata file. Ottawa.

————. 1988. *General Social Survey.* Microdata file. Ottawa.

————. 1982. Canadian Urban Victimization Survey. Microdata file. Ottawa.

Steinmetz, Suzanne. 1981. "A Cross-Cultural Comparison of Marital Abuse." *Journal of Sociology and Social Welfare* 8:404–14.

————. 1977–78. "The Battered Husband Syndrome." *Victimology* 2(3–4):499–509.

Stets, Jan. 1990. "Verbal and Physical Aggression in Marriage." *Journal of Marriage and the Family* 52:501–14.

Stets, Jan, and Murray Straus. 1990a. "Gender Differences in Reporting Marital Violence and Its Medical and Psychological Consequences." In Murray Straus and Richard Gelles (eds.), *Physical Violence in American Families: Risk Factors and Adaptions to Violence in 8,145 Families.* New Brunswick, NJ: Transaction, 151–65.

————. 1990b. "The Marriage License as a Hitting License: A Comparison of Assaults in Dating, Cohabitating and Married Couples." In Murray Straus and Richard Gelles (eds.), *Physical Violence in American Families: Risk Factors and Adaptions to Violence in 8,145 Families.* New Brunswick, NJ: Transaction, 727–44.

————. 1989. "The Marriage License as a Hitting License: A Comparison of Assaults in Dating, Cohabiting and Married Couples." In Maureen Pirog-Good and Jan Stets (eds.), *Violence in Dating Relationships: Emerging Social Issues.* New York: Praeger, 33–52.

Stewart, Donna, and Anthony Cecutti. 1993. "Physical Abuse in Pregnancy." *Canadian Medical Association Journal* 149(9):1257–63.

Stith, S. 1990. "Police Response to Domestic Violence: The Influence of Individual and Familial Factors." *Violence and Victims* 5:37–49.

Stout, Cam. 1991. "Common Law: A Growing Alternative." *Canadian Social Trends* (Winter):18–20.

Straus, Murray. 1990a. "Measuring Intrafamily Conflict and Violence: The Conflict Tactics (CTS) Scales." In Murray Straus and Richard Gelles (eds.), *Physical Violence in American Families: Risk Factors and Adaptions to Violence in 8,145 Families.* New Brunswick, NJ: Transaction, 29–47.

————. 1990b. "Social Stress and Marital Violence in a National Sample of American Families." In Murray Straus and Richard Gelles (eds.), *Physical Violence in American Families: Risk Factors and Adaptions to Violence in 8,145 Families.* New Brunswick, NJ: Transaction, 181–201.

————. 1983. "Ordinary Violence, Child Abuse, and Wife-Beating: What Do They Have in Common?" In David Finkelhor, Richard Gelles, Gerald Hotaling, and Murray Straus (eds.), *The Dark Side of Families: Current Family Violence Research.* Newbury Park, CA: Sage, 213–34.

Straus, Murray, and Richard Gelles. 1990a. "How Violent Are American Families? Estimates from the National Family Violence Resurvey and Other Studies." In Murray Straus and Richard Gelles (eds.), *Physical Violence in American Families: Risk Factors and Adaptions to Violence in 8,145 Families.* New Brunswick, NJ: Transaction, 95–112.

————. 1990b. *Physical Violence in American Families: Risk Factors and Adaptions to Violence in 8,145 Families.* New Brunswick, NJ: Transaction.

————. 1990c. "Societal Change and Change in Family Violence from 1975 to 1985 as Revealed by Two National Studies." In Murray Straus and Richard Gelles (eds.), *Physical Violence in American Families: Risk Factors and Adaptions to Violence in 8,145 Families.* New Brunswick, NJ: Transaction, 113–31.

Straus, Murray, Richard Gelles, and Suzanne Steinmetz. 1980. *Behind Closed Doors.* New York: Anchor Books.

Suderman, Marlies, Peter Jaffe, and Elaine Hastings. 1995. "Violence Prevention Programs in Secondary (High) Schools." In Einat Paled, Peter Jaffe, and Jeffrey Edelson (eds.), *Ending the Cycle of Violence.* Thousand Oaks, CA: Sage, 232–54.

Sugarman, David, and Gerald Hotaling. 1989. "Dating Violence: Prevalence, Context and Risk Markers." In Maureen Pirog-Good and Jan Stets, *Violence in Dating Relationships: Emerging Social Issues.* New York: Praeger, 3–32.

Szinovacz, Maximiliane. 1983. "Using Couple Data as a Methodological Tool: The Case of Marital Violence." *Journal of Marriage and the Family* 45:633–44.

Trevethan, Shelley, and Tajeshwer Samagh. 1992. "Gender Differences among Violent Crime Victims." *Juristat Service Bulletin* 12(21).

Turner, Jan. 1995. "Saskatchewan Responds to Family Violence: The Victims of Domestic Violence Act, 1995." In Mariana Valverde, Linda MacLeod, and Kirsten Johnson (eds.), *Wife Assault and the Canadian Centre for Justice Statistics.* Toronto: Centre of Criminology, University of Toronto, 183–97.

Ursel, Jane. 1994. "The Winnipeg Family Violence Court." *Juristat Service Bulletin* 14(12).

Walker, Lenore. 1989. *Terrifying Love: Why Battered Women Kill and How Society Responds.* New York: Harper Perennial.

————. 1984. *The Battered Women Syndrome.* New York: Springer.

————. 1983. "The Battered Woman Syndrome Study." In David Finkelhor, Richard Gelles, Gerald Hotaling, and Murray Straus (eds.), *The Dark Side of Families: Current Family Violence Research.* Newbury Park, CA: Sage, 31–48.

————. 1979. *The Battered Woman.* New York: Harper Perennial.

Wardell, Laurie, Dair Gillespie and Ann Leffler. 1983. "Science and Violence Against Wives." In David Finkelhor, Richard Gelles, Gerald Hotaling, and Murray Straus (eds.), *The Dark Side of Families: Current Family Violence Research.* Newbury Park, CA: Sage, 69–84.

Warr, Mark. 1985. "Fear of Rape Among Urban Women." *Social Problems* 32(3):238–50.

Wente, Margaret. 1994. "Why the Statscan Tale Needs Debunking." *The Globe and Mail*, December 3, A2.

Wente, Margaret. 1995. "An American Tragedy." *The Globe and Mail,* October 7: D7.

White, Jacquelyn, and John Humphrey. 1991. "Young People's Attitudes Toward Acquaintance Rape." In Andrea Parrot and Laurie Bechhofer (eds.), *Acquaintance Rape: The Hidden Crime.* New York: John Wiley & Sons, 43–56.

Widom, Cathy Spatz. 1989. "Does Violence Beget Violence? A Critical Examination of the Literature." *Psychological Bulletin* 106(1):3–28.

Wilson, Margo, and Martin Daly. 1994. "Spousal Homicide." *Juristat Service Bulletin* 14(8).

———. 1993. "Spousal Homicide Risk and Estrangement." *Violence and Victims* 8:3–15.

———. 1992a. "Till Death Us Do Part." In J. Radford and D. Russell (eds.), *Femicide: The Politics of Women Killing.* New York: Twayne Publishers, 83–98.

———. 1992b. "Who Kills Whom in Spouse Killings? On the Exceptional Sex Ratio of Spousal Homicides in the United States." *Criminology* 30(2):189–215.

Wilson, Margo, Holly Johnson, and Martin Daly. 1995. "Lethal and Non-Lethal Violence Against Wives." *Canadian Journal of Criminology* 37(3):331–61.

Wolfe, David, Christine Wekerle, Deborah Reitzel, and Robert Gough. 1995. "Strategies to Address Violence in the Lives of High-Risk Youth." In Einat Paled, Peter Jaffe, and Jeffrey Edelson (eds.), *Ending the Cycle of Violence.* Thousand Oaks, CA: Sage, 255–74.

Wolff, Lee, and Bryan Reingold. 1994. "Drug Use and Crime." *Juristat Service Bulletin* 14(6).

Wright, Christine. 1995. "Risk of Personal and Household Victimization: Canada, 1993." *Juristat Service Bulletin* 15(2).

Wright, Robert. 1995. "The Biology of Violence." *The New Yorker,* March 13, 68–77.

Young, Jock. 1988. "Risk of Crime and Fear of Crime: A Realist Critique of Survey-Based Assumptions." In M. Maguire and J. Ponting (eds.), *Victims of Crime: A New Deal.* Milton Keynes, UK: Open University Press.

INDEX

Note: Numbers in italics indicate that the only reference to the subject is in a table or figure. Page ranges may contain information in tables and figures as well as in the text.

Self-defence (battered woman
  defence), 191–98, 200, 225
Self-esteem and abuse, 160, 162,
  187, 202, *203*
Self-protection techniques
  (against violence), 83–88
"Self-selection" of respondents,
  38–39
Separation
  why women leave, 189, *190*
  wife assault and, 169–70, 224
  wife killings and, 184–86, 191,
  224
Sex role theory
  dating violence, 111–12, 122–
  24, 223
  violence against women, *4,* 7–
  10, 223
  wife assault, 165–66, 175–76,
  223
Sexual assault
  changes in attitude to, 35–36
  consent and, 118–21
  dating violence (*see* Dating
  violence)
  help-seeking behaviour, 204–6
  legal definitions, 30–31, 118,
  143–44
  marital, 21–22, 142–46, 186,
  190
  pornographic materials, 8
  repeat victimization, 92–93, *94,*
  108–9, 114, *115,* 138–40,
  206, *207*
  reporting to police, 208, 226
  sex role theory, 7–10
  Sexual Experiences Scale, 115–
  16
  statistics, *45, 52–53*
  by strangers, 92–94
  traditional attitudes, xxi–xxii
  trends, 32–37
  university and college relationships, 114–18, 120–21
  Violence Against Women
  Survey, 47–52, *53,* 144, *190*
  women's fear, 62, 79, *80,* 82, *83*
Sexual Experiences Scale, 115–16
Sexual harassment
  concept of masculinity and, 24

continuum of sexual violence
  in, 95–96
fear of crime and, 67–68, 79–
  83, 95–96
indecent exposure, 96
potential for violence unknown,
  67–68, 96, 100
prevalence of, 97–100
sociodemographic factors of
  victims, 100–105
Violence Against Women
  Survey, *71,* 79–83, 97–100
"Sexual predators," 120–21
"Sexual proprietariness," 15, 169,
  185–86
Shame, feelings of, 136, 145, 202,
  203, 208, 226
Shelters for battered women, 133
Simpson, O.J. (trial), xv–xvi, xxi
Situational theories (for violence
  against women), *4,* 10–13
Social control theory (for violence
  against women), *5,* 19–20
Social learning theory
  dating violence, 121–22, 223
  violence against women, 2–7
  wife assault, 2–7, 171–77, 196–
  97, 223
Societal-level theories
  feminist theories, *5,* 21–25,
  158–60, 224
  lifestyle/routine activities, *4–5,*
  15–17, 105–10, 125–28, 224
  resource theory, *5,* 17–19
  social control/general systems,
  5, 19–20
Spousal killings
  Canadian Homicide Survey,
  185
  Danger Assessment Instrument, 185
  risk factors, 183–87, 224–5
  statistics, 179–83
  United States, in, 182–83
  See also Husband killings
Spouse abuse
  definition, 216
Status of man
  evolutionary theory, 13–15
  resource theory, 17–19

Saskatchewan Victims of
Domestic Violence Act, 217–
18
separation, 169–70, 224
sexual assault, 21–22, 142–46,
186, *190,* 206, *207*
social learning theory, 2–7,
171–77, 196–97, 223
statistics (non-VAWS), *45, 51,
137*
types and seriousness of
violence, 134–42, 202
Violence Against Women
Survey, 47–52, *54,* 135–46,
148–58, 160–71, 173–76, 190
when police are called, 204,
206–9, 226
why they leave, 189–90

why they stay, 131–32, 146–47,
187–91, 196, 225
Winnipeg Family Violence
Court, 215–17
"zero tolerance" policy, 214–15
Wife killings
commonalities with nonlethal
violence, 185–86
Danger Assessment Instru-
ment, 185
risk factors, 183–87, 224–25
statistics, 179–84
Winnipeg Family Violence Court,
215–17

"Zero tolerance" policy (on wife
assault), 214–15